Section 27

Section 27

A Century on a Family Farm  Mil Penner

UNIVERSITY PRESS OF KANSAS

Published by the University Press of
Kansas (Lawrence, Kansas 66049), which
was organized by the Kansas Board of
Regents and is operated and funded by
Emporia State University, Fort Hays State
University, Kansas State University,
Pittsburg State University, the University
of Kansas, and Wichita State University

Printed in the United States of America

10 9 8 7 6 5 4 3 2 1

The paper used in this publication
meets the minimum requirements of
the American National Standard for
Permanence of Paper for Printed Library
Materials z39.48-1984.

Library of Congress
Cataloging-in-Publication Data
Penner, Mil.
    Section 27 : a century on a family farm /
Mil Penner.
        p. cm.
    ISBN 0-7006-1196-7 (cloth : alk. paper)
    1. Penner family.   2. Penner, Mil—
Family.   3. Farmers—Kansas—
McPherson County—Biography.   4. Farm
life—Kansas—McPherson County.
5. Mennonites—Kansas—McPherson
County—Biography.   6. McPherson
County (Kan.)—Biography.   I. Title.
CT274.P455 P47 2002
978.1'5503'0922—dc21   2002004928

British Library Cataloguing in
Publication Data is available.

Contents

Illustrations

 # Prologue

Nothing that is can pause or stay
The moon will wax, the moon will wane,
The mist and cloud will turn to rain,
The rain to mist and cloud again,
Tomorrow be today.
—Henry Wadsworth Longfellow

Like a misty morning, the twentieth century is just a memory. But a century of memories becomes a fantastic collage of misty mornings, old cars, family reunions, harvest times, and much more. So it is with Section 27, a mile-square tract of farmland near Inman, Kansas. Its history is common to thousands of square miles of prairie land populated by European emigrants late in the nineteenth century, and yet each story is unique. Each offers its own drama of excitement, bounty, and travail. The twentieth century has passed Section 27 by, but windows to the past tell its story. It is the universal story of the American heartland sharpened by personal accounts of one family's relationship to the land.

Windows — family albums, implement relics, and old barns — that offer glimpses into the story of Section 27 and its community remain, but they are gradually disappearing, especially those pertaining to events taking place early in the century such as breaking sod, the Dust Bowl days, and the Depression. People, buildings, and artifacts from the early Section 27 story are succumbing to the grim realities of time. I, for example, represent the last generation that had a firsthand experience harvesting with a binder and threshing machine. I have made it my mission to explore and record the twentieth-century story of rural America here on Section 27 and its environs.

Our country, our world, is moving away from its rural roots at an ever-accelerating pace. It is not my aim to judge the state of progress, as older people are prone to do, but rather to recall values, customs, and a way of life with close ties to the land. I have a sense that connection to the land and the natural world is essential to a balanced outlook on life. I am very grateful that I had the opportunity to enjoy the mystery of a barn, to love a calf, to catch a lamb, to plow the earth, to feed the chickens, and to experience the miracle of growing things.

I think of my granddaughters, Alyssa, Sofia, and Paulina, as I write. I want to tell them why my generation and I are what we are. I know our perspectives on life often seem strange to them. I am not suggesting that they follow our ways; the young people are wonderful as they are. I just want to let them know that we and the generations before us did the best we could and that we think our lives were meaningful and wholesome. I am often bewildered by the great new world opening up to our granddaughters and their contemporaries, but even though I am at times apprehensive about the future, I am happy for them and wish them well. One thing, however, I would ask of them: remember that all things have their roots in the land. The story of Section 27 exposes the roots of my granddaughters deep in the land.

The contemporary cliché "been there, done that" pretty well sums up my credentials for writing the Section 27 chronicle. I was born on this section in 1929 and have resided on the same farmstead all of my life. On the east half of the section I know each pothole, every alkali spot, and every tree intimately, having cultivated or mowed every square rod of earth and having either planted, nurtured, or trimmed every tree. Hundreds of acres of golden wheat rippling in the wind, blizzards, storms, and floods sweeping over the land, sweaty farmers laboring under the hot sun, and children walking to school down a country road are memories I want to share with you.

For the early years of the century, and even back to the arrival of the Mennonite emigrants, I claim a direct connection with folks who were there. Grandmother Maria Penner made the trek from Russia to Kansas at age fifteen in 1874, and at the turn of the century, she and husband David were the first couple to reside on the Section 27 Penner farmstead. I knew her for twenty-six years. My father, Frank, was born on this farmstead in 1899 and lived here for sixty years. He and my mother, Bertha, both lived to the age of ninety-nine, and both were a source of information.

I want to thank my compadres at Jerry's Café (formerly Ruthie's) for all the information and confirmation I gleaned from them: George Plett, age eighty-seven, grew up north of Section 27 on a hill overlooking the wetlands. Ben Willems, age ninety-two, farmed in the Section 27 vicinity and tells vivid Depression stories. George Becker, age ninety, and his family emigrated from Russia after World War I. They helped my folks at harvest time when I was a little boy. Dave Balzer, age eighty-three and a second cousin to me, grew up on the west half of Section 27. John R. Pauls, age seventy-eight, is a neighbor from across the road.

I've had breakfast at Jerry's three times a week for several years with these gentlemen, and I thank them for being patient with me as I repeatedly led the conversation back to threshing machines and old tractors, dust storms and the Depression. I mention their ages because it's important; theirs is the last generation to have had firsthand contact with the original settlers of the prairie lands. Their recall of old times and their continued vitality amaze me.

Three books have been especially helpful: *The Peter Lohrentz Family, 1811–1980,* by Solomon Lepke Lowen; *A Centennial History of Inman;* and *1888–1988, A Centennial History, Buhler, Kansas.* These books confirmed and expanded my knowledge of family and local history. Geological information was gleaned from Rex Buchanan's book, *Kansas Geology,* the U.S. Department of Agriculture's *Soil Survey of McPherson County, Kansas,* and over fifty years of association with well drillers and conservation technicians. The McPherson County Engineering Department graciously provided the original survey data of Superior Township.

It was my original intention to write the story of the land itself unencumbered by personal history, but I soon discovered that one cannot tell the real story of the land without involving its people and their values. In this book, I prefer to use a broad definition of land that includes all of its flora, fauna, and the weather elements. Thus, in a sense the people are a part of the land, albeit a temporal part. The last word, of course, must come from Section 27. It was here, in some form, long before we who claim to possess it ever drew our first breath, and it will outlive all its future denizens. I have enjoyed my brief sojourn on Section 27.

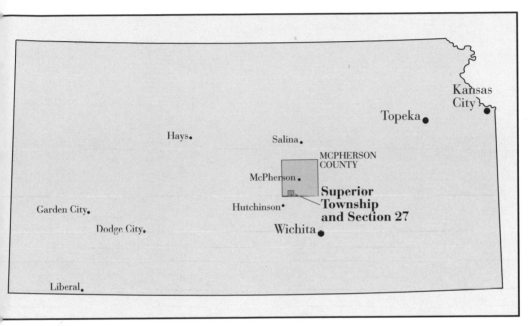

State of Kansas, McPherson County, Superior Township, and Section 27.

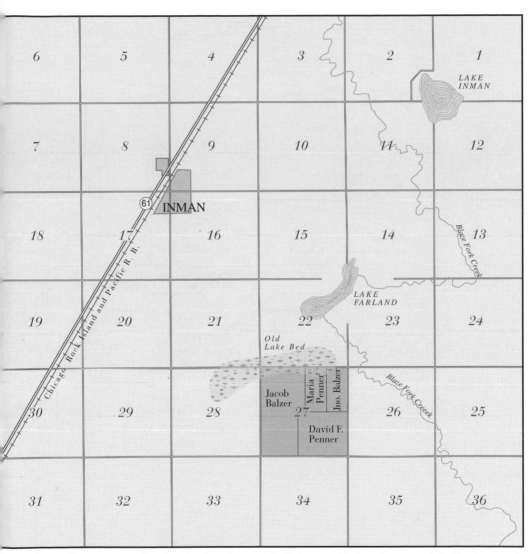

6	5	4	3	2	1
					LAKE INMAN
7	8	9	10	11	12
	INMAN (61)	16	15	14	
18	17	16	15	14	13
19	20	21	22	23	24
				LAKE FARLAND	
30	29	28	27	26	25
31	32	33	34	35	36

Old Lake Bed

Jacob Balzer *Maria Penner* *Jno. Balzer*

David F. Penner

Chicago Rock Island and Pacific R. R.

Blaze Fork Creek

Map redrawn from a 1903 atlas showing locations of the Penner and Balzer homesteads in Section 27 of Superior Township, the town of Inman, Lake Inman, Blaze Fork Creek, Old Lake Bed, and the Chicago, Rock Island, and Pacific Railroad (with state highway K-61 added).

1 🌿 Seeds

For a hundred years of summers, Penner children have picked delicious fruit from Section 27's mulberry grove, staining lips, bare feet, and clothes a deep purple, while generations of mothers sitting out on a porch stemming string beans or shelling peas have exchanged confidences and dreams as they worked. And out in the fields, Penner plowmen have for a century alternately praised and cursed the land's heavy gumbo. Heedless of this temporal intrusion of humanity, great blue herons, symbols of antiquity, sweep majestically, as they always have, over prairie or fruited plain.

Section 27 in McPherson County, Kansas, has been occupied by the Penner family since 1874, when my great-grandfather, David Penner, bought the southeast quarter from the Santa Fe Railroad. For more than a century, this farm in southern McPherson County has been ours to "have dominion over," in the biblical phrasing, per the deed to the land. Bit by bit, virgin prairie and pristine wetlands have been appropriated for the Penner family's home and livelihood. My father, Frank, was born on Section 27 in 1899 and lived there for sixty-one years. For the last seventy years it has been my home as well.

A 1900 photograph in a family album shows Grandpa David F. Penner (there are many Davids in the family) and Grandma Maria in front of a Queen Anne house surrounded by a neat white picket fence. My father is in Grandma's arms, and his older brother, David L., is standing between my grandparents. (Older siblings Peter, Sarah, and Elizabeth are not in the picture.) Though it's not a formal photograph, Grandpa is wearing a suit with a vest and tie. His coat is open, his cap set rakishly, his stance cocky. With his hands in his pockets and his eyes — squinting in the sunlight — looking straight ahead, he appears confident and unafraid. Maria looks

David F. Penner, wife, Maria, and sons,
David L. and Frank, about 1900.

smug and happy. The house — with its fish-scale gables and lattice ornaments, porches supported by turned columns with fanlike brackets,
spindled railings, and shutters — bespeaks prosperity. A cornerstone (which
is still on the farm) is dated 1898, actually denoting a major addition rather
than the original construction. (On a nearby limestone rock, Grandpa had
chiseled his initials — D.F.P. — in a bold, fluid script.) In the background
is an orchard.

My grandparents' private paradise, whether or not they knew it as such,
would soon be transformed by the outside world's swift and forceful
intrusion. Within a few years, gone would be the grapes on the vine and
the horses grazing in the lake pasture. During the exuberant conversion of
the erstwhile Great American Desert into the Breadbasket of the World,
mammoth steel machines would rip the grass and clear the marshes. A
Rambler would replace the carriage in the barn, and a pair of sonorous,
stuttering telephone rings — one long, one short — would summon the
Penners to talk with their neighbors electronically rather than face to face.

Overtaking Section 27 and its people was a world of accelerating change,
but the advance was intertwined with threads of the past — geological, geo-
graphical, religious, romantic, and technological — ambition, disaster,
and even royal attention. The fabric of history in Section 27, as in count-
less other prairie communities, is the seamless joining of past and present.

🌾 OLD LAKES AND BUFFALO GRASS

There is no recorded or apparent evidence of human activity
on Section 27 before surveyors arrived in 1860. No doubt Native Americans and trail scouts had set foot here, but wetlands to the north probably served to isolate the area. What the surveyors found as they drew
the section's perimeter was grassland on the southeast triangle and
marshes in the northwest corner. Being in a transition zone — from tall-
grass to mixed-grass prairie — the land gave forth various types of
grasses according to weather cycles. During prolonged drought, shorter
grasses like buffalo grass and grama grass flourished. Conversely, with
normal (about twenty-eight inches a year) or excessive rainfall, mixed
prairie grasses such as little bluestem, wheat grasses, and even tall prairie grasses — big bluestem, switch grass, and Indian grass — thrived in

Cornerstone from the David F. Penner house on Section 27.

the upland, and prairie cord grass (commonly slough grass) grew in the lowland. Sedges and bulrushes surrounded the shallow marshes. Shallow streams meandered through the section, emptying into the wetlands.

As a young boy in the 1930s, I was responsible for bringing the cattle home from the pasture in the evening, and I recall that the thirty-five-acre unbroken meadow abounded in buffalo grass, not the tall grasses generally ascribed to this area. The buffalo grass was struggling for survival with encroaching common ragweed and something we called wiregrass. No doubt, overgrazing had given the shorter grasses an advantage over the tall grasses.

Our pasture was also pitted with buffalo wallows — irregular depressions about eight to ten inches deep, each covering an area about as long and wide as an automobile. At the time I thought buffalo wallows were ancient history, not realizing that when my ancestors arrived in 1874, the animals (properly called bison) were still being hunted in Kansas. Fanciful stories are told of excursion trains from the East bringing "gentleman" hunters to kill buffalo simply for entertainment, shooting them from trains and leaving them to rot. Whether the story is true or not, someone killed the bison to near extinction by the 1880s.

Columbus Delano, the U.S. secretary of the interior, wrote in his 1873 annual report, "I would not seriously regret the total disappearance of the buffalo from our western prairies, in its effect on the Indians, regarding it as a means of hastening their dependence upon products of the soil and their labors." Historian Robert Richmond writes, "The military and a great many settlers thought the disappearance of the buffalo would mean the disappearance of the Indians, and that is one reason why the slaughter of the animals continued unchecked" (*Kansas: A Land of Contrasts,* p. 141).

It seems that the old prairie still lies sleeping just below the surface. When any of the higher ground — odd corners, ditches, or dikes — is removed from cultivation for ten years or so, a succession of weeds, prairie grasses, and prairie flowers *(forbs)* emerge, ending with buffalo grass, cord grass, bluestem, common milkweed, coreopsis, and Pennsylvania smartweed. After a farmer in the vicinity had his one-hundred-year-old farmhouse lifted from its foundation and moved, buffalo grass greened up the following spring where the house had been. Though prairie flowers were undoubtedly also abundant once, few of the old-timers mention them, probably having regarded them as weeds.

Because the area is so flat, the entire section seems to be at the bottom of the Blaze Fork Valley, varying only five feet in elevation (from 1,440 to 1,445 feet above sea level) except in the southwest corner, where the land abruptly rises to 1,454 feet. A 1903 McPherson County atlas shows part of an "Old Lake Bed" in the northern side of the section and Farland Lake another half-mile north — historically part of a chain of shallow lakes running south from McPherson through Reno, Harvey, and Sedgwick counties.

When Dad was a youngster, in the early 1900s, the Penners called their portion of Section 27's wetlands — about forty marshy acres with a shoreline that contracted and expanded according to rainfall — the "lake pasture." The lake, disdaining manmade rectilinear boundaries, occupied parts of four sections and covered about 145 acres.

Located along the Central Flyway (a major migratory bird route), the chain of lakes was a haven for waterfowl. With migratory shore birds and game birds abundant in season, Native Americans surely used these rich hunting grounds, as did hunting parties from the East once the railroad reached McPherson. Photographs taken in this area early in the century show hunters carrying poles from which hang hundreds of fowl. My father spoke of a "gun clubhouse" just north of Section 27, probably on the north shore of the old lake. Dad objected to what he suspected "went on" there (he disapproved of drinking alcohol and avoided people who did imbibe). Moreover, he considered sport hunting frivolous.

MAPPING THE WILDERNESS

As a legal entity, Section 27 was born, you might say, on November 4, 1860, when U.S. public land surveyors buried a sandstone rock seventeen inches long, ten inches wide, and five inches deep at what they deemed the southeast corner of Section 27. (The sandstone rock now lies under blacktop at the intersection of McPherson County's Arapaho Road and 10th Avenue.) The surveyors characterized the terrain as gently sloping prairie and the soil as second-rate. Now that this once-ungoverned tract

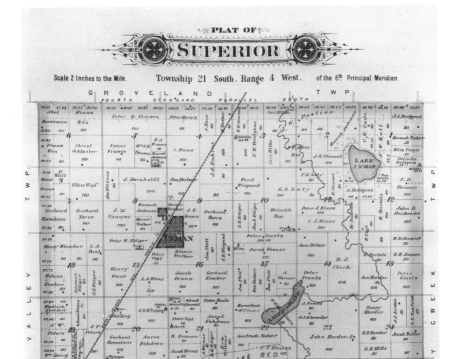

Map of Superior Township from a 1903 atlas. Courtesy of Kansas Collection, University of Kansas Libraries.

had a legal identity, it could be owned and mastered by someone with the money to buy it.

The legal description was "Section 27, Township 21 South, Range 4 West." The southeast corner is 125 miles south of the Fortieth Parallel (the Kansas-Nebraska border) and twenty miles west of the Sixth Principal Meridian. Township 21 South, Range 4 West, was named "Superior Township."

The surveyors used the system originated by Thomas Jefferson, who devised the Land Ordinance of 1785 while he was a U.S. congressman representing the state of Virginia. Previously, the claiming, selling, and buying of land had been in chaos. The 1785 ordinance designated baselines from which to survey, divided the land into townships six miles square, and subdivided each township into thirty-six sections, each section being one mile square (equivalent to about 169 square blocks in the city). Jefferson was president in 1803 when the United States purchased the Louisiana Territory, which included most of Kansas. The following year, 1804, he authorized the legendary Lewis and Clark expedition to explore the region.

Continuing north one mile (eighty surveyor's chains) on that November day in 1860 through the tall prairie grasses, the surveyors buried another rock at the place they designated the northeast corner of Section 27. Here, too, they noted that the land was gently sloping prairie but observed that this corner's soil was first-rate. (The irony of their assessment will become apparent as you read on.) Eventually they placed sandstone "monuments" on all four corners and at the half-mile points along the boundaries.

In this age of paved roads it is hard to imagine what these surveyors experienced here in 1860. Miles and miles of tall prairie grasses, usually without relief of trees on the horizon, made their little horse-drawn wagon loaded with meager supplies and monument rocks seem insignificant. No doubt a few men accompanied the wagon on saddle horses. As the wind bent and swayed the grasses like ocean waves, the men must have felt like sailors in a lifeboat at sea. On the other hand, approaching Section 27 they may have encountered a bare and ravaged plain where thousands of bison had nibbled the grass short and created a dust bowl as they wallowed in the ground to free themselves of insects. Section 27's buffalo wallows attest to that possibility.

In spite of crude instruments — a theodolite and chain — and extremes of weather (days of one-hundred degrees plus, winds up to seventy miles per hour, torrential rains, and near zero-degree blizzards are usual in Kansas), these surveyors were quite accurate, although not perfect. In the late 1970s when I was measuring land for pivot irrigation systems, I discovered where they had placed their margin of error. In Superior Township, most quarter sections measured nearly a full 160 acres as they should if you included the road on two sides, but when we measured land in the northern tier of sections, we found the north-south measurements to be considerably shorter. This adjustment allowed the surveyors to place township boundaries on the proper lines.

A few months after Section 27 was surveyed, in January 1861, Kansas became a state. The nation was on the brink of civil war. Buffalo Bill, only fourteen, was riding the Pony Express trail. People were being bought and sold even more casually than Section 27 would be bought and sold. Only six miles north of Section 27, cursing teamsters were cracking their whips over oxen and mules that pulled freight wagons along the Santa Fe Trail. On the steppes of Russia, farmers of German descent — Catholic, Lutheran, and Mennonite — were prospering. My paternal grandfather, David F. Penner, was conceived on those prairielike steppes in 1860.

🔥 MASTERS OF THE LAND

Permanent settlement in McPherson County was gradual. The Fuller ranch, founded in 1855, was a stopover on the Santa Fe Trail where it intersected the Running Turkey Creek in eastern McPherson County. Otherwise the area was virtually uninhabited by Europeans until the late 1860s, when Swedish immigrants settled in the northern part of the county. At about the same time, Civil War veterans and small groups of settlers from the East claimed land in Superior Township under provisions of the Homestead Act of 1862. Other would-be settlers were deterred by a belief that the region was uninhabitable. Lieutenant Zebulon Pike and Major Stephen Long had explored the area decades earlier and characterized it as a "desert." They considered the lands west of the Missouri River fit for cattle grazing and little else. Long and Pike predicted that the wasteland would be a permanent barrier to both eastern settlers and western intruders. An atlas published in 1822 included Long's map of the Arkannsa Territory with a bold inscription "Great Desert" across the land between the Missouri River and the Rocky Mountains. Section 27 was included in this ominous appraisal.

In my schoolroom in the 1930s, there was an old geography book that referred to the Great American Desert. I knew little of geography, so the mystique of a desert in my own state was intriguing. Little did I realize that I was living on the "desert's" eastern boundary. Presciently, the nonexistent desert's perimeter foreshadowed the 1930s Dust Bowl.

What eventually spurred mass migration into the prairie states were various acts of Congress granting vast tracts of western land to states along proposed railroad rights-of-way. The states then issued patents to railroad companies for alternate sections of land on strips up to forty miles wide as an inducement to lay track all the way to California.

To convert the land to dollars, the railroads sought purchasers who would not only buy the land but also produce freight to be shipped by rail. They saw the thousands of disenchanted German farmers in Russia as part of the solution to their dilemma, promising them rich soil, flowing streams, freedom, and unlimited potential for prosperity.

Thus it happened that Section 27, Township 21 South, Range 4 West — so recently uninhabited and uncharted — was passed from the president to explorers and surveyors, through the hands of Congress and the railroads, to nomadic farmers who spoke no English but were eager to build new lives in this free and fertile land. The real estate abstract for Section 27 details this step-by-step transaction from the United States Congress, the State of Kansas, the Atchison, Topeka, and Santa Fe, Great-grandpa David Penner, and finally down to my wife, Verna Lee, and me.

🔥 IN SEARCH OF FREEDOM

Dominion over Section 27 would have evolved very differently had it not been for Catherine the Great, czarina of Russia in the latter part of the eighteenth century, and the embattled Ukrainian-Crimean region of southwestern Russia. The area was famed for its fertile soils, and the czarina made attractive colonization offers of productive farmland and religious freedom to Catholics, Lutherans, and Mennonites in Prussia and Poland.

Mennonites, once known as Anabaptists, trace their beliefs to the Reformation led by Martin Luther in the early 1500s. Unlike the Lutherans, however, the Anabaptists practiced adult baptism, separation of church and state, and pacifism, and refused to take an oath. Though persecution by the established church included torture and martyrdom, the sect — which had originated in Switzerland — proliferated, spreading first to Holland, where Menno Simons (an erstwhile Roman Catholic priest) unified the denomination eventually named after him.

Being both pious and remarkably capable, the Mennonites found that their destiny turned on a paradox. Reputed to possess an unusually strong work ethic, to value simplicity, and to be excellent farmers, the Mennonite people were invited by kings and rulers throughout Europe to develop agricultural lands, only to be exiled on religious grounds a generation or two later. The pattern repeated itself from 1525 to 1874 in Holland, France, Germany, Poland, Prussia, and Russia as the Mennonites efficiently developed, drained, and reclaimed land, usually prospering for a time and taking their Dutch culture with them wherever they lived.

When the Russian czarina promised religious freedom and perpetual exemption from military service if the Mennonite farmers would develop the land on the steppes of southwestern Russia, they emigrated from Prussia where they had turned swamps into farmland and had enjoyed such prosperity that the powerful begrudged them their success. In the Dutch polders and in Prussia's Vistula delta, they had acquired an affinity for draining wetlands that later had great significance for Section 27.

The first difficult years in the Ukrainian-Crimean region gave way to prosperity, and the area became known as the breadbasket of Russia. Orchards and mulberry trees surrounded Mennonite villages; entrepreneurs built mills and developed machines — including a thresher in 1853 — that contributed to their productivity and prosperity; and wheat was revered almost as greatly as the Bible.

In the 1860s and 1870s, however, the historical cycle recurred and the Russian government began to renege on the promises of the czarina, long dead. Russianization of language and education, taxes, and military service threatened. So in 1874, like many other Mennonites, Lutherans, and Catholics, most of the inhabitants of the Ukrainian village of Alexanderwohl sold their possessions and began their journey to America. They traveled in two groups. One, led by Elder Jacob Buller, crossed the sea in the *Cimbria*. The other, led by Dietrich Gaeddert, traveled on the *Teutonia*. Both groups settled in Kansas, the Buller group near Goessel.

The Gaeddert group, bound for the vicinity of what would become the town of Inman, arrived in nearby Hutchinson in the middle of October 1874 after a journey of three months. Winter was approaching, and the Atchison, Topeka, and Santa Fe Railroad supplied a large immigrant house for the settlers. Some families stayed there until spring, while others hurriedly built temporary frame, adobe, or dugout houses.

LANDOWNERS

Dietrich Gaeddert was my great-grandfather; his son, David, was my maternal grandfather. In Gaeddert's entourage were David Penner and his son, my paternal grandfather, David F. Also in the group were Maria Lohrentz, who later married David F., and her parents.

McPherson County records confirm that on October 21, 1874, David Penner purchased the southeast quarter of Section 27 for the sum of $1,260 and in 1885 also bought the northeast quarter. David also bought land on Section 35, where he built his first farmstead. Exactly when the Penners came to live on Section 27 is unknown. My father told me the land was originally used as pasture and hay meadow.

Teutonia passenger Peter Balzer bought the other half of Section 27 and also half of Section 35. The original connection between the two families is unclear, but later three Penner sisters married three Balzer brothers. (The hedgerow between the two farms must have had some pretty big gaps.)

There is an old shack on the Section 27 farmstead that now sits empty and dilapidated. It was constructed with square nails, framed with full-dimension two-by-fours, and covered with drop siding and a wood-shingle roof. Its outer dimensions are ten by sixteen feet.

When I was young, Dad used the building as a shed for tractor oil and grease. One day I asked him about it — how old it was and who had built

Claim shack on SE ½, Section 27, purchased by David F. Penner in 1874.

it. He said that it once was a chicken house. Inferring from his use of the word "once" that there had been other uses, I persisted in asking about its origins. Finally he told me it had been there when the Penners bought the land in 1874, adding rather condescendingly, "Grandpa said there was just a cattle herder living there." Apparently it was something the Penners didn't like to talk about.

The State of Kansas had issued a patent for the land to the Atchison, Topeka, and Santa Fe Railroad dated April 6, 1873, which is the earliest record of ownership in the county records. But who would have bothered to build such a structure on railroad property? Distinctive characteristics of the lumber indicate that it must have been shipped in by rail. Newton would have been the nearest and earliest terminal in 1872. Could someone have claimed the land through the Homestead Act and were his rights usurped by the railroad? The shack's dimensions are those of a house required to prove up a claim, and stories have survived of "squatters" residing in the county prior to the railroad patents.

Could my father's reluctance to speak about the shack have originated in his grandfather's sense of guilt about claiming what he had bought in good faith from the Santa Fe? We'll probably never know.

🔥 PLANTING AND REAPING

Of greater consequence for the prairie than even the Mennonites' piety were the kernels of hard red winter wheat the wanderers brought from Russia. The story is that many of the immigrants had allocated precious space in their steamer trunks to meticulously sorted seeds of Turkey Red wheat. This story may be a bit of folklore as suggested by historians, but growing up in the Mennonite culture I find it almost implausible to think that they did not do so. Remembering my mother exchanging flower seeds and roots with her sister or recalling my father's telling of the immigrants bringing the mulberry seeds for trees still growing on our farm, the story seems possible. However, it is highly improbable that the minuscule quantities of wheat brought in steamer trunks could have been the basis for the hard winter wheat industry.

After its hardiness became apparent, Bernhard Warkentin, a Mennonite miller in Harvey County, imported thousands of bushels of Turkey Red for seed stock (today virtually all strains of winter wheat carry DNA from the Russian steppes). Of course, there are many other people and institutions that deserve credit for establishing wheat as a major crop in Kansas. What is important to the Section 27 story is that for over a hundred years wheat has been an almost romantic and yet a very real economic influence on the land and its people.

By the turn of the century, only twenty-six years after the settlers had arrived, the prairie's natural contours were marked by fence rows and hedgerows. Rectilinear fields of grain, straight roads with bridges across streams, neat farmsteads surrounded by shade trees and orchards, and gardens yielding produce from foreign seeds reflected the Dutch and Mennonite cultures. Domesticated creatures edged out wild ones: horses pulled plows on weekdays and buggies to church on Sundays, and docile cattle grazed over vacated buffalo wallows. Tall cottonwoods grew along Section 27's south boundary. (The last two survivors were bulldozed by a McPherson County road crew in 2000.)

In a new round of building, the simple houses, barns, schools, and churches were replaced with larger, more functional structures. A utilitarian rationale of expediency overcame the Mennonite belief that anything beyond the basics was sinful pride. Now families were larger, requiring two-story houses, and a parlor, reserved for Sundays, was viewed as a simple necessity rather than a luxury. Flourishing crops must have granaries, and more horses, cattle, pigs, sheep, chickens, geese, and ducks called for bigger barns with haymows. No wonder Grandpa David F. appears jaunty in that 1900 photograph.

At the turn of the century, steam engines — powering locomotives, stationary machinery, and a few cumbersome tractors — augured the unbelievable mechanical and technological revolution that would soon sweep the prairie lands. The pioneers never dreamed that midway through the century their proud barns would be anachronistic or that electricity, central heating, and indoor plumbing would put their showy new houses to shame.

On Section 27, the twentieth century dawned full of promise. The Penner and Balzer households had plenty of growing boys, water in the well, wheat in the bin, and sod left to break.

2 🌿 Breaking the Sod

Breaking the sod changes the land forever. When my predecessors on Section 27 broke the sod, it broke a natural cycle that had taken millennia to perfect.

After the great travail of the Ice Age, the land had finally become relatively stable. For thousands of years, Section 27 lay as a plain of silty clay in which grasses and forbs grew, died, decayed, and grew again. In the process, a thick, rich layer of humus developed, anchored by woven masses of roots reaching deep into the soil. This luxuriant biomass supported and enriched an ever-more-diverse cycle of plant and animal life, and the prairie became an immense storehouse of the sun's energy.

When David Penner and innumerable other settlers broke the sod, they tapped this energy and introduced a new element in the evolution of the prairie. For some, breaking sod was akin to a sacrament, but for most, it was a matter of getting on with the work of ensuring a livelihood and gaining prosperity.

Today, breaching land altered only by the elements is an experience unavailable to most. In the early 1980s, however, Stan and Virginia McCone built a sod house near Sanborn, Minnesota (I met them while gathering material for *Prairie: The Land and Its People*). There were many reasons behind their decision to live as their ancestors had; one of those reasons was simply to know what it had been like to live as pioneers.

"It's quite a feeling," said Stan, "plowing sod that has never had a plow in it . . . and the little flowers down there. . . . It gives you the feeling of trespassing. [The sod] just rips and cracks and pops, and it comes out in ribbons."

"We got done [building the house] in the fall," Virginia added, "and we had all kinds of little blue flowers . . . delicate little blue flowers growing out of the wall."

When I broke the last sod on Section 27 in 1959, I wasn't concerned with the ecological impact of plowing original grassland, and I doubt that Great-grandpa David ever thought about it either. He had come to America to build a home and community. For me, breaking the sod was an economic issue, but for him it was a way of life.

 IT WASN'T EASY

Because of their religious beliefs and cultural practices, David Penner and his family had left their prosperous farm and comfortable home in the Russian Ukraine, had traveled by train and steamship for months, and had finally reached the remote and comparatively desolate grassland called Kansas. The family, wintering in a communal immigrant house until after the wheat could be planted, was warm but far from comfortable.

Piecing together stories from my father and other older men who knew the immigrants firsthand and deductions made from personal experiences with the tall prairie grasses and plowing sod, the following scenario may well have occurred. On a drab October morning in 1874, David stood alone, scythe in hand, facing acres and acres of tangled prairie grasses higher than his head. This was not what he had so eagerly anticipated. On the high seas his vision of America had not included swinging a scythe at these dry, twisted grasses before him. He felt every bit of his forty-three years as he contemplated the immensity of the job ahead of him, but there was urgency in the cold wind from the north. This was no time for reflection. Already it was nearly too late to sow the Turkey Red wheat he had brought from the Ukraine.

Like the other Mennonite farmers, David had hoped to plow, harrow, and sow before the unfamiliar winter set in. They had not anticipated the dense grasses and forbs that rebuffed their walking plows. The tall prairie refused to roll under in the furrow. There was talk of burning the grass, but there was no way to control a fire once it started. David finally decided to cut a small field of grass for hay and then follow with the plow. After a few hours of backbreaking work with the scythe, he determined that a horse-drawn mower would be one of his first machinery investments. (Family records show that fellow *Teutonia* passenger Peter Lohrentz purchased a grass-mowing machine on arrival in 1874.) For several days David, his wife, Sara, and their children cut, raked, and hauled hay to the spot where the barnyard would be. As they worked, Sara observed that some of the "weeds" — Maximilian sunflowers, pitcher sage, and goldenrod — were pretty.

Days later, David stood once more in the field, now with his hands on the plow, the reins wrapped around his shoulders. This was the moment he had been waiting for as he faced a field of grass stubble and the rumps of two draft horses.

The plow was a walking plow with a ten-inch cut. Experienced though he was, plowing the sod was no simple thing for David. The horses were unfamiliar; they couldn't understand his Low Dutch "giddyap" and "whoa." They had never pulled a plow, and the roots in the sod were tough.

The prairie was so quiet he could hear the roots snap as the moldboard turned the sod into continuous ribbons. Hour after hour David followed the horses, guiding them by twisting his shoulders to put pressure on the reins. As they got used to the plow, the work took on a rhythm punctuated by creaking leather, snorting horses, and snapping roots.

While David rested the horses at the end of the field, there were other sounds to listen to, some unfamiliar, like the call of the meadowlark. Thousands of honking geese flew in giant V formations and a soaring hawk screeched, while below, monarch butterflies hovered over a milkweed and the aroma of fresh earth was strong and promising.

The earth was a problem, though. When David pulled and twisted the cut sod to break off a clod, the roots clung to the soil, refusing to separate. He resolved that the next day the entire family would work in the field to rake and pound the unyielding ribbons into a seedbed. Much work remained before even a small crop could be put into the ground.

Turkey Red and its genetic offspring have prevailed on the Kansas prairies since that first moldboard turned the sod. Small fields were broken in 1874, and more followed as manpower and horsepower permitted. Even so, my father, Frank Penner — whose earliest memories of the farm dated back to 1905 or so — talked of unbroken pasture and hay meadows with streams of clear, shallow water running slowly but constantly throughout the year.

By 1900 walking plows had been replaced by riding plows, either sulky plows (one moldboard) or gang plows (more than one moldboard). At best, one man with a gang plow and five horses could plow three or four acres a day. Since David and his son, David F., farmed without hired help except at harvest time, 160 acres would have been the most they could have had in cultivation — a fraction of the 480 acres David had bought on Sections 27 and 35.

It wasn't until the big gasoline tractors came on the scene that the Penners and the Balzers got serious about breaking all the sod on Section 27. In my father's memory, the giant plowing tractors ushered in the glory days of the Penner farm. In his latter years, no matter how the conversation started, Dad always ended up talking about the old Hart-Parr or Avery tractors. (Previously, the only self-propelled power source had been the steam tractor — cumbersome, dangerous, and expensive to operate. Although some steamers were used to plow sod, most were threshing engines.)

In 1905 or 1906, Grandpa David F. purchased a nine-and-a-half-ton 22-45 Hart-Parr tractor. (A predecessor, the 1903 Hart-Parr, is displayed at the Smithsonian Institution in Washington, D.C., as the first successful farm gasoline tractor.) David F. had the courage and foresight to see this machine's potential, and he was wise enough to understand that his boys — Peter, David L., and Frank — needed an incentive to stay on the farm. David F. had enrolled in a Hart-Parr traction-farming correspondence course in which this sincere (if naive) flight of fancy appears:

> There is a moral influence about an engine that is hard to explain. Nevertheless, it is a fact that ownership of an engine gives a man more interest and pride in his farm. The wife takes a new pride in the farm and all its work. Many a young fellow has fully made up his mind to quit the farm, but when his father bought a new tractor the boy took a new interest in the farm and its problems and stayed.

The first farm tractors were almost unbelievably crude, but in the eyes of a farm boy riding a sulky plow in July with horseflies tormenting, this breathing hunk of cast iron must have been as much excitement as a Mennonite could tolerate.

 THE SODBUSTER ARRIVES

Usually, when a new tractor was delivered to a farm, a representative from the factory arrived with it to explain its peculiarities. In 1904, even Henry Ford and the Wright brothers had only elemental knowledge of mechanical things; little wonder that low-tension magnetos and primer cups mystified farmers. The anticipation of breaking sod by just steering a tractor was powerful, but the reality of that huge machine sitting on a railroad car in Inman waiting to be unloaded must have been awesome. My father often related vivid memories about the Hart-Parr's arrival. The following description, with details from a Hart-Parr owner's manual, is an attempt to convey his enthusiasm.

There it was — cold and dead — how could anyone bring it to life? Father and sons gazed at the massive machine, each no doubt with different emotions. Peter, almost twenty, would have been exuberant, ready to grasp the one-thousand-pound flywheel and start up the tractor. David L., eleven, and Frank, seven, would have climbed and explored while their father, David F., conscious that others were watching, stepped up onto the flatcar with the expert from Charles City, Iowa.

The expert checked the fuel tanks, the water tank, the oilers, and the grease cups. Satisfied with the inspection, he opened the starting relief valve one turn, the gasoline cock, and the air cock on the side of the fuel float-cup; pressed down the float pusher until gasoline overflowed through the air cock; set the timers for late ignition; filled the priming cup with gasoline; squirted some gasoline down the air-admission pipe; set the controlling lever clear forward; and closed the battery switch. Then he turned the huge flywheel. Silence.

Once more he spun the wheel. The engine coughed and sputtered. A few more squirts of gasoline, a turn of the flywheel, and the engine boomed a few quick bursts, hissed twice, and settled into a cadence — boom, hiss, hiss, boom, hiss, hiss, boom.

David F. was in turmoil. How would he remember all those steps, and what order they went in, and then have the courage to spin the big wheel and let go if it started? Peter had read the instruction book a hundred times, hoping the expert would turn to him and say, "Well, son, it's all yours." Now the engine was making the flatcar shake, and the expert was busy closing the relief valves, advancing the timers, and closing the carburetor air cock. David F. couldn't hear a word the expert was shouting over the engine noise, but Peter and David L. were nodding in comprehension.

David F. was impatient to get the tractor unloaded, but the expert was waiting for the engine to warm up. When he thought it was warm enough and running evenly enough, he opened the kerosene cock and closed off the gasoline, explaining that it was cheaper to run kerosene. Suddenly the engine began to pound. David F. was terrified that the tractor would break up in full view of all the skeptical onlookers. Calmly the expert reached for the water-regulating valve and opened it one notch. The pounding and shaking continued. He opened it another notch; it calmed somewhat. One more notch and the engine returned to its normal cadence — boom, hiss, hiss, boom, hiss, hiss, boom.

To Peter's enormous disappointment, the expert climbed onto the operator's platform alone, shifted into forward gear, and pulled back on the control lever. With a lurch, the gears engaged and the tractor rolled forward onto the unloading ramp. When it began its descent, there was no stopping the tractor. (It would be twenty years before tractor makers considered brakes essential.) Even the expert had an anxious moment when he spun the steering wheel frantically to avert disaster. Still, the left rear wheel missed the last twelve inches of the ramp and thudded onto the soft ground. The tractor intimidated David F., and he motioned for Peter to ride with the expert during the two-and-a-half-hour drive to the farm.

The tractor had only one forward gear, and top speed was two-and-a-half miles per hour. "Reverse" was achieved by planetary gears in the belt pulley. As the tractor rolled, road dirt sifted through the huge external gears, which clanged and rumbled in protest. The engine was a horizontal cross-mount two-cylinder that turned at 280 revolutions per minute. Many early engines were distinctive for their hit-or-miss governor system. When the engine reached the appropriate rpm, the ignition switched off briefly until more power was needed, hence the boom, hiss, hiss, boom exhaust cadence. The steering, like that in earlier steam engines, was a crude chain and bolster.

Life with this giant had its ups and downs. It did indeed pull an eight-bottom plow through unbroken soil at an impressive pace, and it was ideal for fields a mile long. Plowing with this early rig was a two-man operation, one man on the tractor, another on the plow. Dad recalled that the plowman would often nap for twenty minutes while the unit chugged to the end of the field. Responsible for lifting the plow bottoms out of the ground before the tractor turned at the end of the field, the plowman would rise from the platform, walk back to the long levers, and push them down to lift the bottoms. If he was comfortable napping on a bouncing floor only two feet wide with sharp coulter disks slicing the sod just beneath, then he napped.

But getting the beast started and keeping it running was troublesome. You had to learn just how much gasoline to squirt in the primer, and the amount varied with the weather and the tractor's mood. Often the final recourse was prayer or cursing, depending on the tractor operator's religious inclination. Either method usually worked, inasmuch as it allowed time for the gasoline in the cylinders to vaporize.

Though no one realized it for years, dust was an engine's archenemy. The open air intakes were located right where the wheels kicked up the greatest amount of dust. Because neither factory nor farmer understood the problem, there were frequent, costly, and time-consuming repair jobs in the fields, where dust was ever present.

Soft spots in the fields were especially hazardous. If the heavy machine began to sink, the lugged steel wheels would dig fiercely until the tractor could stop. The Hart-Parr manual suggested chaining a post to the wheels and driving up, adding a caution not to drive too far or the post would crunch the fenders. Another remedy was for the operator to bury a "deadman" some distance ahead, attach a cable to the wheel and the deadman, and wind his way out.

 PROGRESS

The following year, the Balzers bought a newer model, a Hart-Parr 30-60. (David and Albert Balzer, third generation cousins, told me this tractor did the original grading of North Main Street in Hutchinson,

The Balzer family's 30-60 Hart-Parr tractor
plowing on Section 27 in 1908.

Kansas.) With most of the starting problems resolved and having considerably more power than its predecessor, the 30-60 was the envy of the Penners. It boasted jump-spark igniters (spark plugs), whose idiosyncrasies were described in a Hart-Parr correspondence course:

> Let us suppose we have a conductor with a gap in it which can not be entirely closed. That gap of air is a regular gate. An ordinary current can no more get across than can an ordinary cow jump or smash through a high plank gate. But when a very high-tension current comes along it will smash right through that gap of air like a mad bull would go through the plank gate.

The writing style may have been rustic, but Grandpa knew what it meant.

A thorough knowledge of a plow was important also. A plow bottom has numerous components. The cutting edge and point are the *share.* The *moldboard* above the share turns the soil over; the *landside* rides against the furrow wall; and the *frog* is another name for the plow bottom's framework. The shares, experiencing the greatest amount of wear, needed frequent attention. A set of shares lasted barely a day, so every day the plowman replaced the shares and took the used set to a blacksmith, who heated them to cherry red and then beat the cutting edge to a fine point with a hammer (later a trip hammer). Blacksmiths were prized in wheat country, and farmers depended on them to keep things running smoothly. Their work required great strength and skill. A 1901 Kingman Implement catalog, for example, advised farmers to make certain the blacksmith heated the plowshares to cherry red, but not beyond. Until 1887, Section 27 had its own blacksmith, who lived and worked in the tiny village of Farland on the southwest corner. (In 1887, Farland's buildings were moved four miles north to Aiken, later named Inman.)

By the end of World War I, most of the sod had been plowed in McPherson County, with the exception of some wetlands and pastures used for livestock. Farms were highly diversified until the 1950s and early 1960s when they became more focused on intense specialized enterprises. Until midcentury most farms had a mix of livestock and poultry, requiring pastures, hay, and feed crops. Horses were on the decline after tractors became common.

In 1959, I finished the job my great-grandfather had started eighty-five years earlier. My wife, Verna Lee, and our three small children lived in our own little house on Mom and Pop's farm. We were happy, but money was scarce, and most of the farmers in the area were trying to squeeze more money out of their land by converting pastures to wheat fields. I didn't like milking cows, so I was easily persuaded.

On our thirty-five acre pasture, buffalo wallows were still visible, and paths cut by the hooves of cattle and sheep radiated from the bridge where the animals entered every morning. Our little boy, Murray, loved these dusty, crooked trails, running his heart out, fearless, in spite of his grandma's concern about his safety with the sheep buck being in the pasture.

I don't remember whether I consulted Dad first, but one day I started plowing the remaining sod with our M Farmall tractor and three-bottom plow. The furthest thing from my thoughts was the significance of obliterating virgin sod. I was too busy admiring the way my plow turned the ribbons of earth, contemplating the challenge of preparing a seedbed among the clinging roots, and imagining the black soil as bushels of wheat in the bin. The plow pulled much harder than usual because the roots held the soil so tightly, so I shifted the tractor to low gear (still moving much faster than the Hart-Parr). My mind on the work and the potential income, I sliced heedlessly through wallows and paths until Murray came into view, running on his beloved paths one last time, tears streaming down his face.

I subjugated the last of the sod on Section 27, except for one small triangle. Less than half an acre remains, and I guard it zealously.

3 🍃 Wetlands

Section 27, now fertile farmland, once lay beneath an ancient sea. Eons later, when the ocean had long since evaporated, a river flowed there. Then the river, too, was gone, but it left behind an underground lake and a marshy wilderness. The sea and its legacy — aquifer and marshland — drew the destiny of Section 27 with greater force than the dogged efforts of farmers, politicians, or developers. Call that force what you will — God or physics — it has challenged, outwitted, and rewarded those who made Section 27 their home.

🍃 ANCIENT INHERITANCE

Before the age of the dinosaurs, more than two hundred million years ago, the area in which Section 27 lies was a great inland sea. When the sea evaporated, it left a thick salt bed, four hundred feet deep in places. For millennia, winds and rivers deposited minerals and soils over the salt, forming a new landscape.

On that archaic terrain, the Smoky Hill River, rising in Colorado, turned south and flowed through what is now McPherson County into the Arkansas River. Section 27 lay in the Smoky Hill River Valley until, a million years ago or more, floods diverted the river northeastward to join the Kansas River system. Alluvial and windborne debris eventually covered the old valley south of the new channel, but a watercourse survived underneath — as the Equus Beds — and on the surface — as the McPherson Valley Wetlands. (Equus is the Latin word for horse. The Equus Beds were named for fossilized horse bone fragments found in core drilling samples.)

OLD LAKE

When federal surveyors established Section 27 in 1860, the south-eastern two-thirds was prairie and the northwestern part was wetland. On early maps, the wetland — straddling the intersection of Sections 21, 22, 27, and 28 — was called "Old Lake Bed." Furthermore, Old Lake was a link in a chain of lakes and marshes extending south from two larger lakes north-west of McPherson, the Big Basin and the Little Basin. Old Lake was about thirteen miles south of the Big Basin, and more lakes dotted the country-side all the way to what is now the city of Wichita.

In wet years Old Lake was two to four feet deep, but there was very little open water. Aquatic plants crowded in from all sides, and sedges and bul-rushes pushed toward the center. American lotus, with its large umbrella-like leaves, pale yellow flowers, and nutty fruit, seemed to float on the ponds it inhabited. Surrounding the lake and its profuse vegetation was a dense perimeter of cord grass. Meandering shallow streams from the up-lands replenished the lake throughout the year.

I like to imagine Section 27 as it must have been when it lay undisturbed for centuries. Spring and summer rains would turn the wetlands glisten-ing green, the wind sweeping over the prairie, raising and bending the grasses, each wave chasing another unimpeded by fences or plowmen. In the fall, green would give way to amber as frost sent plant nutrients underground. Then the muted autumn colors would yield to wintry white, and savage blizzards would subdue the faded grasses. Meanwhile the little prairie creatures — mice, muskrats, beavers, mink, and more — would sleep snug and secure under their blanket of snow, tangled grass, and earth.

When the lake was frozen and snow-covered, there would be silence, broken occasionally by the scream of an eagle or the call of a coyote. If the winter was dry and mild with ice seldom covering the water, geese would return to feed in the wetlands.

In early spring, thousands of migrating waterfowl — whooping cranes, sandhill cranes, pelicans, blue-winged teal, mallards, giant Canada geese, and shorebirds of all kinds — used Old Lake and the surrounding ponds and marshes as a stopover en route to their breeding grounds far to the north. Larger animals, too, were populous — bison, elk, antelope, wolves, coyotes, bobcats, mountain lions, and even grizzly bears, though there were few deer.

At daybreak, as mist rose from the water, a redwing in the rushes would gurgle "o-ka-lay." More voices would join the chorus — geese rising noisily off the water and a jackrabbit's cry as a coyote made its last catch of the night. Soon a meadowlark would pipe and a muskrat would splash. Midmorning clouds would portend thunder and rain. A sandpiper, just arriving from Argentina, would trill its delightful song.

⚜ FIRE AND STORM

Life for the resident prairie fauna was often difficult and dangerous. Temperature extremes, drought, and mosquitoes were annual hardships to be endured, but tornadoes, hail, floods, and fires could be devastating.

Fire was both a blessing and a curse. The Native Americans set fires, as a cultural practice, to remove the smothering grass residue and promote the growth of early grass in the spring. They may also have used fire to flush out bison and to fight enemies.

The prairie was vulnerable to fires set by dry thunderstorms. Lightning could easily find a target among thousands of acres of dry grass. On the other hand, without fires there would have been no prairie; the impending forests would have advanced unimpeded.

To prairie people — settlers, travelers, and Indians — fire was a fearsome thing. To be caught in its path was terrifying. Tall, dry grasses are easily ignited, and a grass fire generates its own momentum. Sucking up air, it creates a draft that propels the flames over land faster than a human can run. Fingers of fire, actually burning leaves, point to the sky and reach over unburned terrain to ignite another conflagration.

⚜ DREAMING OF DRY GROUND

When David Penner and Peter Balzer arrived in October 1874, they never imagined how the salt beds and the subterranean water would both vex and enrich their community. For them, the land promised lush pastures and acre after acre of wheat. They envisioned prosperous farmland dotted with homes, schools, and churches.

As Penner and Balzer inspected their wetland real estate at the north end of Section 27 for the first time, they were surprised, almost shocked, by the tough slough grass rising above their heads. Wiry panicles clawed at their faces as they breasted their way through the tangle — stumbling, surging, and stumbling again as the dense undergrowth tugged at their feet. They quickly learned why the grass, with its serrated edges, was called ripgut. "Yankee" farmers had told them, however, that if mowed early in the season, slough grass would make fine hay and that it was good roofing material for sod houses.

At Old Lake, among the bulrushes and sedges, the farmers saw long-legged shorebirds pushing their bills into the muddy lake bottom, but the men's thoughts were elsewhere. Before them was a challenge like the one their forefathers had confronted before transforming Prussian marshes into farmland. "We will drain this water," David Penner and Peter Balzer resolved.

🌿 WHOSE WATER?

The Penners and the Balzers prospered, though the wetlands remained. By the turn of the century, David F. Penner was managing the east half of Section 27, and his brother-in-law, Jacob Balzer, farmed the west half. They built bigger, better houses and barns than their fathers had built, and they plowed more sod. They used the slough grass (more accurately, prairie cord grass) for pasture hay, but the dream of draining those provoking marshes endured.

About a half-mile north of Section 27, on the shores of Lake Farland, the McPherson and Inman gun clubs had built clubhouses and boathouses and had set up a windmill. McPherson hotels brought hunters in from Kansas City by train and organized excursions for them. The hunting around Lake Farland was considered the best in the valley. In an old newspaper article, Hugh Riddell, an old-timer in the area, recalls how two hunters went out to the lake, each with two double-barreled shotguns. Each man fired his guns once, and they picked up ninety-six ducks. Market hunters shot game by the thousands and shipped the fowl east in barrels. The Mennonite elders, all teetotalers, feared the influence of all these "English" strangers and suspected that liquor was being consumed on the club premises — another reason to drain the marshes.

As the Penners and Balzers dreamed of plowing the wetlands, a Harvey County entrepreneur from Alta Mills was taking action. John Schrag, the son of a Swiss Mennonite miller, had his eye on draining the two-thousand-acre Big Basin, and he started buying land in the area in 1901. Eleven years later he began the drainage project, unconcerned about its consequences for Section 27 some thirteen miles downstream on Blaze Fork Creek.

A fifteen-foot ridge impeded the outflow from Big Basin into the Blaze Fork. Using an elevating grader pulled by a steam tractor, Schrag built terraces above the basin to intercept water headed toward it. He succeeded in diverting the runoff from about twenty thousand acres into the Blaze Fork Creek before it entered the Big Basin. But digging through the fifteen-foot ridge to drain the basin itself was too big a job for the grader. In 1916 Schrag built his own steam shovel, making the wheels out of cottonwood logs and using a boiler shipped in from the East. The unit was propelled by a block-and-tackle system anchored to a hedge-post deadman.

Soon water was running directly from the Big Basin into Blaze Fork Creek.

🌿 MAN AND MACHINE VERSUS NATURE

Schrag's project, of course, caused great consternation downstream. Adding more then twenty thousand acres to the Blaze Fork watershed created a potential flood problem. The downstream farmers, midway between the Big Basin and just north of the Mennonite settlement, formed Drainage District No. 1 and took legal action, fighting their battle all the way to the Kansas Supreme Court, but losing. In self-defense, they widened channels and built protective dikes, worsening the situation for their neighbors even farther downstream.

In 1919 professional engineers drew up plans for Drainage District No. 2, a comprehensive channelization, drainage, and diking project in the Section 27 vicinity. Section 27's David F. Penner and Jacob Balzer were heavily involved in this project. In 1920 canals and dikes were built in order to control flooding — an ultimately unsuccessful effort, at least during unusually wet years. (The flooding problem has never really been solved. Every once in a while, in Brigadoon fashion, Lake Farland and Old Lake reappear, and the people in hilltop Inman once more see the shimmering waters of the wetlands in the early morning light.)

Meanwhile, Penner and Balzer had begun their own drainage projects. Their large tractors, used for plowing the sod, were also ideal for pulling elevating graders to make ditches, roads, and dikes. A road and bridge were built through Old Lake in the northwest forty acres of Section 27. (The bridge is still there, high and dry, in a wheat field.)

David F. had replaced the old Hart-Parr tractor with a model 40-80 Avery tractor, a ponderous twenty-two-thousand-pound hunk of iron. The drive wheels were taller than a man. The Avery's highly touted features included an opposed four-cylinder "Draft Horse" motor and a sliding-frame two-speed transmission. To shift the huge exposed gears, the operator had to slide the engine in the frame with a long lever. Advertisements vaunted the exposed gears' advantages, one being that problems were easy to spot and repair before they grew serious. "Many young boys and girls can run Avery Tractors," boasted the ads.

Armed with determination and powerful equipment, the Penners and the Balzers drained Old Lake into the new drainage canals built by District No. 2. Soon fields of wheat, oats, and barley replaced most wetlands.

In the process of draining the wetlands, the original Blaze Fork Creek was channelized — deepened and straightened — and dikes were built to contain excess water. The project was controversial in the community, and the peace-loving Mennonites were drawn into angry confrontations and lawsuits. The dikes were especially irksome. When they failed, as they often did, they created hardship at stress points. When they stood, high water flooded previously unaffected land downstream. The height and stability of the dikes were hotly contested. Many district meetings opened with prayer and degenerated into strife just short of fisticuffs.

🔥 PUNCTURING THE PRAIRIE

By 1929 Frank was the master of the Penner domain. I was born that year, Frank and Bertha having been married in 1928. The Great Depression loomed, but in McPherson County oil was booming. During my childhood, when the family drove to church on Sunday mornings, we'd see

Penner's 40-80 Avery tractor pulling one of the excavators
that dug drainage ditches on Section 27 in the early 1920s.

a forest of oil derricks on the eastern horizon. Section 27 was never endowed with an oil well, but the test drilling here brought problems of its own.

It was the ancient layer of salt, three hundred feet underground, that caused the trouble. To locate oil, workers drilled small holes reaching into the salt layer, dropped explosives into them, and detonated the explosives. By analyzing the recorded echoes, oil explorers could gauge the potential for profitable oil production. Drillers located the test holes on the corners of sections when they suspected oil might be present. Unfortunately, the core holes on the northeast and northwest corners of Section 27 and on all four corners of Section 22 admitted enough water to dissolve portions of the salt bed, creating unstable caverns and ultimately producing sinkholes. The oil explorers denied responsibility, but the patterns here and elsewhere in Superior Township were conclusive.

One day, maybe in 1935, when we were out riding in the family's maroon Chevy, Pop and Mom were talking about the sinkhole problem. As we made the uphill grade on the northeast corner of the section and crossed a little bridge there, it was easy to see why they were upset. The sinking of the land was obvious at this spot — the corner that the 1860 surveyors had declared first-rate land. In 1920, Drainage District No. 2 cut a drainage canal through the hill at this intersection, and now there was a growing pond on the west side of the road where the oil explorers had drilled.

Pop mentioned Uncle John's proposal to pump out the water, find the core hole, and plug it. Pop approved the idea, but Mom thought it was "foolishness" (probably because Uncle John had thought of it). Nevertheless, the plan went forward. Cofferdams were built, a pump set, and a hole dug — all to no avail. The landmark became known as the Big Sinkhole. Almost as large was the Little Sinkhole, a mile west on Section 27's northwest corner.

During the ensuing ten years, the sinkhole grew dramatically. The little bridge on the hill, and the hill itself, dropped into a seven-acre depression. The bridge railings barely poked out of the water. Drainage District No. 2 sought to contain the area by building dikes around it, but every two or three years a larger circle of dikes was needed to surround the expanding depression.

The continued sinking was a big problem for Pop and other farmers because the system of dikes designed to protect their farmland often failed when the Blaze Fork and Big Basin watersheds received a lot of rain. One low spot in the dikes would defeat the system. To make matters worse, the sinkholes were too deep to drain via drainage channels.

THE INVISIBLE STREAM

A more manageable water source was the derelict Smoky Hill River channel known as the Equus Beds, but it wasn't until the 1950s that farmers understood the irrigation potential of this underground river. Wells one hundred to two hundred feet deep yield water at one thousand gallons per minute, enough to irrigate a quarter section (160 acres) of farmland. Where wheat had been the principal crop, irrigation made corn, with its much higher yield potential, the crop of choice.

The Equus Beds proved unique in their ability to replenish themselves. The Ogallala Aquifer in western Kansas and most other underground water sources are not rechargeable, but the flowing underground Equus Beds absorb rainfall from their watershed. Though not infinite, the water supply in the Equus Beds can be managed to balance supply and demand. The city of Wichita, fifty miles southeast of Section 27, relies heavily on Equus Bed water.

Abundant underground water, like oil, was localized in the area, however. Would-be irrigation farmers soon discovered that some had it and most didn't. Only a narrow margin of land on the east side of Section 27 has water available in irrigation quantities. At present, the northeast quarter of Section 27 is under irrigation.

SATURATION POINT

In the midfifties, Section 27's eighty-year Penner-Balzer dynasty started to erode. Fourth-generation heirs sought livelihoods beyond the farm, and names like Schmidt, Klassen, and Ediger began to appear on the abstracts. I took up the ancestral calling to develop and drain, subjecting land in McPherson, Reno, and Harvey counties to bulldozers and earth movers, practicing soil conservation, and developing the land to its maximum agricultural potential.

Growling, smoking diesels and clanking steel tracks were the tools my helpers and I used to terrace, clear, and level the land. The decrepit claim shack on our Section 27 farmstead housed barrels and barrels of oil, grease, and supplies for the tractors and trucks departing daily to the job sites. When we had squeezed the land dry, the McPherson Valley Wetlands were no more.

Like my Dutch dike-building forebears, I felt a great sense of accomplishment when dry land emerged from my efforts. In southeastern Reno County, a speculator, who had purchased forty marshy acres for a song, asked me to drain the land. No problem. Three hours of work with a crawler tractor and a pull scraper, and the water was running into the channelized Blaze Fork. The speculator was delighted. A "worthless haven" for ducks, geese, and turtles had tripled in value, and all it cost him was one hundred dollars for tractor time.

Ironically, it was the bulldozer that aroused my sensitivity to the natural world. Years ago, while I was digging into the embankment of a salt-water disposal pit, a mother badger attacked my dozer with courage and ferocity in defense of her den. Undaunted by her massive opponent, she bit into the steel. Nearby, slimy muskrats and snapping turtles the size of basketballs tried to hide in the cord-grass perimeter, and redwings screamed from their homes among the cattails as my tractor forced them into a wheat field.

For a while these furry, hard-shelled, or feathered creatures were mere diversions as I built ponds, terraces, and shopping-center parking lots. But gradually I learned their identities, observed their habits, and appreciated their resilience. I began to enjoy and even sympathize with them. Newly aware that the mother badger was crying for her young, the redwings were angry, and even the stoic turtles grieved when I drove them from the marsh, I began to question my species' right of eminent domain.

4 🖋 Lake Valley

Lake Valley School, as most people remember it, was nowhere in the vicinity of either a lake or a valley — which just goes to show how reality and memory don't always agree.

It was a hot day in August 1874 when a few people gathered in the Farland Post Office on the southwest corner of Section 27 to organize and name a school for District 67. Mandated by law, the meeting was an irksome task for the handful of busy settlers and hunters living in the district.

The school was to be near Farland. The county school superintendent, who was at the meeting, suggested choosing a name that identified a local landmark, as other county schools — Pleasant Ridge, Prairie View, Little Valley, and Happy Hollow, for example — had done.

The settlers were probably in no mood to argue. More than likely, one farmer or another spoke up: "I see a lake, what do you see Jed?" and Jed, catching the drift, might have replied, "That sure is a lake, and I see a valley." All that was left was for a third district citizen to shout, "Done. Lake Valley it is. Saddle up, boys." And in 1874, from the slight rise on Section 27's southwest corner, the settlers could indeed see Old Lake shimmering under the August sun less than a mile north and, to the east, the broad, ill-defined Blaze Fork Valley.

The school didn't remain in Farland for long, however, because it was too far from the east side of the district for children to walk. In 1878 the Lake Valley schoolhouse was moved one mile east, to the southeast corner of Section 27. Eight years later the school moved again — another half mile east — to its final location. Here the lake was out of sight, and the valley was indistinguishable under cottonwoods, hedgerows, orchards, and farmsteads. The final ironic affront to the name occurred in the early 1900s, when the Old Lake was drained.

At the turn of the century, Lake Valley was one of a multitude of one-room schools spread across the plains. Determining a district's size was simple: schoolchildren should walk no more than two and a half miles if they "went around the road"; the distance was shorter if they "cut across the field." Students from eight sections walked or skipped; rode horses, buggies, or bicycles; or were on occasion carried through sunshine, rain, or snow to Lake Valley.

My uncle, Peter Penner, was in the class of 1903 — the first class to graduate from Lake Valley School. In those days, the land preempted education; children were needed to work on the farm, which is probably why there were no earlier graduates. Even when school terms were only five or six months long, young people stayed home when there was work to do. By 1926 Lake Valley had a seven-month school year, and later, when I attended school there, the school year spanned almost eight months, September into mid-April.

Mennonite settlers soon were in the majority, not only in District 67 but also in large portions of McPherson, Reno, Harvey, and Marion counties. Even so, the Mennonites feared, just as they had in Russia, the undermining of their closed community with its language and structure. The environment in the United States was unique for the Mennonites. Historically, their migrations had taken them to isolated regions where their autonomy was encouraged. In the United States, however, the Mennonites had purchased most of their land from the railroads, which owned only alternate sections along the right-of-way. Between the railroads' forty-mile-wide checkerboard blocks were lands that, according to the Homestead Act, were open to settlers who could "prove up" their claims — and those settlers tended not to be Mennonites.

Thus, much of what the Mennonites had found objectionable in Russia was equally problematic in the United States, or more so. It would prove to be more difficult, in this country, to control their education, community mores, and native language. Schools and townships in central Kansas had been organized just before the immigrants' arrival in October 1874.

Lake Valley School's 1908 student body and teacher.
Frank Penner is second from the left in the front row.

English language schools and churches of other denominations already had a foothold, and roads and bridges were in the public domain.

In the early pioneer days, some Mennonite groups conducted German-speaking schools in private homes in the Inman/Buhler vicinity. Few survived into the twentieth century. Dietrich Gaeddert taught German-speaking classes in his home for some time, but this apparently was not a long-term effort since he served on the Union school board prior to his death in 1900. Lake Valley and some other public schools offered a three-week German language school every spring until the early 1930s.

Located near the Hoffnungsau Church, the Hoffnungsau Preparatory School offered secondary level classes in German with a gradual transition to English by the time it closed in 1929. This school started in 1907. The curriculum centered on religious education and included history and mathematics.

🌿 NEW WORLDS

The women and men who taught in the isolated one-room schools were genuine heroes. They arrived early to light the stoves and stayed late, leaving only after their janitorial work was done, the blackboards cleaned, and offending "after-schoolers" had been sent home. Not only did they teach eight grades, but they also often taught students much bigger and stronger than they were — reluctant pupils who saw absolutely no value in education.

My father wasn't much of a writer, but in 1979 he put on paper his recollections about his first year in Lake Valley School — 1904. He mentions that the teacher prayed and they all sang to start the school day. Discipline was the rule. "When the teacher called for the first grade to come forward to recite, the students picked up their work; on the count of one they turned their knees into the aisle, on two they stood up, and on three they marched to the front," my father wrote.

There was another side to discipline, however. A neighbor recalls that, during his grade-school days in the 1920s, a young female teacher had such a hard time contending with recalcitrant farm boys that the school board ended the term early and hired a man to regain control. On the first day of the new session, the big boys took one look at their new teacher, a small mild man, and snickered, eager to renew their mischief. They tested the teacher with all manner of misconduct, but the little man just carried on, seeming not to notice. Finally the boys jumped out the windows and ran away.

The next morning the boys arrived late, whooping it up until they saw the teacher's piercing eyes riveted on them. Uneasily they glanced at each other. Deliberately, the teacher rose from his chair. "Boys, I have something to show you," he said, reaching under the desk and pulling out a pistol. "We may have to shoot a couple of you," he added calmly, "but we will have discipline!" The rest of the school year was uneventful.

More typical may have been my school days during the Depression and the early 1940s. One Monday, when I was six (I know it was a Monday because the washing machine was running), Mom dressed me in new overalls, combed my hair, gave me a black lunch pail to carry, and took me outside just as an older girl with a long pigtail wrapped around her head came through the mulberry hedge. I knew her slightly. She was Rosella Balzer, a seventh-grader, who lived with her folks on the west half of Section 27. Mom simply told me to go with her. Rosella grasped my little hand and we walked to the road. I wanted to run home, but Rosella's grip was firm.

At the road we met another girl and a boy on a bicycle. Farther down the road we met two older boys. This was beginning to be exciting. Finally we arrived at a big white house with lots of children playing on swings, a merry-go-round, and a teeter-totter. I'd never seen so many children having fun. A young woman came out of the house carrying a red, white, and blue cloth and hung it on a tall pole. That really got my attention. She went back inside but soon reemerged, ringing a hand bell. Suddenly all the children disappeared into the white house. I was scared and turned to run home. The lady caught my hand, led me into the house, and showed me where to sit — on a bench behind a little desk. Some of the children were talking, but suddenly I couldn't understand a word. The lady rang the bell again, everyone was quiet for a moment, and then all the children stood and pointed to another red, white, and blue cloth. In unison, they droned something utterly incomprehensible. The teacher spoke, and I thought she was praying, as in church. Then everyone sang. I understood none of it.

It was a terrifying day, though the teacher, Miss Pauls, was very kind. She explained to me in Low Dutch that I was in school and that I soon would learn to speak English as the other children did. To this day I have no idea why Mom and Pop didn't tell me about school or acquaint me with the English language. As first-generation American Mennonites, my parents used the Low Dutch vernacular in everyday conversation; High German was the "church language." I was not at all acquainted with English.

Miss Pauls taught all eight grades, a total of twenty-three students. Our first grade had six children (the largest class in Lake Valley history); several classes had only one student each. School was in session from nine to four.

The memory of my first few weeks at Lake Valley School is an unhappy blur, but dear Miss Pauls brought me through the trauma. It was the Little Gingerbread Boy in a tattered Bobbs-Merrill primer that brought me the first glimmer of what school was about. The six first-graders were seated on recitation benches near the teacher's desk. As Miss Pauls read the story aloud, showing us how her spoken words, the pictures, and the printed words fit together, understanding dawned. The picture of the fox leering as the Gingerbread Boy said, "I can run, I can run, and I can run away from you," ignited a spark in my mind. The magic of that moment has never left me, and I wasn't the least bit alarmed when the fox's long snout snapped off the Gingerbread Boy's head a page later. I was so elated by my new awareness that I thought it was funny.

Later that year Miss Pauls introduced me to the school's small library. I'll always remember the first book I took home — the story of a little boy's journey to dreamland. By the warm light of a flickering kerosene lamp, I read the book to the very end. The last page showed the sleepy boy riding a white pony up a steep mountain trail to a castle silhouetted against a starry sky, and even then I had a sense of what it meant to aspire to something — I didn't yet know what — that was as high as the stars.

EARTHY LESSONS

I learned much that year that wasn't in the curriculum, the basic stuff of life that my small friends already seemed to understand. One morning that fall we lower-grade boys were playing near the school's horse barn when Johnny said, "Let's play stallion and mare." Even the way he said it in Low Dutch was full of intrigue. "Walter and I will be the farmers. Peter, you be the stallion, and the rest of you are mares." I was used to hearing the Dutch words for mare and stallion in reference to our draft horses, but never had those words insinuated so much.

Each boy glanced furtively toward the schoolhouse, then the "mares" dropped down on their hands and knees. I stood by, hands under my overall bib, watching as they crawled around pretending to eat grass. Johnny went to a school buggy and came back with a small horsewhip.

I was a little afraid. Some instinct told me I was witnessing something primal, something little boys were not supposed to know about. Johnny opened the barn door a little, then herded Peter, the "stallion," into the barn. The stallion wasn't docile; he reared and bucked, and once I heard him kicking the barn walls. I peeked through another door. Johnny made a big show of bravado, snapping the whip as he maneuvered the wild stallion into a stall. Walter had gone into the barn, and he and Johnny were talking, using words Uncle John often used before Pop made me leave the room. The "farmers" came out of the barn and circled the mares, studying them carefully. Johnny occasionally flicked one on the rump with the whip to turn "her" around.

Johnny glanced at the schoolhouse once more, then resolutely chose a mare and drove her into the barn. The mood was electric. The other mares became little boys again, and we all raced into the barn. Johnny slammed the door shut. Like a master showman, he brought the snorting stallion out of his stall. The stallion rushed at the mare, and it was deathly quiet as he mounted her and made a few humping moves with his pelvis. Suddenly it was over and the stallion and the mare became two embarrassed little boys.

Gravely Johnny turned to me and asked, "Would you like to play horse?" I was too petrified to run. Fortunately, the school bell rang. Five innocent little boys ran to the schoolhouse. I knew I had witnessed something I would later identify as "carnal knowledge," but I wasn't at all sure what it meant.

 BUGGY LUNCH

Gradually I settled in to the somewhat comfortable but still bewildering routine. I liked Miss Pauls very much. She sensed my confusion and went out of her way to help me. I literally believed everything she said.

Once during a lesson in "health habits" she said coffee wasn't good for us. I was middle-aged before I ever drank coffee; every time I was offered any, I thought of Miss Pauls.

Two old one-horse mail buggies carried almost half of Lake Valley's twenty-three pupils to school every day, rain or shine. That close-knit buggy group dominated the school. All the other boys in my class — Johnny, Peter, and Menno — and one girl, Esther, rode to school on these buggies with older brothers and sisters. Two older boys, Frank and Nick, made a great to-do about driving, but the reality was that the old horses knew the way. Indeed, in cold, wet weather the front buggy window was closed and so mud-spattered that no one could see the way. When the buggy arrived at the school, each of the passengers jumped out and did his or her assigned task — holding the horse's head, unbuckling buckles, or carrying a can of oats into the barn. Johnny always made a show of hitching up, acting as if he were in great danger when he reached under the horse's belly, though none of the old horses had lifted a hoof that high for years.

I soon learned that if I wanted to eat lunch with my new friends I had to race out to the buggies and squeeze in to find a place to sit, usually on an overturned oat can. It wasn't the most pleasant eating environment, among five sweaty little boys, the strong fragrance of horse manure, and the mud on the floor. In subsequent years, some teachers would insist that we eat in the schoolhouse.

Buggy lunch topics ranged from cowboys to tractors (whose was biggest) and cars (Chevy versus Ford). Two of the boys claimed to have a cowboy cousin. I didn't have much to say because I didn't know what a cowboy was, our tractor wasn't the biggest, and my folks drove a Pontiac. One philosophical discussion I recall was whether or not you could drive a nail into your head far enough to make it stay. They said a boy at Big Lake almost had enough nerve to make it work, but his head got too bloody.

Miss Plett, my second- and third-grade teacher, used a discipline system that terrified me. For each infraction we got a red flag; the limit was five red flags. She never spelled out the consequences, but I assumed the worst. Actually, whenever anyone got close to five we started over. One of the things she required was a health habits chart on which we recorded that we had brushed our teeth, combed our hair, and washed our hands.

I think Miss Plett was the teacher who had us memorize the "Star-Spangled Banner." As a test, we had to recite it. I don't remember how well I did, but I'll never forget Johnny's attempt. He stepped up and stuttered for a while, clearly in deep trouble. Finally he blurted out, "I can't say it but I can sing it." Picture a scared, tongue-tied boy in overalls, reaching for the high notes in our national anthem. It was worse than you can possibly imagine, and the worse it got, the harder he tried, taking a deep breath and starting all over again. Miss Plett almost lost her composure and finally interrupted, "That's all, you may sit down."

In the lunch buggy, we would speculate about the new blue Ford that would often appear after school was dismissed. Young as we were, it was difficult to envision why a young man would call on a teacher.

NATURE CALLS

By the third grade, school was familiar and comfortable. Children from our neighborhood walked to school unless it was raining or snowing. In the winter we bundled up, wearing three-buckle overshoes to get through the mud and slush. Entering the little vestibule, we'd stomp our feet, creating a terrible mess. The teacher arrived at school in the morning clean and fresh; by the time she helped a dozen children remove overshoes dripping with mud and barnyard manure, she was almost as dirty as we were. The boys and girls had separate cloakrooms in which to hang their coats and set their lunch pails. Drinking water was outside at the pump, and we had two new WPA outdoor toilets on opposite corners of the school ground. Our common drinking cup hung on the pump. I always put my lips near the handle for sanitary reasons. The girl's toilet apparently was a two-holer, though I wouldn't have dared to check for sure. One day at third recess I heard a chubby little girl calling to her swifter friend, "Save a hole for me."

It was Mr. Epp, my fourth- and fifth-grade teacher, who aroused a love of nature in me and I'm sure in others as well. He was a sort of flatlander's Ichabod Crane — a slender man, still a bachelor though his hair was thinning, a good storyteller, and a strict disciplinarian (although not as severe as the hapless Ichabod). His car, made in the early 1930s, was typical for a teacher in those days — a blue Chevy coupe with a rumble seat and yellow wheels. He parked it in the school's horse barn every day, and I can't help but wonder if some of the women he courted weren't put off by the aroma in that Chevy.

If Mr. Epp had a fault, it was his forthright sensitivity to the natural world, not considered a manly attribute in the Lake Valley District. No matter, he would often talk about the birds and animals he saw en route to school. One morning he became so enthralled looking at the countryside that he crashed his little Chevy coupe into Mr. Siemens's new Ford. Elma, Mr. Siemens's daughter, was in my class, and the situation was a little touchy.

Mr. Epp marveled at the hedgerows, fields, and pastures he passed every morning. As he described them, nondescript dusty roads became avenues of beauty and adventure. In the spring he would organize a bird-sighting contest, recording the birds we saw and the dates next to our names on the blackboard.

My sixth-grade teacher was the most academically qualified ever to grace the halls of Lake Valley. Unfortunately, everyone knew about her background, which worked against her in the Dust Bowl era during the Depression. She was from back East, her father was a professor, and she had an especially thorough education — psychology and stuff like that. The poor woman didn't have a chance.

Nobody told us to be mean, but we overheard enough adult whispers to know that our elders were skeptical. She got off on the wrong foot by insisting we eat lunch in the classroom and that we take twenty minutes to do so — an eternity when for some of us lunch consisted of several slices of rye bread spread with lard. Actually, I was delighted to get out of the buggy rat race, but I had a hard time acknowledging that to myself. Johnny, Peter, and Menno were my role models; I so wanted to be like them. I was even self-conscious about my lunch bucket, which was different from theirs. Mine was large enough to carry a Thermos bottle with hot chocolate or juice that I'm sure Mom lovingly made for me. The other boys had small, oval, red or blue boxes, no Thermoses, and not much food.

Miss H. must have been very lonely. She boarded at a nearby neighbor's place and, having no transportation, walked to school every day, where she was met with suspicion and sometimes hostility. Unfortunately, we felt somewhat justified in some of our pranks, but she never lost her temper and actually taught us a lot that year.

On one occasion she disciplined one of the older boys, probably Walter, by making him stay inside during recess to study while the rest of us went outside. We were determined to give Walter some moral support. Our schoolhouse, like most, had a row of tall windows on the north side to illuminate the classroom. Since Lake Valley had a shallow basement, it was set on a high foundation, making it impossible to peek in from the outside. We all got together and pushed one of the buggies under the windows so some of the older boys could climb up and see what Walter was doing. Right about then, Miss Linbeck, the county school superintendent, drove up, and the rest of us shared Walter's fate.

Once, after one of the big snowstorms (more common in the past than today, it seems), there were three-foot snowdrifts along the hedgerows not far from the school. Some of the boys had been trapping and selling jackrabbits, and they saw a golden opportunity to cash in. Jackrabbits would hide in a hedgerow during a blizzard, and as the snow accumulated, they would maintain a tunnel and an air vent under the snow. After a storm you could see where the rabbits were hiding by finding the vent holes.

The day was bright and warm, so at noon recess we grabbed all the baseball bats we could find and hustled out to the hedgerows. This was a new experience for me and probably for most of the other boys, but a primitive herd instinct overcame our inhibitions. I didn't know what to expect until someone shouted, "Here's one," and smashed his bat into the snow. Sure enough, he dazed a jackrabbit and finished him off with a few more blows. Like a bear that smells blood, we were frenzied and there was no stopping us.

A jackrabbit is no cuddly bunny. It is six to nine pounds of kicking, screaming, biting fur and long ears. Since we were short of bats, some of us would just dive into the snowdrifts above the air vents. I was like a little poodle when I finally caught one; I didn't know what to do with it. They were usually under about two feet of snow, so it was quite a battle, with those big legs kicking desperately. I never managed to hold onto one, but the boys with the bats were making hay, and what a sight they were — blood, guts, mud, snow, and fur all over them. I've never seen a bunch of happier boys.

Suddenly, reality hit. We heard the school bell faintly tinkling almost a half a mile away and took off running, dragging rabbits by legs and ears. When she saw us, Miss H. nearly went into shock.

Yes, we had occasional lapses in decorum, and I don't regret them. Like cream rising to the top, those memories are the first to return. In reality, though, discipline was seldom a problem, even for Miss H. The no-talking-or-whispering rule followed me through eight grades, and it was rarely broken. There was no time for idle chitchat. If your assignments were finished, you could always listen to other classes reciting their lessons. I recall traveling vicariously all over the world as I listened in on geography and reading lessons. Romance and tragedy fired my imagination as I heard about Evangeline and Gabriel passing each other by and about Rip Van Winkle, whom time passed by. I caught the humor of Miles Standish's vain courtship and the deacon's fateful masterpiece. I fearfully crouched in the apple barrel with young Jim Hawkins as John Silver and his cohorts plotted mutiny. The Bobbs-Merrill readers used in the 1930s were treasure troves of classical prose and poems. Hawthorne, Irving, Longfellow, Poe, Stevenson, and many other American writers were familiar to Kansas's grade-school students of that era.

 CYCLES

We always had a fifteen-minute recess in the morning, an hour at noon (including lunch), and fifteen minutes more in the afternoon. For the first four or five years, only the boys played ball — softball in the fall and spring and basketball in the winter. The court was outside, but we did have two goals. Because of the dirt floor, there was always standing water at the free-throw line after rain or snow.

I think girls were finally allowed to play ball because we needed them. Mr. Epp arranged for us to play a few other schools, and in order to field a nine-person team of kids old enough to compete, we had to include the girls. When it came to playing basketball, where only five were needed, it was mortifying for me to sit on the sideline when Esther was chosen to play.

At the most we played only two or three extramural games a year. They were impromptu affairs, no doubt arranged by phone the night before. (There was no phone at the school.) To haul us to the games, the teacher would drive one car, and one of the fathers would take another, each loaded with up to eight or nine children. Our mothers, of course, didn't drive.

I must have been in the sixth grade when I finally got my bicycle. I had been begging and praying for a bicycle for years because my friends often rode their bikes to school. They were cheap bicycles, I later realized, with no extras and narrow tires, but all I cared about then was being just like the other boys. Every day as we walked home from school, I wondered whether Pop might have bought a bike for me. If the old pickup was standing outside in the yard, I would run to it and peek in the bed, always naively expecting to see a new bike.

One Saturday it happened. Pop had been to Buhler to buy groceries, and I heard him explain to Mom that Pete Dyck, the local "Honest John" trader, had traded a pig for a bicycle that wasn't selling because it was too expensive for most people. Then he turned to us — my sisters, Marvella and Rachel, and me — said he had a surprise for all of us, and led us outside. Having heard the word bicycle, I raced ahead and jumped up on the truck fender. What I saw made my heart tumble clear down to my toes. Not only was it a girl's bike, but it also had balloon tires, a handlebar basket, a rack over the rear fender, a chain guard, and some fancy knee action spring on the front wheel. I knew what Johnny would have to say about me riding a girl's bike with all that junk on it. But Pop didn't notice how mortified I was. He was busy explaining that it would be my bike to begin with, but that as Marvella and Rachel got older, they could ride it also.

I learned to ride the bicycle at home, thinking maybe my friends would never know that I had a girl's bike. Often I would give my sisters a ride on the back carrier. That was my big mistake. Pop got the idea that Marvella and I could ride to school together on the bike. Naturally, that is exactly what we did, and my fears were fully justified.

 FINALS

Pop was on the school board when I entered the seventh grade. Miss H. had decided to teach elsewhere, and Pop was involved in hiring a new teacher. I overheard talk of how teachers' salaries were going up, and it was hard to find good teachers for small rural schools. Pop was determined to get the best teacher possible for us, though his main criterion was

Milferd and Marvella Penner
on the way to Lake Valley School in 1939.

firm discipline. Lloyd Miller was said to be the best teacher in the county, so Pop invited him to our farm. I immediately sized him up as a no-nonsense teacher and started worrying about the next school session. Pop and Mr. Miller talked awhile, but when they got down to the salary issue and Mr. Miller asked for the preposterous sum of $110 a month, I breathed a sigh of relief.

The board finally hired Rosella Dyck, a local girl just out of high school. Due to the teacher shortage, high school graduates who took a three-month college course were permitted to teach. I think they paid her eighty dollars a month.

I liked Miss Dyck. She was very pretty, and she turned out to be a terrific teacher. Any skills she lacked were made up for by her ability to create in us a desire to learn. After the noon hour she would read to the whole school for about twenty minutes. For us, having no television sets or movie theaters and few radios, books like John Fox Jr.'s *Trail of the Lonesome Pine* opened up a window into a world of romance and adventure we had never dreamed of.

Since my introduction to the library in the first grade, I had been working my way through the collection. When I had read every book, Miss Dyck suggested that I start on the encyclopedias. I actually did read the "E" volume because it had the fewest pages.

Our graduation examinations were a hurdle we faced with mixed feelings. For some eighth-graders, graduation meant the end of formal education and passage into the real world. Cousin Elmer opted to quit school, but his admirable work ethic, manual skills, and entrepreneurial spirit carried him very well through life. I remember Mom and his mother talking about Elmer's abilities and wondering what there was to gain by more book learning.

My classmates and I expected to go to high school, but for most of us it just seemed to be a way to mark time before we became farmers. Uncles and cousins told me how lucky I was that, as the only boy in the family, the farm would be mine. The girls would have their inheritance, but the operation of the farm itself was virtually guaranteed for me. All I'd heard and read about exotic lands, history's heroes, and romantic adventures would be forgotten. Ironically, I had finally found my niche in school. I took great pleasure in social studies, reading, and — surprising even myself — arithmetic. Grammar and spelling, however, were forever difficult.

Miss Dyck guided us through the final-exam period. Failure was a possibility. We all knew people, mostly boys, who had had to repeat the eighth grade, so we took the state-administered tests very seriously. My classmates and I voluntarily, but according to custom, stayed after school every day for a month to review what we had learned. Surprisingly, I scored in the county's top 10 percent.

I have never regretted my one-room-school education. We learned the basics — reading, writing, arithmetic, and geography — but we gained much more: the love of learning, open minds, and a sense of responsibility. What more could we have asked for?

5 🌿 Lady of the House

The land has been called "Mother Earth" for many reasons. One of them surely must be the ways in which the land creates and produces bounty for its children. Nowhere was that metaphor more fitting than on Section 27 in the early twentieth century.

Tradition still held that women existed for the purpose of baking pies, sweeping floors, mending socks, feeding chickens, and enlarging the family census. "Baking pies" included picking the fruit and packing it into one-quart glass jars as well as preparing the meals that went with the pies. That included frying chicken and preparing mashed potatoes, which meant butchering roosters and digging potatoes.

"Sweeping the floor" was broadly defined as "keeping house" — making beds, dusting curtains, filling lamps with kerosene, and so forth. "Mending socks" naturally required washing, ironing, and folding the laundry first.

The chickens, however, were a family responsibility. The man was to furnish mash and grain, haul manure, cull the chickens, and maintain the chicken house. This left scattering feed and gathering eggs — and, worst of all, putting feisty broody hens in a little cage to cool them down — to the women and children.

The matter of the household census was very delicate. It concerned both romance and duty, the latter being prevalent inasmuch as large families were the norm in the community. They were also a source of pride, especially for fathers. Great-grandpa Dietrich Gaeddert (who led the Alexanderwohl migration to Inman, Kansas) fathered twenty-six children by two wives (having been widowed). Great-grandpa David Penner and his wife, Sara, had four girls and one boy (my grandfather, David F.).

Sons and daughters were loved and cherished, but boys were economic assets as well. Working in the fields, from shocking oats to driving tractors, was considered improper for ladies until the 1950s, as were construction and barnyard chores. (This was not true in all households.)

🔥 WE HAD THE BEST FARM

My mother, Bertha Gaeddert Penner, became mistress of the Penner household on Section 27 in 1928. Born on a Harvey County farm in 1899, she had five sisters (Anna being closest in age) and three brothers. All the children worked hard, but, to Bertha, household chores were a natural and pleasant part of life, and she always would cherish the memories of her childhood.

Dietrich Gaeddert (the father of twenty-six) was Bertha's grandfather. She had known and been fond of his second wife, Helena. "She was a good [step]grandma, although some of Grandpa's children were about as old as [she] was," Bertha wrote in a short memoir. "They [Dietrich and Helena] also had children, so it was a big family with many grandchildren."

In fact, the stone house (Dietrich's and Helena's home two miles east of Buhler, Kansas), which Bertha barely remembered, must have almost burst at the seams when all the grandchildren came to visit. "She [Helena] always invited us for the holidays," Bertha wrote. "I especially remember the Christmas she had a big kettle of borscht ready." The borscht simmered on "a big stove in the kitchen, which had a dirt floor." The stove was located in the center of the house so it could heat all the rooms. Bertha was quite impressed with the house because "it had a front door so you could open the upper half and leave the lower closed."

Bertha's maternal grandparents, Henry and Sarah Regier, built the house in which she grew up. Newly arrived from Ukraine in 1875, Henry and Sarah and their children lived in a grain bin until the house was finished (eight miles east of Buhler).

"It was quite a big two-story house," Bertha wrote. White with light-blue trim, it had a combination dining room–kitchen and a "big pantry with a cellar door in the floor. We were always reminded never to leave the cellar door open." The first floor also housed a bedroom, utility room, "and a parlor that was used only when guests came." Upstairs, there were three more bedrooms off the hall, in which there was a closet used only to store fifty-pound sacks of flour.

As had been the Mennonite custom in Europe, fruit trees surrounded the house. "East of the house was an orchard with apple, apricot, and plum trees; to the south were peach and cherry trees; [and in the] southeast corner was a walnut grove. West of the house were six very big mulberry trees and a playground where we played dare base, horseshoe, and blackman."

It was a child's paradise, and though she had no idea there was any other way to live, Bertha knew how fortunate she was. "When I was young I thought we had the best farm," she wrote. "[There was] a big pasture with a stream of water that flowed into the Turkey Creek. Here under the big cottonwoods the coyotes howled in the evening, that always scared me."

But there were peaceful evenings, too. "Some nice evenings we would sit on the porch. Across the creek our cousin, John V. Regier, had a new phonograph. He would set it close to the open window and play it real loud so we could hear it too. He sure had to play the song 'Red Wing' that was a most popular song at the time."

Farm children have always been given chores before they can acquire a taste for leisure. Bertha and her siblings were no different. "When we were old enough, we fed the chickens and gathered eggs. This we liked to do. Sometimes we had over one hundred eggs a day. Sometimes Anna and I would sit at the east barn step in the shade and watch the chickens. A few would go to the field during the day, but for feeding time they would always come back. We gave names to those that came from the field. A pretty rooster was 'Wild Jim' and a gray hen was 'Minnie.'"

Bertha and her sister Anna were constant companions. "We had two slatted corn bins under one roof with a driveway in between to unload corn. We pretended we each lived in one bin, which was supposed to be our house. We each had a telephone made of spools from thread and store string. It worked when we talked loud enough. Once, toward evening, Anna and I climbed on a strawstack. I guess it must have settled already — at least we could get up quite high. We either played church or school. We sang, 'O Beulah Land, Sweet Beulah Land, as on the highest mount I stand.' I think we had a great time."

Pop used to brag that Bertha had gone to school in Paris, and in fact she had — Paris School (District 28, Harvey County), where her favorite subject was spelling. She completed eighth grade there in 1915 and three years later attended the nearby Hoffnungsau Preparatory School for several years.

🔥 RIVALS

Frank and David Penner were closer than most brothers. They worked together on the farm, played in the Lake Valley Band, and talked about girls. They talked a lot about Bertha Gaeddert, each remarking about how beautiful she was.

In fact, both young men were infatuated, and on the same day that Frank worked up the courage to send Bertha a letter, David talked to her at a picnic at Halstead Park and she agreed to go out on a date with him. David didn't discuss the matter with Frank, who knew only that his brother had stopped talking to him about girls. Before Frank figured it all out, it was announced that David and Bertha were getting married.

The wedding took place on June 14, 1925. It was the custom for fathers, with equal measures of authority and generosity, to place their sons on farmsteads belonging to the family. Peter, the oldest son, had been provided for with a quarter-section farm six miles from the home place. David and Bertha would have a quarter section with a house and barn just northeast of Section 27. How Bertha, with the light of new love in her eyes, viewed this austere dwelling — a small, square, hip-roofed house flanked by two scraggly mulberry trees, a small, unpainted barn nearby, and wheat land as far as the eye could see — we can only guess

Bertha's relationship with the Penner family wasn't all sunshine and roses. Grandma Maria was abrasive and demanding, and Bertha was not one to easily let go of an affront. As a rule, however, she kept her feelings inside, which was also traditional. It was many years before she confided to my sister Marvella that Maria had given her and David a tongue-lashing one Sunday for visiting Bertha's mother instead of spending time with David's relatives.

On an October day, when David and Bertha had been married for sixteen months, they were getting ready to go to an auction with David's sister, Sarah, and her husband, John Unruh, when David complained of "the grippe" and urged Bertha to go without him. He seemed a little better in the afternoon, but that night he became very ill. A neighbor who shared the couple's party line helped Bertha call the doctor and numerous family members. The diagnosis was grim: David had infantile paralysis — polio. He died the next day.

As tradition dictated, Grandpa David F. took charge, appropriating the young couple's land and farm equipment and returning it to the family resource pool. Bertha, understandably, was deeply hurt.

A widow at twenty-six, Bertha found work as a housekeeper for the Uterback family of Newton. Briefly she experienced an upper-middle-class urban existence, living amid modern conveniences such as central heat, electricity, and plumbing. She spent weekends with her widowed mother on the home place. Her brothers would take her to Burrton where she would board the Arkansas Valley Interurban Railroad for the commute to Newton. (The AVI provided one-coach electric-powered passenger service from Wichita to Hutchinson via Newton from about 1917 to the mid-1930s.) During this interlude, Bertha learned to see the world from a different perspective than that of most rural women of the time, and the experience stayed with her for the rest of her life.

Less than eighteen months after David's death, Bertha married Frank. Her welcome back into the Penner family left much to be desired. Personality clashes and old customs gave new cause for resentment.

The wedding was planned for the evening of March 18, 1928, but David F. pulled another of his autocratic maneuvers. The wedding day dawned fair but soon turned overcast, the wind shifted, and a blizzard threatened. Without consulting anyone, least of all the bride, David F. rescheduled the wedding, reserving the church for the early afternoon and informing most of the guests by phone. The Gaedderts, however, had made arrangements that couldn't be changed — food and flowers, for example — and guests coming from a distance were already on their way. Bertha was furious at the alteration in plans. It was an offense she never forgot.

Yet so reluctant were both Bertha and Frank to talk about their deepest thoughts and feelings that I was a grown man before she ever mentioned her short marriage to my father's brother, and the two had been married for sixty-five years when Frank finally confessed to his son-in-law Randy that he had been sweet on Bertha before she married David L.

FAMILY LIFE

Under a cloud of resentment, Frank and Bertha moved into the Queen Anne house on Section 27 with David F. and Maria and their unmarried daughter, Elizabeth. The Penners were set in their ways and gave Bertha little opportunity to express herself. When she ventured to turn the dial on the battery-powered radio, her mother-in-law responded with a stinging rebuke: Only Maria and Elizabeth were to choose the station. It was yet another indignity Bertha would remember, and her resentment grew like an abscess until she finally opened her heart to her daughter Marvella years later.

Fortunately, a house in Buhler was under construction, and when it was completed the elder Penners and Elizabeth moved in. Though Bertha was now mistress of the house, Maria's shadow stayed to haunt her. Every day in every room, Bertha knew exactly what Maria would say must be done (although Elizabeth had done the work, mechanically asking Maria each weekday morning what kind of pie to bake that day).

The house had many places a ghost could hide — long halls, two stairways, and a lot of small, dark rooms. Like the family, the house had grown in size and affluence. The original end-gabled one-story house had become the northwest wing of a much larger and more elaborate two-story T-shaped addition with ornate end and center gables, built in 1898. The old part now housed the kitchen and a summer kitchen, outside of which the water pump sat on a large concrete slab.

We lived in the Queen Anne house until I was six. Every morning we sat in bentwood chairs at the square kitchen table for breakfast and morning devotions. Rachel, the baby, sat in a high chair, occasionally dropping food on the floor or flipping her dish and coating her face and hair with cereal. I can still see the kitchen stove, a range and oven combination of light blue and white porcelain with chrome trim. Nearby were kindling — either corncobs or shingles — and a few bigger sticks of wood in a basket. Mom often complained about the stove not drafting properly, so Pop was always experimenting with chimney extensions. On the other side of the table was a large oak cabinet, which had a built-in flour bin, assorted cupboards and drawers, and a white porcelain work surface.

For devotions, Pop would read a Bible passage and then lead us in prayer. Until the 1940s, devotions were in German. He read by the light of a kerosene lamp — in fact, there were kerosene lamps throughout the house — since we had no electricity.

From the kitchen, a dark hallway led to the parlor, the dining room, bedrooms, and a stairway closed off by a paneled door, which was stained deep red with a faux wood grain, typical of the craftsmanship throughout the house. The men of Maria's family, the Lohrentzes, were acclaimed woodworkers, and their influence was apparent both on the exterior and in the interior decor of the house.

Rising from the parlor was an exposed stairway with a curved banister and turned balusters, also finished deep red. The parlor, ornately carpeted in gold with a red floral design, was reserved for Sunday company and visits from the preacher.

THE MAYTAG

The summer kitchen was for hot-weather cooking and for doing laundry. It held milk buckets, brooms, and overshoes, a rendering kettle for heating wash water, and a black summer cookstove. Washtubs hung on the wall above the bench they were placed on when in use. On another wall were cupboards full of empty canning jars and washpan-size blocks of homemade lye soap. A cream separator, used twice a day, was kept handy near the door. And in the corner was the washer, a gray square-tub Maytag beside a hole in the wall for the engine's flexible exhaust pipe.

The Maytag and the washtubs were pressed into service on Mondays, which were frenzied days for my mother. Custom and peer pressure imposed the weekly ordeal called "washday" — a patchwork of lye soap, wood fire, boiling water, gasoline vapors, and dirty overalls.

Washday was serious business. A housewife's reputation depended on the early-morning appearance of fluttering shirts and dresses on the clothesline for the neighborhood to see. In nearby Buhler, a Mrs. Janzen — a neighbor of Aunt Justina (called Tina) — always got her wash out first. Mom and Tina figured she must have been doing some getting ready on Sunday, which, of course, would have been highly reprehensible. (Occasionally, when bad weather threatened on Sunday evening, Pop would bring in kindling and firewood for the big wash kettle, but I assumed it was permissible by the same exemption that allowed farmers to milk cows on Sunday.)

There was something soothing about the peculiar rhythmic sound of the washing machine engine. I remember playing in my sand pile one washday morning, winding the spring on my green toy Caterpillar tractor and watching it climb over the little hills I'd made in the sand. Across the road, the neighbor's Maytag thrummed in the cool quiet of the summer morning. I felt a little lonely, and the industrious churning of that engine not far away was good company.

Mom had trouble starting our Maytag that morning. She often had to fuss around with the fuel mixture and the spark plug — in semidarkness, since she didn't want to get the kerosene lamp too close to the gasoline. Mom was no mechanic, but she could use the spark plug wrench that was standard equipment with Maytag washers. It was very irksome for her to hear the neighbor's engine firing while hers refused to start.

Even after the engine was popping and belching in cadence, washing was a major chore. Mom had to feed kindling and firewood under the big black kettle, and I helped her carry buckets and buckets of water to fill the giant kettle. The suspenders that held up my overalls sometimes slid off my shoulders when I struggled with a heavy bucket in each hand filled with water from the windmill pump across the yard. We used the windmill water when there was a good breeze. Otherwise the water came from the hand pump on the back porch.

The hand pump was a marvelous thing. It seemed to create water on its own. Generally you had to pump the handle fast a few times, the pump rod squealing in protest, to bring the cool water gushing out in spurts. If you pumped really fast, you could make water squirt up out of the rod packing. Mom hollered at me so loud when that happened that I wondered if the pump might explode.

Almost as wonderful as the hand pump was the rain barrel, heavily tarred inside, that Pop set up to catch runoff from the roof in summer. All we had to do was open a spigot to use the water, which, lacking the mineral content of ground water, was soft and clear. On warm days, the aroma from the rain barrel was wonderful. I always associate the fragrance of rain barrel water with finding out that Mom was going to have a baby because it was near the rain barrel that an older neighbor boy and I were playing when he told me. I didn't believe him at first, but he said he could tell by looking at her. I supposed babies must be as miraculous as hand pumps and rainwater.

When the water in the big kettle was hot enough, Mom poured the water into the washer and filled the washtubs, pulled down off the wall and set on the bench, with cool rinse water. A quick kick started the engine, and a pull on the lever jerked the agitator into motion. I watched the roiling water, the wet clothes slurping through the wringers and Mom flipping the roller levers, but I kept my distance. Mom had told me many times about the naughty boy who didn't listen to his mother's cautions and caught his arm in the ringer. She painted a graphic picture of the wringer pulling and pressing the little fingers, seizing the elbow, and stopping only at the armpit.

After making sure her youngsters were where they belonged, Mom carried the clean wash out to hang on the line. The laundry had to be dried, no matter how cold, hot, or windy it was. Sometimes she wore overshoes; in our gumbo, the mud clung to your shoes till you could hardly lift your feet.

If the weather cooperated, the wash would be dry in the early afternoon. We all took great interest in the drying process, in view of how hard Mom had worked to get the wash on the line. All manner of mischief was possible — the dog could pull the sheets down, the cattle might get out and run under the clothesline, or, more likely, the wind would snatch a flapping bedsheet and hurl it across the yard. Mom would almost cry if a clothespin worked loose and dropped a Sunday shirt into the dust.

I was the washday hero on one occasion, one early-spring day mild enough so we could open all the windows. I was playing alone outside while Mom eavesdropped on the party line. It must have been the year Pop cut down the mulberry hedge because I could see clear to Inman, so the dust cloud was still a distance away when I saw it rolling toward us from the northwest. During the Dust Bowl days it didn't take much wind to stir up huge brown billows. I screamed at Mom in Low Dutch, *"Sea windijch, sea stuffijch!"* ("Very windy, very dusty!").

Bertha Penner and son, Milferd, in 1929.

Mom slammed the receiver onto the hook, grabbed a big washpan, and ran outside as fast as she could. She saved the white things first, her fingers snapping clothespins off the line, furling the laundry, thumping it into the pan, carrying it into the house, then running back to the line, all the while keeping a watchful eye on the darkening sky. Doors were banging and curtains flying by the time she got the last batch safely inside.

Laundry that was washed on Monday naturally had to be ironed on Tuesday. Mom sent us kids to another room when she filled the blue Coleman gasoline iron with exactly one measuring can full of white gasoline, pumped up the pressure, and, after checking several times to make sure everything was just right, applied the match.

PROVISIONS

There was no leisure to be had the rest of the week either. There were peaches, plums, corn, apricots, beets, beans, and tomatoes to be canned; apples to be dried; the garden to be hoed; chickens to be butchered; and an unending agenda of other responsibilities that went along with "baking the pies" and "sweeping the floors." Time had to be found for mending clothes and sewing the girls' dresses alongside preparing regular meals. Cooking for threshing crews and preparing for holidays were periodic responsibilities piled on top of the regular chores, according to the season.

Without intending to, Mom made butchering chickens a dramatic production. First we scattered feed on the ground. Greedily the chickens came running, oblivious to the threat to one or two of their number. Mom looked the roosters over, picked one, and shrewdly snared him by one leg with her chicken hook. A bucket of boiling water and a hatchet waited at the chopping block. Two large nails, about two inches apart, protruded from the block to hold the rooster's neck. Sometimes Mom calmed the frightened rooster, showing us how if she rocked his body back and forth gently the head would seem to float in place. Then, not wanting to prolong the ordeal any longer than necessary, she deftly held the neck between the nails, and whoosh! The hatchet in her other hand came down.

Then the fun began. For a while, a decapitated rooster doesn't know he's dead. He struggles, and kicks, and may actually run away — for a short distance. Usually, Mom got the rooster's neck into the funnel-like device that channeled its blood onto the ground before the bird had a chance to escape. Plunging it into boiling water loosened the feathers for pulling. True, the last moments of the condemned rooster's life weren't especially pretty, but it was easy to forget all that when you bit into a scrumptious drumstick.

Mom rarely got away from the farm except on Sundays, for morning services and afternoon visits, usually with relatives. Two or three times a year the family went to Hutchinson to buy shoes, yard goods, and maybe a suit or a dress for special occasions. On Sundays, women of Mom's generation wore hats to church, in stuffy black or dark blue with a feather or ribbon to brighten it up a little. Annually Mom fretted about needing a new spring or winter hat.

Pop normally went to Inman or Buhler once a week to trade cream and eggs for groceries. He'd hand the clerk at Abe's Store the list that Mom had made. Once or twice, as Pop and I were leaving for town, Mom waved us back before we were out of sight to add another item to the list, and then we'd be on our way again.

Traveling door-to-door salesmen sold Mom notions, seasonings, and specialty items. The Watkins man sold vanilla, of course, but also spices and even liniment. The Raleigh man and Ola Lorentz, the McNess man, also called on a regular basis. The salesmen, invariably smiling, carried wire display cases filled with intriguing bottles and packets, from patent medicines to condiments. Mom purchased from them, but she was always wary of the ones she didn't know, keeping the screen door latched until it was time to exchange money for products.

If she was overcautious, there was a reason. It was the era of Bonnie and Clyde, the young Texas couple who murdered twelve people in a two-year killing spree that ended in 1934. A killer named Earl Young was said to be on the loose in Kansas, and the *Hutchinson News* had been carrying stories and pictures about the fugitive. One afternoon I was playing in a drainage ditch next to the driveway when a strange car drove into the yard. Of course, Mom was "not home." She always hid and kept the children quiet if strangers showed up when Pop was in the field. I peeked through the bushes as the car drove off, and the driver was the spitting image of Earl Young.

 MOVING UP

In 1935 the folks started planning a new house. Mom had been keeping house in the Queen Anne without electricity, plumbing, or central heat. One of the few modern appliances we had was a refrigerator — cooled, paradoxically, by a kerosene heater. A big tank on the top held a solution that, when compressed by the heat, pumped cold air into the refrigerator. Every Saturday night, Mom used the ice-cube trays to make ice cream.

Pop, who had taken correspondence courses in architecture, did the drawings according to Mom's idea of the perfect house. She especially wanted large windows over the kitchen sink to look out on the sunrise. I fondly recall watching Mom and Pop look at pictures of new homes in a catalog. The one I liked best had a roof over the entrance so low to the ground that a boy could easily climb up. If Mom had known my motives, she would have eliminated that style from consideration immediately.

Mom and Pop had a wonderful time together planning the house, one of three "modern" dwellings in the neighborhood. When completed, it had a full basement, electric lights (but few outlets), running water, a bathroom, and a big furnace in the basement that could be fueled with coal or wood. Three extra bedrooms were on the second story. Soon after we moved in, Pop and Mom invited the school board and their families over for the regular board meeting. Three of my friends, whose fathers were also on the board, headed straight to the bathroom, much to Mom's consternation since they opened the faucets and flushed the toilet over and over. Indoor plumbing was quite a novelty.

"Modern" by 1930s standards still left a lot to be desired. The old Maytag was installed in the basement, adding stair steps to Mom's washday circuit. To make up for the inconvenience, Dad replaced the gas engine with an electric motor.

The central forced-air furnace was also a dubious improvement. It did a wonderful job of heating the entire house, and its mouth could accommodate a twelve-by-eighteen-inch log (which eliminated a lot of wood splitting for Pop), but feeding the beast was heavy work for Mom. An ash box under the grate had to be cleaned at least once a week. When we burned coal instead of wood, clinkers (fused incombustible coal residue)

Part of the original Penner house being moved away.
The new 1936 house is in the background.

would clog the grate. Pop would help with the furnace chores when he was in the house, especially in the mornings, but he had cows to milk, animals to feed, and enough farm tasks to keep him outside almost all day. Thus most of the furnace tending was up to Mom.

At night, the dampers were closed to lower the fire so there would be some hot coals left to restart in the morning. In the morning when I heard the grate rattling, I knew the house would soon be warming up and Mom would be expecting us downstairs.

In the basement near the furnace was a six-by-fifteen-foot room for firewood and coal storage. Pop and I would go to Inman to get coal, loading it into our International pickup truck from an open rail car. When the car was almost full it wasn't a bad job, but shoveling coal out of a nearly empty car required tossing the shovelfuls over the high sides. Returning home, we shoveled coal into the storeroom through the basement window, covering everything on the first floor with a fine layer of dust.

A cheaper source of fuel was wood from hedges or trees — mulberry or cottonwood. Mom preferred the hedge and mulberry logs because they were smaller and actually put out more heat. One year Pop made a deal with someone in the nearby sandhills to fell and cut up cottonwood trees on shares. To fell the trees a two-man handsaw was used to slice through the trunks. Once the trunks were down, Pop had rigged up a drag saw with a Cushman engine to saw them into two-foot lengths. Then the real work began. Being two to three feet in diameter, the logs required a lot of work with sledgehammers and wedges to split them into a manageable size.

No matter how much work was involved, Mom appreciated having a nice place to do the laundry and being warm throughout the house in winter. She soon found that the morning sun flooding through the double kitchen window was too bright during part of the day, and she requested an adjustable awning so she could see the sunrise but block some of the light as the day progressed. She'd sing gospel songs as she dried dishes and watched the sunrise, and she loved to note where the sun was on the shortest and longest days of the year. The sun came up over Harry Siemens's farm two miles to the southeast on the shortest day, she said. Unfortunately, on the longest day, the barn obstructed her view of the first summer dawn. Nevertheless, Mom had many happy moments in that house, and it was hard for her to say goodbye to it when she and Pop retired to a new house in Newton.

Bertha Penner died November 20, 1999, just shy of her one-hundredth birthday. Had she lived another month or so, her lifespan would have touched three different centuries — the nineteenth, the twentieth, and the inscrutable twenty-first.

6 🌿 Higher Education

Mom wanted me to go to college and become a preacher, like her cousin Albert. She assumed that a good education would loosen my ties to Section 27, but everyone else knew I would become a farmer. Why question it? I was Frank Penner's only son, and the transfer of the farm to me was only a matter of time. Uncles who seldom spoke to the younger people reminded me at every opportunity how grateful I should be.

Until I reached high school, it didn't occur to me that I might have something to say about my future. Once that realization struck, throughout high school and my short college career I vacillated between wanting to be a farmer and wanting something else (to tell the truth, I never seriously considered becoming a preacher).

I entered Inman Rural High School just twenty-four years after Grandpa David F. helped organize the school district. I was fourteen, it was 1943, and World War II was raging overseas. There were no school buses; nearly everyone carpooled. I showed up on the first day riding scrunched down in the back seat of an old Model A Ford driven by a neighbor girl, hoping no one would see me. It was mortifying to be chauffeured by a girl, and an "English" girl at that.

My familiarity with the high school was limited to a few music lessons I had taken there as an eighth-grader. Pop had played the baritone horn in the Lake Valley band and wanted me to learn to play the instrument. For a while he tried to teach me himself. We would practice in my bedroom, Pop sitting beside me on the bed. First he'd lubricate the horn valves, removing them one at a time, spitting on them, working them up and down, and finally screwing the tops down. Then he'd play a few simple tunes, and finally he would give the horn to me. Once in a while, through the accumulation of saliva, I managed an agonized bugle call.

Pop quickly saw the wisdom of turning my music education over to a professional — his friend Mr. Reimer, one of Inman High's best music instructors. Without explanation as usual, Pop took the horn and me to Mr. Reimer at the high school one day. Pop and Mr. Reimer talked awhile, and then Pop said he was going to trade eggs for mash in town while I learned to play the horn.

I was nervous, but Mr. Reimer put me at ease. First he gave me a music aptitude test — a few dozen questions on a mimeographed form. Whatever I lacked in musical ability was disguised by my natural ability to do well on multiple-choice and true-or-false tests. My score, Mr. Reimer reported to Pop on our next visit, had tied that of the smartest and most talented student musician at Inman Grade School.

When I finished the test, my lesson began. Mr. Reimer explained in great detail how to purse the lips on the mouthpiece to produce the sound. With his coaching, I managed a few squawks.

After he dismissed me with the admonition to go home and practice, I walked out of his classroom into a labyrinth of hallways and doors. The school day was over, but a few kids were still wandering around, apparently oblivious to the bumbling eighth-grader dragging the big horn case. When I finally found the front door, Pop wasn't there. I waited a long time, feeling awkward, though, apart from a girl in a cheerleading outfit and boots (whom I watched with unabashed interest as she strode down the hall, pleated skirt swinging), there were few people in the building. It was almost dark when Pop's pickup finally appeared.

❦ THE SOUND OF SILENCE

Mr. Reimer eventually drilled me to the point where I could play a recognizable rendition of "Lightly Row." When I started high school, being his student and scoring well on the music aptitude test meant that I was automatically enrolled in the band and glee club — an aberration that illustrates the untrustworthiness of test scores. Mr. Reimer had no illusions about my ability by then, but he had resigned and there was a new music teacher.

I got through several months of band before someone caught on that I wasn't actually playing the instrument. It happened one winter morning when I had left my horn in the old Ford and the moisture in the valves froze it up. In band I tried faking it as usual, but the valves wouldn't budge, and my awkward pantomime caught the director's eye.

In glee club I stuck it out by just mouthing the words for the whole school year. Mom was so proud of me when we performed religious songs in our occasional public concerts.

Academically I was a good student. I loved world history class and I loved the teacher, Miss Romine. When we studied the ancient Sumerian and Egyptian cultures, I began vaguely to understand the dimension of time through history. So enthralled was I with the textbook that the pages were embedded in my memory like photographs. During tests, I simply "read" the pages stashed in my mind.

The academic side of school lifted my spirits and my confidence. What's more, in general science class I sat next to the prettiest girl at Inman High, and she actually talked to me. In fact, we sat in the back row whispering continually about everything under the sun, and we still managed to maintain high grades.

Pop and Mom had never talked to me about "growing up" — hormone changes or dating or physical attraction. I was content just talking to girls until our first freshman class party, a campfire wiener roast at Lake Inman. There was a new kind of excitement in the air. Boys and girls weren't just friends anymore; something more subtle and complicated was going on.

One of my friends confided that he was going to ask a girl if he could take her home. He was excited about the prospect of sitting close to her in the car and maybe doing "more." It was bewildering. My world was changing, and I wasn't ready.

School seemed different after that. There was the in-the-know group, appearing poised and confident in budding relationships, and there were the rest of us, still perplexed by unfamiliar feelings.

In catechism class at church, when the preacher raised the subject of "boy-girl relationships," he got my attention, though he began his remarks by saying that we were too young to understand the sanctity of marriage. Who, I wondered, was thinking of *marriage?* God (he went on), the loving Father, had already chosen a mate for each of us, and in due time we would find each other. Being a true believer, I accepted what the preacher said, though apparently it meant I should wait until marriage to explore these new feelings. Meanwhile, the general science girl dated and went to wicked places like roller-skating rinks. For a while I retreated to Section 27, going to school and participating only in activities I was coerced into, such as football.

SAVING FACE

I had never seen a football game in my life; I didn't know anything about the sport, but my friends encouraged me to play. Some of the seniors had been drafted to serve in the war, so there was a shortage of football players, especially for practice fodder. It was an educational experience, though I'm not sure I would call it playing.

I was in for a series of shocks, the unfamiliar experience of getting naked with about thirty other boys being but the first. I couldn't help noticing the difference between the sopranos and the basses. Then there was the "jockey strap." I had no idea how to put it on or why. They told me it was to protect the "family jewels." But as unaccustomed as I was to the locker room routine, when we finally put on our shoulder pads and laced up our cleated shoes, I felt the machismo elation that has motivated athletes to excel since long before the first Olympic games in ancient Greece.

The regular coach, like nearly every other *real* coach, was in the army. Our substitute, Harry, was a local businessman. Pompous Harry loved to blow his whistle and act gruff. He had his favorites; the rest of us were just stuffed in the line for the first team to batter. Harry never explained the basics of the game; he just drew play charts, which many of us found totally mystifying.

I was a left guard. The first-team right guard — really a nice guy the rest of the time — wore a big smile every time he creamed me. My one moment of glory came when the coach had us second-stringers running down the field with the ball, zigzagging as actual opponents would, while first-team players tried to tackle us. When my would-be tackler came at me, expecting to crunch me to the ground, I focused on his jaw and stiff-armed him, as I'd heard Harry instruct the first-stringers. Down he went. I beamed, expecting praise, perhaps a promotion to halfback. Instead, Harry blew his whistle and berated me for decking the guy. This was tackle practice, he said.

The first team really wasn't much better than us tackling dummies. Pretty Prairie High School beat us 96 to nothing.

Fortunately, football and band weren't the school's only extracurricular activities, and I came out of hiding to take a part in an all-school play. It was the best thing I could have done, breaking me out of the tight circle of Dutch boys and introducing me to many English students.

A petite blonde senior and I were cast as a sister and brother, and she actually became something of a big sister, encouraging and guiding me to master my inhibitions and set aside my stiff Mennonite demeanor. I made other friends in the cast, too, and ended up having a wonderful time.

Things were looking up — football season ended with a whimper, I enjoyed my classes, and the play had given me new confidence. The only thorn in my side was the peach fuzz on my chin, one of the many things Pop hadn't warned me about. An older boy named Don virtually stalked me, teasing me about my beard, chanting "Beardy, Beardy," and encouraging other kids to do so, too. Finally, after this had gone on for months, Pop gave me a safety-razor kit and showed me how to lather up.

With that coming-of-age hurdle behind me, I was almost sorry when my freshman year ended, knowing I would miss my friends during the summer. But I was happy to be back in the farm routine, mostly doing tractor work, which I loved.

 SUMMER FIELDS

More than anything, I liked to mow alfalfa. Pop had rigged up a seven-foot power-takeoff mower for our Case tractor, so mowing, raking, and baling alfalfa were among my summer tasks. The scent of newly mown hay is just as it's described in bad poetry; there is no getting around it. It is simply wonderful to be in the midst of acres and acres of luscious green, with yellow and white sulfur butterflies floating above purple flowers and honeybees buzzing on a perfect day in June. The heady aroma gradually changes from pungent succulence as the cutter bar slices the green stems to the softer fragrance of curing hay. I never put these feelings into words, but they were there, just like the awakening hormones.

So seductive were Section 27's attractions, I often wondered why I should bother diagramming sentences when this beautiful world was calling me. My friends, whom I saw only on Sundays in the summertime, considered high school nothing more than a rite of passage — a time to have fun, play games, see girls, and learn enough to keep their teachers minimally satisfied. Some of the boys, especially those who lived in town, got together to play ball, drive around, and who knew what else, but Pop had biased me against such activities as being frivolous and leading to worse things — playing pool, for example, or drinking beer.

THE FUTURE FARMER

Pop rewarded me for the summer's work with an old, barely running Model A Ford. I had hoped for a better car, but since almost all the other kids drove Model A's I was satisfied, especially when Pop told me he had arranged for me to haul our bunch to school. My carload included Joyce — the English girl who had driven me to school the previous year — Bertha Neufeld, my friend Delbert, and Delbert's twin sisters, Edna and Elva. Those poor girls, huddled in the back seat, suffered in silence when I barreled recklessly down muddy roads claiming I was "scaring ditches." One problem with the car was that the floorboards were partially rusted out, so when we charged through a water hole the water squirted up into the car. It was crowded in the car, but I got twenty-five cents a month per person.

At that time Model A's were only about fourteen or fifteen years old, and no car built before or since has been as durable (though on mine, the brakes were shot). Of course, you could always stop a Model A by downshifting real fast — from high to second to low and into reverse if necessary. I stopped that way for three years with only one crash: entering the school parking lot with a load of boys, I realized too late that the lot was a muddy, slimy mess. I did the downshift maneuver and slowed to about ten miles per hour, but the car skidded, sideswiped Harvey's Model A coupe, and hit the steel posts guarding the sidewalk. In a modern car it would have meant disaster, but Model A's were tough, and since Harvey's car was the same color as mine, you could barely see where I had hit it. Harvey said that if his dad noticed the scratches he would say he had skidded into a ditch. My car was unscratched, but on the way home from school — I was going about fifty on a muddy road with my load of kids — the car began to bounce violently and there was a horrendous metallic clang. The front bumper had fallen off and we had driven over it. I put it back on at home and all was well.

One cold day when I started the motor, it backfired and burst into flames. Grateful for the shed's earthen floor, I opened the hood and threw dirt on the carburetor. Fast as I was, the fire had gotten hot enough to blister the paint on the adjacent gas tank. (A Model A's fuel tank was just behind the motor.)

My friend Leland had a sporty blue 1936 Ford with musical horns. He usually drove when we went uptown to the drugstore for ice cream or a four hundred (milk, chocolate syrup, and lots of ice) at noon. Pop had started giving me an allowance of five dollars a month so I could take my turn buying treats.

A big part of my education for the remaining three years of high school was vocational agriculture, imperative for future farmers. The instructor, William Brown, was a large, deliberate, slow-talking man. He was imperturbable, and whether or not you learned anything was strictly up to you. Some learned a little, some learned a lot. I fell somewhere in between because I learned quickly without much effort.

Mr. Brown would stand in front of the class and lecture, absorbed in his subject and aware of little else. Squirrel, a star student who sat near the front of the class, had the amazing ability to absorb Mr. Brown's slow discourse on dairy cows while turning his back on the teacher and telling the rest of the class barnyard jokes.

Vo-ag was two hours a day, five days a week — three days of class work and two of farm shop, where we engaged in such activities as basic blacksmithing, acetylene welding, rudimentary woodworking, and firing .22 bullets in a vise with a hammer. Mr. Brown probably wasn't as unsuspecting as he seemed. More likely he was just tolerant of our shenanigans.

Part of his demonstration of acetylene welding emphasized the importance of maintaining a steady flame. Whenever he got to that point, someone would nonchalantly step on the hose and cut off the acetylene. Mr. Brown was patient for a while, but finally he turned knowingly to the guilty party and gave him a withering stare that ended the acetylene supply problem. Meanwhile, without our quite realizing it, we were learning. After all, you had to know what the proper flame looked like in order to snuff it at the critical moment.

PIGS

Everyone in vo-ag had a home project — raising chickens or pigs, growing vegetables, or doing something else agricultural. Pop and I never discussed it, but somehow he learned that I needed a project. So he went to a sale and bought me a sow. Soon baby pigs became my home activity. It didn't require much effort on my part. We mixed the sow in with our other pigs and, lo and behold, one day she had piglets.

I must have missed some of Mr. Brown's instructions while listening to Squirrel's jokes, so I didn't realize we were supposed to be keeping a record of our expenses. When it was time to turn the records in, all I knew was what we paid for the sow and received for the little pigs, so that's what I reported. Because of my ignorance, my project ended up being the most "profitable" one in the group.

Since I was in the hog business, it seemed only logical to build a small A-frame hog house for my shop project. I went over to the lumberyard a few blocks from the high school and told Mr. Wiederstein that I was going to build a hog house. He looked me over and asked who my father was. After I told him, he asked for my bill of materials. (Mr. Brown had mentioned a bill of materials, but Squirrel had been telling a good joke right then.) Mr. Wiederstein got very serious, looked down at me, and said he didn't have time to talk to boys who didn't know what they wanted. I tried to explain that I was building an A-frame and that it would be for only one pig, but he scooted me out and told me to come back when I knew what I wanted. I resolved to listen to Mr. Brown in the future. Meanwhile, I had a serious problem.

The next morning, without further explanation, Pop told me to take the pickup, go to the lumberyard after school, load up my lumber, and haul it to the school shop. Mr. Wiederstein had a twinkle in his eye when he asked for my bill of materials, but gratefully I saw the lumber laid out and ready to load.

I planned to start working on the hog house right away, but in spite of my best intentions, I got sidetracked. My friends and I decided to build a big wooden sled (some hog house lumber went into it) to pull through the snow with our Model A's, and Mr. Brown showed us how to make good rope by stringing binder twine on a twister device and spinning the handle. When Bertha Neufeld told her father that we were making rope in school, he put a ball of binder twine in my car, expecting me to make rope for him. I had good intentions about that, too, but the ball of twine just sat in my car.

It was still there when we took a field trip to see some pigs near Buhler. I drove a carload of boys, and one of my passengers was John Dale, the acetylene hose stomper, who made any event more interesting. For some reason I thought nothing of it when he asked, as we were barreling along, if he could tie one end of the twine ball to the window crank or when, a few minutes later, he said he was hot and asked if he could open the window. Then, in the mirror, I saw Mr. Neufeld's binder twine trailing behind us, all one-thousand-plus feet of it. The other boys thought the prank was hilarious, but my sense of humor failed me when I saw cars almost a quarter mile behind us lurching crazily to avoid being flayed. At that point I did what had to be done: I pushed the foot-feed to the floor. If you've never been treated to the spectacle of an old Ford carrying six boys hollering in unfettered glee and sporting a tail a thousand feet long, you've missed something.

By the end of the school year I had cut up some lumber and built a floor for the hog house. Pop ended up hauling everything home. He hammered out a hog house in a day and said I could paint it. (My children finally painted it in the 1950s.)

Later I found out that the previous year some senior boys had built a hog house and asked Mr. Brown to inspect it. The moment he was inside, they slammed the door shut, nailed two-by-fours across it, and ran off to the next class.

 EDUCATION ON THE ROAD

We took field trips almost every week and always made an annual excursion to the Kansas State Fair in Hutchinson. One year it was my good fortune to ride in Mr. Brown's car, a black 1937 Chevy. At the fairgrounds, to our surprise, Mr. Brown led us past the horticultural exhibits and headed straight to the stock car races in the grandstand. I had never seen anything so inspiring. One driver in particular, Emory Collins, was phenomenal; he seemed to be able to make his car stick to the curves at terrific speeds.

More memorable still was the trip back to Inman. It was getting dark, old Highway 17 was full of twists and turns, and Mr. Brown wasn't done teaching for the day. "Let me show you boys what makes Mr. Collins a winner," he said when we approached the first bend. "He steps on the accelerator when he gets to a curve." Every time we reached a twist in the road, Mr. Brown stepped hard on the gas and intoned, "Boys, do you feel the wheels taking hold of the road?" Luckily, there was only so much speed the old Chevy could crank out.

Coyote hunts and crow bombings were also part of our field trip education. These activities were rather loosely organized.

In the wintertime coyote hunters, traveling in pickups carrying dogs, would scour the countryside searching for coyotes. When they spotted a coyote they released the dogs to run them down. Mr. Brown apparently thought it would be educational to watch the process.

On our coyote hunting expedition we had a hard time finding the hunters, who were purportedly somewhere north of Inman with pickup trucks and dogs. Ray, who had a load of boys in his dad's 1941 Ford, told Mr. Brown he'd scout out the hunters. Mr. Brown drove north, Ray raced (at ninety miles an hour) around the perimeter of the section, meeting Mr. Brown's car at the next corner. This went on for some time — until Mr. Brown recalled that it was Ray who had told him about the "hunt" in the first place.

It was at the crow bombing site that Mr. Brown's stoic demeanor crumbled. Crows were becoming peskier by the day. Following regular routes, thousands would sweep over our farm every morning, stopping to pick through our feedlot, then continuing their northeasterly flight. Late in the afternoon they made a return journey, finally roosting in catalpa groves near Hutchinson. They were such a nuisance that some state agency decided to set off shrapnel bombs in the catalpa trees at night. A ten-acre grove south of Buhler was the first site chosen for the state's experiment in pest management. The next day our class went to view the wretched outcome. What a sight — thousands of dead and wounded crows blackened the ground.

There happened to be intense rivalry between the Inman and Buhler high schools in those days, especially in sports and Future Farmers of America competitions. The vo-ag instructors sponsored the FFA chapters, and Mr. Brown took the responsibility seriously. He observed the rituals faithfully, at every meeting — an owl figure perched near him — chanting, "I sit here by the owl, a symbol of wisdom." FFA chapters always entered exhibits at the state fair. The Inman chapter's displays usually did very well, but the Buhler chapter was gaining on us. Mr. Brown and his Buhler counterpart, Mr. Johnson, were not friends, to say the least.

On the day of the crow bombing field trip, Mr. Brown was for some reason especially perturbed with Mr. Johnson — so perturbed, in fact, that at the catalpa grove he pulled a wounded crow out of the carnage, headed for Buhler, drove to Mr. Johnson's house, and threw the poor bird on his rival's lawn. After that, he reverted to his usual behavior — deliberate and unruffled. His personality was dry and his teaching techniques were unimaginative, but they worked.

Inman High was blessed with many excellent teachers and one standout, Mr. Matthews, who taught American history and Constitution and coached boys' basketball. He knew his academic subjects well and tolerated no nonsense in class, unlike Mr. Brown with his easygoing way. Though he had never coached an athletic team, Mr. Matthews replaced our basketball coach in midseason and was so effective that the following year his team won the state championship.

Boys who didn't qualify for the basketball team took gym class. Maybe we didn't have the skill and coordination of the basketball players, but under Mr. Brown's tutelage we did learn the rudiments of gymnastics, boxing, and wrestling.

One day during my sophomore year a husky kid named Mark accosted me in an empty hallway and said he was going to beat the s____t out of me because I was a C.O. Most Mennonites were indeed conscientious objectors, opposed to war and obliged as a matter of principle to refrain from armed combat. But I understood how Mark felt; his brother was in the navy. So I didn't argue with him, though I hadn't thought much about the issue. I was trying to come up with a reasonable response when Mark drew back his arm and aimed his fist at my jaw. Almost without thinking, I did as Mr. Brown had instructed in gym class, raising my left arm like a boxer. All the kinetic energy in Mark's striking arm was unleashed on my elbow, at which point he turned and ran. The next day he came to school with his hand wrapped up, telling everyone he had broken his hand in a fall on the ice.

Although I managed to acquit myself respectably in football practice and a hallway scrap, I wasn't a fighter or an athlete. My interests were literary. There were so many great books even in Inman High School's limited library collection that I tried to read a new book every day or two. One of my favorites was Richard Halliburton's *Royal Road to Romance,* an account of the adventures of a young college graduate (Halliburton) who thumbed his nose at tradition to roam the world on a shoestring. He climbed the Matterhorn in the winter, swam the Panama Canal (duly registered as the *S.S. Halliburton*), dove into a sacred sacrificial pool at Chichén Itzá (a sacred Mayan archaeological site in Mexico) alone on a moonlit night, and followed routes taken by legendary heroes. Halliburton might have embellished his fascinating history, which he recorded in a series of books written in the late 1920s and early 1930s. Nevertheless, there is no question that he was remarkably bold (he perished in the Pacific on a one-man voyage from California to Hawaii), and I found his tales very inspiring. They certainly aroused my desire to experience life outside the perimeter of Section 27.

As early as grade school I had longed to be a writer, though I had no idea what "being a writer" actually entailed. The Halliburton books magnified that ambition, and I took advantage of opportunities for creative writing in my English classes. I always earned A's for my work, unless mechanics — grammar, spelling, punctuation, and so on — were factored into the grade. I hated grammar and argued with my teachers about the need for a farm boy to know the difference between an adjective and an adverb. Still, teachers praised my writing. Unfortunately, because I was either obtuse or immersed in Mr. Brown's pragmatic vo-ag perspective, I failed to understand that grammar and syntax were essential skills for writers. Thus the dream, which had begun as a goal, soon became nothing more than a fantasy.

The deck was stacked against Mom's ambition for me also, it seemed. Between my father's wish for a Penner to carry on the Section 27 legacy and my own lack of confidence in my ability to decide otherwise, Pop's intentions seemed certain of fulfillment.

7 The Way We Were

Like most transplanted cultures, ours quickly became a hybrid of old and new, tradition and circumstance. In the 1930s, Section 27 was still quite isolated in many ways — by our language (Plautdietsch, a unique Dutch dialect commonly known as Low Dutch or Low German) and by our peculiar piety, among other things. Yet we shared with other Depression-era Dust Bowl dwellers the economic and agricultural woes that bankrupted farmers and townspeople alike.

As children do, I saw life on Section 27 as the norm. We lived at the center of the world and everything outside was "foreign." Six miles east of us was Turkey Creek, said to be the boundary between the Russian and Swiss Mennonites (who originated in Switzerland and also came to America in 1874). There was a story about one of the old patriarchs taking his young grandson to the top of a windmill, pointing across Turkey Creek, and saying, "Boy, over there is the land of the Philistines; stay away from their girls." Which side of Turkey Creek they were on is irrelevant; the world was pretty small on both sides.

As I grew older, I began to notice that the rest of the world lived differently than we did. How odd it was to see a man plowing on Sunday, a policeman smoking a cigarette, a boy wearing short pants, a man with a beard, another man wearing a suit when it wasn't Sunday and there was no funeral. Sin and strange people were all around. (General Conference Mennonite men seldom wore beards in the 1930s.)

In the 1930s and 1940s, surrounded by acres and acres of wheat fields and pastures, our farm was seldom visited by outsiders, especially during the four months when there was no school. For days at a time I had only my sisters, Marvella and Rachel, and Pop and Mom to talk with.

If we were lonely, we didn't know it. We talked to the farm animals, we read the daily *Hutchinson News,* we had a telephone and, later, a radio, and we made weekly trips to town. Church and Sunday visits and special occasions, such as weddings, brought the families together.

◖ PRIPS AND PANCAKES

Weddings were beautiful affairs, formal and highly entertaining. At the Hoffnungsau Church, the bride and her entourage wore elaborate gowns, the groom and his attendants wore new Sunday suits, and the wedding march was played on a grand piano. The boys customarily sat in the front row of the balcony, the grand piano right below us. If we leaned over the railing, we had a bird's-eye view of the piano and pianist. At one wedding the pianist, a rather buxom woman, wore a dress that, while perfectly proper, was unusually revealing when viewed from directly above. As her performance grew more and more emotional, she leaned and swayed, the neckline of her dress moving in and out with her phrasing. As word spread about the scenic vista below, some of the (other) boys actually came quite close to falling over the railing.

A wedding always meant a feast. After the wedding, before the boys were allowed in the church basement to eat, there was usually a lot of running around among the parked cars. Confrontations and fights often ensued. I had a distant cousin called Red who was bigger than I was. Red had it in for me, and if he was around, I had to be on my guard all evening.

It was worth the peril, though, because we got to eat all the baloney, cheese, zwieback, sweet pickles, and sugar cubes we could handle. When the time came, we rushed to the basement stairs, creating a bottleneck like pigs crowding through a hog house door at slop time. The servers were high school boys and girls paired at random. They were too absorbed with each other to notice how often they replenished our platters of baloney and cheese, and we were so busy gorging ourselves with slices of heavily frosted sheet cake and bricks of half-vanilla, half-strawberry ice cream that we barely had time to stuff sugar cubes into our pockets.

The sugar cubes were there for the coffee and prips drinkers. Many of the older people drank prips, a hot beverage made from roasted cereal grains. I watched as grownups poured cream and dropped sugar cubes into their steaming cups, which they did more lavishly at festive occasions. They'd stir the mixture for a while, then pour some into a saucer, pick up the saucer with both hands, blow on the liquid to cool it, and slurp with abandon. Someday, I told myself, I would learn to drink like that.

The shivaree the night before the wedding at the bride's home offered a tacitly sanctioned outlet for creative mischief. Some shivarees went beyond the unspoken limit, especially if the groom had been an aggressive shivareer in the past. Amazing feats of strength and daring were performed; a wagon or chicken coop might be placed on the peak of a barn or a car placed up on blocks. All it took was for someone to suggest putting the plow in the middle of the yard and the heavy four-bottom plow would appear like magic. Then someone would say, "Let's trip it." Old farmers will understand the problem this created for the bride's father. The only way to "untrip" a mechanical-lift plow is to pull it about thirty feet, tripping the lift lever as the plow rolls forward, all the while plowing an unwelcome furrow in the middle of the yard.

The pancake shivaree took place some evening after the wedding when the young couple was cozily involved in the bedroom. With great fanfare — horns blaring and much banging on doors and windows — the "guests" demanded admittance and a pancake supper. While the couple fried pancakes, the friendly visitors crumbled crackers in the bed or got canned goods out of the cupboard and soaked off the labels. At one springtime shivaree, paper bags full of fluttering moths were released in the house.

There were plenty of other special occasions to provide diversions for us boys. Our neighbors, the J. P. Balzers (women didn't seem to have first names back then), invited us to their golden anniversary celebration. Close as they lived, I barely knew them, but I was aware of a little tension between them and my folks, apparently having something to do with J. P. being a preacher in a church that was a bit different from ours. I heard the folks talking about revival meetings, which Pop didn't have much use for. (We had been to a revival meeting once. The wind was blowing, the tent flaps were fluttering, and the preacher was saying we should come up to the front before we went to hell. Then a lot of men gathered money from the congregation. Pop muttered about collections all the way home.)

Nevertheless, we went to the golden anniversary gathering, and we boys had a great time. We didn't have to go to the service, so we spent the evening, with its long summer twilight, sliding down the roof of an old shed in our Sunday suits. We really shined up the seats of our pants. I think it was Waldo who hit a nail and ripped his trousers wide open.

 SUNDAY RULES

On Sundays we went to Sunday School and services at the Hoffnungsau Church. Sunday was supposed to be a day of rest, but there were exceptions. You could milk cows and feed the livestock, for example. It was acceptable to throw hay down from the loft into the mangers but not to start a tractor to haul hay in from the field. Similar principles applied in the house. Mom wouldn't go to the garden to pick tomatoes, but it was permissible to fix an elaborate meal for Sunday company or prepare a dish for a potluck dinner at church.

Children's play was supposed to be more restrained on Sundays. One Sunday afternoon at the Martens farm, we boys had begun an energetic game of cowboys and Indians when Mr. Martens put a stop to it, though I wasn't sure whether he objected because it was Sunday or because we were pretending to shoot each other.

The Sunday rules were so mundane that they were seldom addressed in sermons or catechism classes. The usual forum for debates about what was acceptable was the Sunday school class. Was it wrong, someone asked, to use the tractor on Sunday for emergency tillage when the wind came up and caused the fields to "blow"? There were those who believed that if you hadn't anticipated the problem on Saturday, you must wait until Monday to address the problem.

One Sunday in February, Pop was put to the test when a cold northwest wind came up and soil particles began to roll in the dry field of wheat west of our house. The wheat was sparse, and on Saturday, when the wind had been calm and it had looked like rain, there appeared to be a chance of saving the crop. We went to church Sunday morning, and by the time we got home, dirt was beginning to pile up along the mulberry hedge. Good steward of the land that he was, Pop was in agony. Not only was he losing part of his wheat crop but he was also losing precious soil and it was getting colder. By Monday the frozen soil would be too hard to chisel. Pop put water in the Case tractor, hitched up the duckfoot (that is, the field cultivator), and went to work — without, it seemed to me, endangering his immortal soul.

I was about thirteen when Pop let me drive home from church one Sunday. He was sitting beside me in the Pontiac, talking to Mom in the back seat, when I passed a slow-moving car. When Pop realized what I had done, he was angry and mortified. I had broken a Sunday rule; what's more, it was an older couple from our church driving the slow car.

❧ SOCIAL GRACES

It was customary on Sunday to visit relatives and friends. Sunday visits reflected your standing in the pecking order, and the folks were a little insecure on that score. Discussions about the visiting situation usually began in the car on the way home from church. (It was one such conversation that had occupied Pop's attention when I passed the older couple in the car.) Since the Sunday visits were practically the only social activity Mom engaged in, she was very particular about them. Her mother, her siblings, and (grudgingly) Pop's mother and siblings had priority. Thus, there was little time for friends, probably accounting for the folks' insecurity about their social standing.

Sunday afternoon visits always included *faspa,* a traditional four o'clock light meal. The standard fare for Sunday *faspa* was zwieback with lots of homemade jelly, cheese and baloney, home canned fruit, and cake for dessert. Zwieback are a unique dinner roll made by squeezing the dough into two round globs and putting one on top of the other. An expert zwieback baker, my wife's sister Ruthanna, says the difference between plain rolls and zwieback is that zwieback lack milk and eggs and the dough is firmer. Shaping the dough and setting one atop the other properly appears to be an art difficult to master.

Faspa was also served to threshing crews and men working in the fields. Maybe it is somewhat similar to a coffee break except with more substance. Supper on the farm came at a later hour, usually after dark when chores were all done.

The Sunday visitation discussions would often continue throughout dinner. (In rural America the three regular meals are generally referred to as breakfast, dinner, and supper.) Finally, Mom and Pop would reach a decision. Then Pop would go to the telephone, listen to see if anyone was on the line, and say, "Line 12 busy?" to make sure the party line was available. If nobody answered, he would ring Central by turning the telephone crank.

Central — the operator — always listened in on conversations "to make sure the connection was good." Calling a relative was safe but requesting anyone else's number was risky. Asking to be connected with the deacon's phone, for example, could set off a chain of speculation: "Who do they think they are?" "They must be having a problem." "Since when have they been friends?" Mom, especially, hated placing her affairs in a public forum, and we never knew just how public it might be. There were twenty-one farms on line twelve, and anyone could be listening.

When Pop got through to whomever he was calling, his side of the conversation — carried on in Low Dutch — went something like this: "Hello, is this by Siemens? . . . That was a fine rain yesterday. . . . Oh, we had almost two inches. . . . What are you doing after dinner? . . . Yes, I will also an afternoon nap have. . . . Would you for *faspa* like to come over? I think last time we came over to you. . . . Yes, that was a few years back."

The negotiation would continue for a while, carefully balancing friendship and obligation. It was far preferable to be the one receiving a call rather than risk having your call considered an imposition. Worse yet was the dilemma that arose when Uncle Dave (Mom's brother) was bringing his family over and Uncle John (Pop's sister's husband) called.

If someone was coming over, Mom's day of rest would no longer be restful. There would be no nap. She had to check the parlor, dust the buffet in the dining room once more, put the extra leaves in the big round table, and run down to the basement to get the best-looking jar of peaches out of the pantry. While Pop was getting ready to take his nap, Mom would complain that the zwieback were a little too brown because the phone had rung at the wrong time. Pop would wake up just in time to usher the guests into the house.

I was six or seven, when a family, I'll call them the Joneses from Buhler, came to visit. The afternoon began like most, with the usual praise for the house (we were in the new house by then) and the parlor furniture, followed by obligatory conversation about how well the hens were laying and how low wheat prices were. Then Mr. Jones surprised everyone by saying that "in these end times" it wasn't surprising, and probably didn't matter, that egg and wheat prices were down.

I had been getting ready to go outside, and I was in the next room when Mr. Jones began his oration. "Yes," he continued, "the end of the world is near. All the signs are pointing to the coming of the Great Day." Pop protested mildly, pointing out that the Bible says no one will know when the end comes, but I was already scared.

Mr. Jones quoted Scripture about famine, pestilence, earthquakes, and "rumors of war." Pop kept trying to change the subject, but Jones was on a roll. He touched on the Depression, the great dust storms, and the wars in Ethiopia and Spain. He talked about cannons booming and said that one of these days "the heavenly host would come out of a great white cloud, trumpets blaring." Some of us, he added, would be "caught up in the air." I had heard enough and ran off.

MATTERS OF FAITH

What Mr. Jones had said continued to bother me. One warm night, when the windows were open, I heard cannons booming in the distance. I had been asleep and woke up in a cold sweat. Still I could hear it clearly, the random firing, maybe the guns in Spain. Finally I fell back to sleep.

The next morning there were no guns booming, but I heard them again a few days later when the weather changed suddenly. In the late afternoon, great white clouds built up in the east, the wind became dead calm, and the cannons were booming under those towering clouds; I was terribly afraid. I looked up at the awesome clouds, lit by the setting sun, and expected to see Jesus and the heavenly host in shining robes descending from the white billows. I waited for the sound of the golden trumpets. Then I saw Pop, calm and serene, going out to the barn with the milk buckets. Jesus did not come that day.

If I had had a different kind of relationship with my parents, I might have told them how troubled I was. Instead, I had to wait in agony until the realization dawned on me that on days when there was only a light east wind the booming of the huge single-cylinder oil field engines five miles away was clearly audible.

Sometimes there were Sunday evening visits, but church doings took priority. There were, for example, monthly C.E. meetings. Christian Endeavor, an ecumenical organization, sponsored both Junior C.E. and Senior C.E. An elected committee gave us musical assignments and topics to study. Some of the members read the long, tedious papers they had prepared citing dozens of Scripture passages. "A pooling of mutual ignorance," someone once called these readings. All discussions related to one of two themes — that our faith was pleasing to God and that all around us there was a lot of evil to watch out for.

Other Sunday evenings were given over to missionaries on furlough from the heathen world. It was interesting to see the slides taken in foreign countries and hear the stories about heathens worshiping idols and cows. Clearly, said the missionaries, the heathens were in desperate need of our Gospel. The commentary explained that and the slides revealed great poverty — half-naked people living in thatched huts and having only dismal roads to travel on. It was possible, we were told, to teach these poor creatures the basics of building nice houses for the missionaries, and with patience the heathens could be taught to be good servants in those houses.

Sometimes, on weekday evenings, there would be rehearsals for church programs such as Children's Day and Christmas Eve. It was during the Depression, and people took care not to drive unnecessarily, so we carpooled with neighbors and were instructed to stand at the road when our ride came by. Henry Neufeld would drive up in a yellow-green 1936 Plymouth, already loaded with kids, and my sisters and I would start a second layer of passengers.

At church we lined up according to height and practiced singing and marching to the front of the church. One Christmas I had to be one of the magi. Mom was proud of me, but I hated every minute, especially since I had to sing — alone, in my toneless voice the second stanza of "We Three Kings" as I marched through the church in my crown and purple bathrobe.

Once a month the women's sewing societies met for quilting and other needlework. The items they made were sold at an annual auction to raise money for missionaries overseas. Mom's generation of women didn't drive, so one of the men would drive her and the other neighboring women in the Senior Sewing Society to the church. A younger group called itself the Happy Hour Circle, blithely unaware of the name's early evening barhopping connotations. The younger women were emancipated enough to drive themselves to church.

❦ BLOOD AND GORE

Men, however, had more social outlets than women did. One annual winter activity was the rabbit hunt. From the late 1930s into the 1950s, jackrabbits were a menace to crops, gardens, and trees, so the farmers organized rabbit hunts to eliminate them. One, in which I took part, started right across the road from Section 27. Men and boys piled into the back of a farm truck and, as the truck drove around the section, jumped off at about two-hundred-foot intervals.

Depending on the hunt rules, we armed ourselves with either clubs or shotguns. Once a section was encircled, we walked toward the middle, making as much noise as possible. Rabbits and even coyotes ran ahead of us into the entrapment circle. Nearing the center of the circle, for safety's sake, we could shoot only back, away from the circle, not into it. That meant finishing off a multitude of cornered rabbits with clubs. Hundreds of rabbits would be slaughtered, their carcasses bought by a mink farmer as meat for his animals. The hunts never seemed to diminish the rabbit population, but disease and the changing agricultural environment have almost eliminated the flop-eared creatures. Now I miss them.

Equally intense was the annual hog butchering ritual. It was a labor-intensive project, and my folks and aunts and uncles helped each other. Hog butchering took place in the winter; the meat wouldn't spoil and there was less work on the farm. Usually two or three other couples came to help at dawn, eager to get to work and equipped with buckets, pans, aprons, and knives. If Uncle George were in the crew, he'd bring his .22 special to shoot the hogs.

Pop would fill the rendering kettle with water and place kindling and firewood under it the night before, lighting the fire in the morning before going out to milk the cows. Mom would prepare dinner ahead of time and set out the paraphernalia to clean the casings in the basement. Near the shop where the men would be butchering, a block and tackle hung from a tree over the scalding barrel.

The hog, or hogs, to be butchered were already penned. Pop sometimes made a wire bit to put in the hog's mouth to guide it out of the pen. Uncle George would be waiting, and as soon as the hog stood still, facing him, he fired. One shot always did the job. With a small red dot between the eyes and (I thought) a look of stunned disbelief, the hog fell over, its knees buckling. One of the other men would approach, carefully (in case one of the hog's legs should kick), and slit the jugular with a long knife.

The men would roll the hog onto a sled and pull it to the block and tackle. Then came the dangerous part, when the men ran to the house to get boiling water from the rendering kettle — always debating how much water was needed in the barrel to scald the hog — ran back to the block and tackle, hoisted the hog, and dipped it repeatedly into the water. After they scraped the hog to remove all the hair, the real butchering started.

The men disemboweled and quartered the carcass and carried the meat into the shop, where it was processed on hygienically clean tables. The women put the intestines into large dishpans and carried them to the basement, where they scrubbed them and turned them inside out to use as casings for the sausages.

It was customary to be solicitous about preferences. "Frank, do you want a lot of bacon? How do you want the hams trimmed? Do you want the head cleaned? A lot of cracklings, Bertha?" The pace was fast and furious until noon. By noon, the men were nearly done with their part, with only the sausage meat left to grind and a great deal of cleaning up to do. One or two of the men joined the women to stir lard in the rendering kettle and keep the fire going. The sausage stuffing began midafternoon, and before long there was meat sausage, liverwurst, and headcheese.

By *faspa* time everyone was ready to taste the results of their hard work. It was undoubtedly the most caloric meal of the year, with the assorted meats including spareribs still hot and dripping fat from the rendering kettle. If my sisters and I arrived home from school in time for *faspa,* we got to taste the goodies. Once when I took a big bite of headcheese, my teeth closed on something metallic. "That's the bullet I put in the brain," Uncle George laughed. I never ate headcheese again.

From then on, cracklings — bits of fatty meat that remained after the lard was rendered — and liverwurst were breakfast staples. Mom squeezed as much grease from the cracklings as she could with a little hand press and then heated them. Big dollops of blackstrap molasses disguised the fatty taste. And nothing was more delicious than liverwurst on coarse rye bread.

🔥 FAMILY TIES

The family was always together at breakfast. The hour and the menu varied with the season, but we would all be there at the appointed time. The same was true of the other meals except when we were in school. Pop believed firmly that the family must be together at mealtime. When his children grew up and married, Pop would assess our family harmony by asking, "Do you all eat together at the same time?"

My parents' way of life was simple and their values straightforward. Harmony and integrity were important. Pop never mentioned money as something to strive for. He was naturally concerned, during the Depression, about the price of wheat — at one point it dropped to twenty-five cents a bushel — but the folks made do, and Pop had been prudent enough to be out of debt when the hard times began. He waited to buy until he had the cash, he believed that money should come from hard work, and he had no use for "speculators" who, as he believed, profited by taking the farmers' hard-earned money. In fact, he blamed the speculators for the Depression and said it was dishonest to make money without working for it.

Pop was an independent thinker. He openly questioned dogmatic biblical interpretations of Creation, for example, and the Second Coming. Still, his values were basic and uncomplicated: do not smoke or drink alcohol; respect women; work hard; be honest. Greed bothered him more than anything else. He criticized farmers who bought more and more land; once you have enough to support your family, he believed, you should leave the rest for younger farmers. He didn't mind working alone for hours at a time. For Mom's part, between her housekeeping and child-rearing responsibilities and the availability of line 12, she was busily occupied most of the time.

Mom and Pop — for that matter, all the Penners and Gaedderts — were very private people, never openly emotional. For all I knew, my sisters and I were the products of immaculate conception; I recall my parents embracing only once. Looking back, I see evidence of their affection for each other, but it wasn't apparent to me as a child. They bickered some, usually about Pop's expenditures for the farm. Mom didn't approve of the silo, for example. Her brothers didn't have silos, and she didn't know why we needed one.

When Pop had polio, however, it was especially hard on Mom because of his brother's (Mom's first husband) death from the same terrible illness. She was unusually tender with us children when she tucked us into bed and said a prayer, but she was in anguish. Uncle John and Aunt Sarah drove to Newton and brought Mom home after Pop was admitted to the hospital. When they came home I knew that something was horribly wrong when they walked in the door. The only explanation us children received was that Pop was in the hospital.

Aunt Lizzie moved in with us, and Mom was grateful in spite of past differences. One morning a man from the county board of health knocked on the door. When Mom opened it, he stepped back quickly as if she could infect him just by looking at him. Keeping his distance, he said that we were "in quarantine," that I would have to stay home from school, that nobody who wasn't already there could enter our house, and that the house itself must be fumigated. Then he asked Mom to shut the door and stay inside, but we could hear him pounding on the house. Eventually, we went outside to see what the pounding had been about. He was gone and there was a big red sign on the house that read "WARNING: Infantile Paralysis." A day or so later, a man in a Model A coupe drove up, but, apparently seeing the sign, he jammed on the brakes, shifted into reverse, and backed out of the yard as fast as he could.

Warning or no warning, a young neighbor, Jake Pauls, came over twice a day to do the chores. Uncle John often drove Mom to Newton to visit Pop, but she could see him only through a window. One time I was allowed to go along. It was a shock to see Pop in bed, weakly waving at us.

After Uncle John fumigated the house, I went back to school. I usually walked to school, but one bitterly cold day Aunt Lizzie offered to drive me.

I declined; she, however, said that if I felt it was too cold, to come back for a ride. Well, I ran halfway to school, then decided it was too cold and ran home.

I don't know how long Pop was in the hospital, and I have no memory of his homecoming. He had been one of the lucky ones; polio often damaged the muscles used for breathing, and those so afflicted were placed in iron lungs. Pop regained most of his strength, but damage had been done that would disable him in later years.

Polio became a nationwide epidemic, creating a general fearfulness that closed swimming pools and curtailed attendance at public events. Young and old, rich and poor suffered. Many became permanently disabled, and many died. Later we would learn that the disease had crippled President Roosevelt. No one knew what caused polio. Two horses on our farm had died just before Pop became ill, and we thought that flies might have carried the plague from beast to man.

The medical breakthroughs that were just a few decades away were of no use to us. Childhood illnesses were a lonely ordeal. There wasn't much that a doctor or anyone else could do about them. Mom and Pop would make the diagnosis, sometimes with the aid of a telephone call to Dr. Johnson in Inman. If you had spots, you had measles, larger spots were chicken pox, a red rash meant scarlet fever, and swelling in the neck indicated mumps — all of which must simply be endured. More serious were a deep, breath-stealing cough and a high fever, signs of whooping cough, pneumonia, or even diphtheria. For these symptoms a doctor would come to the house and offer grave looks, genuine concern, and vile potions.

We were aware of two kinds of measles, the "real" measles and the three-day measles. I had them both. When I was sick with the "real" measles, I had to stay in the bedroom with the shades drawn for several weeks.

My first encounter with a doctor had nothing to do with illness. One night, after my sister Marvella and I had gone to bed, we heard a great commotion. Peeking out the bedroom door, I saw an old man with a black bag and heard someone clattering around in the kitchen. Pop saw me and told me to go back to sleep. The next morning a woman we had never seen before — who had been responsible for the clattering — told Marvella and me we had a baby sister. Mom seemed to have disappeared, but the woman

Frank and Bertha Penner's children in 1948:
Marvella, Milferd, and Rachel.

stayed, making frequent trips to the guest bedroom in answer to the baby's cries. Finally that afternoon Marvella and I got to see Mom and the baby.

Pop told us that "Siemens's Ann" (a way of referring to people in the Low Dutch vernacular, as in "Neufeld's Peter") would be staying with us for a while. The man with the black bag, Pop said, was Dr. Johnson, who had "found" the baby. I couldn't understand why Mom had to rest in bed when Dr. Johnson was the one who had done all the work.

Mom wanted to name the baby Bertha Francis, but Pop wanted to name her Mary after Grandma Maria Penner. So they named the baby Rachel.

8 🌿 The Farmstead

The tall prairie grasses were gone from Section 27 by the 1930s, when I was a little boy. Every acre had succumbed to the plow or the cow. On our half of the section, thirty-five acres were in heavily grazed pasture, about five acres were in farmstead, and the rest was in cultivation. My parents owned the southeast quarter, Grandma Maria owned the northeast quarter, and the Balzer family still farmed the west half. We grew wheat, oats, barley, alfalfa, and kaffir corn; milk cows, beef cattle, pigs, chickens, ducks, and sheep were the livestock enterprises. We used horses to pull some farm machines until 1937.

The Penner farmstead, located to this day where Grandpa David F. built the Queen Anne house in 1898, is at the center of the south boundary of the Penner half section. For as long as I can remember, the driveway has run northeast for a few hundred feet before turning due north for another three hundred feet, where the building sites begin. The dogleg is there to accommodate a diked ditch that enters Section 27 at a northeasterly angle, runs north for about a quarter mile, then turns east toward the Blaze Fork. The ditch was dug in 1921, not for wetland drainage but to carry water from a seven-thousand-acre watershed west and south of Inman. The Penner farm is noted for its curved driveway, a rarity in a community that is rectilinearly oriented.

Remaining from the pioneer days are a double-row mulberry hedge planted to produce silkworms, three bur oaks (the patriarchs) near the windmill well, and the old claim shack. The mulberry hedge might well have been planted the very first year, in the fall of 1874. Pop recalled his grandfather saying they had brought the seeds from Russia with the hope of raising silkworms. Mulberry trees are native to Kansas, but I believe the

The Penner farmstead viewed from the east, about 1955. Note Mil and Verna Lee's cottage on the far left, sheep coming home from pasture on the far right, the mulberry hedge on west and north perimeters, and the Balzer farmstead in the upper center.

story that these seeds came from Russia. Further proof is the fact that many of Section 27's mulberries bear white fruit, which is not a native species. As a young connoisseur of mulberries, I soon discovered that we had three varieties — purple, white, and pink, with the white mulberries being the sweetest. Going barefoot under the mulberry trees was a squishy purple mess.

The mulberry hedge has been cut to ground level at least three times. I have observed during my seventy-year watch that uncut mulberry trees in a hedgerow die, but cut trees rejuvenate. The first cutting I remember was in the mid-1930s. Pop hired a crew that used a horizontal buzz saw mounted on a Ford Model T frame. Several men pulled the thirty-inch unguarded saw blade, pivoting on an eight-foot arm, into the tree trunk. Two other men used long poles to push over the cut trees. After chain saws came along, the job was much easier.

Twice I have cut the hedge by myself, and in the process I have come to feel responsible for those trees. It is almost a sacred bond. As I see the golden chips rolling out of the chain saw's kerf (the groove cut by the saw), I know that I'm stealing life from the venerable tree, but that with the coming of spring, new life will sprout from the old root. It gives me a sense of connection with my grandfather and great-grandfather, though from what Pop told me I imagine it was young David F. who bent his back to plant the seeds and manned the hoe to cultivate the growing trees.

Mulberry logs make good firewood. When I watch them burn, I think of the little seedlings sprouting on a treeless plain; the sparks and pops call to mind generations of little boys and girls picking juicy berries.

No one knows exactly when the three bur oaks were planted, but they show up in photographs taken at the turn of the century. Nearby were the windmill and a stock-watering tank. When we hauled alfalfa hay to unload at the north end of the barn, the hayrack would pass between and under two of the oaks. It was fun to ride at the very top of the load, cradled deep in the sweet-smelling hay and feeling the strong oak branches sweeping overhead.

When the county rebuilt our road in 1936, two cook shacks parked under these oaks. Men from Lindsborg, who boarded there with their teams, used horse-drawn drag scrapers to build driveway approaches and install culverts. A drag scraper was essentially a steel pan with a cutting edge, a hitch yoke, and two wooden handles. A man lifting the two handles as the horses pulled would draw the cutting edge into the ground. When the pan was full he would release the handles and guide the horses to the dump area, where he would again pick up the handles and give the pan a quick flip, unloading five hundred pounds of dirt. Ninety-two-year-old Ben Willems, a Ruthie's Café regular, remembers McPherson County paying him $3.20 a day ("a fabulous wage") for team use and labor at about that time.

Pop never said much about what the farmstead was like when he was young, but one day when we were drilling post holes along the county road, he mentioned that cottonwoods had once towered along our side of the road all the way to the farm east of us. At the turn of the twenty-first century, only two trees and one stump remained of this once proud row. By the spring of 2000, McPherson County bulldozers had removed even those.

❦ THE CHOSEN PLACE

As related in an earlier chapter, the claim shack — still standing, though very fragile — was on the premises when Great-grandpa David bought the land in 1874. The shack's presence might have drawn his attention to the spot as an ideal place to build, though it seems strange that a solitary cattle herder would in effect choose the site that has been the Penner farmstead for more than 125 years. The faint outline of a streambed meandering across the farmstead hints at what might have been the reason for his preference. Maybe, late one spring afternoon, the herder came across the clear stream, a welcome sight after a day spent pushing his way through tall grasses. He may have tethered his horse and spent the night there, beguiled by bullfrogs singing bass in concert with their higher-voiced cousins, refreshed by the sounds of fish splashing and ducks settling down for the night. However idyllic it might once have been, the placid watercourse was replaced in 1921 by a manmade ditch that, when it flows at all, spews muddy floodwaters.

In 1939 Pop decided to build a machine shed where the claim shack was. The claim shack had been "built around" — expanded on one end and with a lean-to patched onto the west side. Part of the addition was a corncrib, which Pop didn't need; the rest was an implement shed with a dirt floor, though the shack and corncrib had wooden flooring.

Pop loved farm machinery, and protecting it had high priority. He used the implement shed to store a combine header, a binder, grain drills, and an old side-crank Wallis tractor. It was quite dark inside, there being neither windows nor electric lights. The darkness and the greasy dirt floor, which chickens and who knows what other animals had stirred and scratched to a manure-rich powder, were irresistible to a barefoot boy. Eventually, though, Pop razed everything except the claim shack, which he moved about sixty feet west.

BASIC STRUCTURES

The heart of any farmstead was the barn. Our barn was quite large — eighty by twenty-eight feet with a twelve-foot lean-to. It was unique in that each end gable had a rain hood and large doors at haymow level about eight feet wide and twelve feet tall at the peak. Inside, at the roof apex, was a steel track with a carrier for lifting hay up into the barn and carrying it to the middle.

The original barn had been just forty feet long, but it grew as the farm prospered. By the mid-1920s, the barn could handle twenty horses. The original portion had heavy wood floors set on floor joists supported by limestone rocks. The space beneath the floor was a haven for feral cats, skunks, possums, and other critters.

An undated photograph shows the original barn with painted trim around the windows and doors, a fanciful ventilator, and turned gable ornaments. As was true of the Queen Anne house, the ornate frills had disappeared by the 1930s. The original barn had a carriage room that later served as a garage. Common when the barn was built (but rare today) were arrow-straight full two-by-twelve-inch timbers twenty-eight feet long used as ceiling joists. Supporting members were four-by-six-inch wood posts. I remember the barn as a light gray, though I wanted it to be red like my friend Johnny's barn.

Times were tough for everyone, but much more severe for people who were less well prepared than Pop was. The folks had no debts, and, living on a diversified farm, they were practically self-sufficient. In fact, economic conditions were in some ways advantageous for Pop because he had money in a bank that remained solvent. Labor was cheap, as were many building materials, so Pop made major improvements on the farm, constructing not only the elevator but also a machine shed and a new house. He also expanded the chicken barn and bought machinery. He was frugal, but he believed in doing everything well, and everything he built was ample and stout. Not one to gloat while others were suffering, Pop understood that success was to some extent a matter of luck. In part because of the Depression, he refused to borrow money at any time during his farming years, possibly passing up some excellent opportunities. Still, the best years the folks had financially were during the Depression.

Pop's pride and joy was his grain elevator, a thirty–by–thirty-two-foot tin-clad granary with an inside elevator to carry grain from the pit to the bins. Pop designed and built this state-of-the-art structure in 1930, just as the Depression began. A large single-cylinder stationary engine set in a corner powered the elevator. A system of flat belts and line shafts applied power at the top of the headhouse thirty-five feet above the floor. The building shook when the International engine cranked up and the pulleys began to turn.

Like the early Hart-Parr tractor, the elevator engine, with two huge flywheels, was a hit-or-miss affair. It would fire only when the governor called for power. A hole in the wall led the exhaust outside, so everyone could hear when Pop was elevating or cleaning wheat. Under full load there were 240 solid beats a minute. When the elevator cups ran empty, the engine would coast for a time, going hiss, hiss, then suddenly fire a loud bang when the flywheels lost their momentum.

The elevator belt carrying the buckets had to run at a precise speed to spill the grain properly when it reached the top. Pop loved to talk about how he figured this out, considering engine speed and pulley diameters through a series of jackshafts to reduce the headhouse pulley speed to the required revolutions per minute. It wasn't a difficult engineering feat, but Pop wasn't an engineer. He had an eighth-grade education and had taken a few drafting lessons through correspondence.

HIGHJINKS

One summer day a Lake Valley classmate came to spend the day with me. His name was Menno, and his folks had dropped him off without warning. I could see that Mom wasn't too happy about it.

To entertain Menno, I took him into the elevator. There were wooden bins on either side of the inside drive, and upstairs were more uncovered bins full of wheat. For a while we had fun just walking barefoot in the wheat, but that activity soon lost its appeal and we looked for something a little more exciting to do. We thought it would be fun to go up to the third level and jump into the wheat. Then we looked up at the headhouse platform and decided to jump from there.

When we climbed the ladder to the top and looked down, almost twenty feet, the view was scary. We went back down a level and jumped down into the wheat, but the lure of the greater height was irresistible. We stood, teetering on the brink, then backed off several times like novice divers on the high board. I was way too scared to jump. Menno probably was, too, but a boy has his pride.

After vacillating for an hour, Menno shouted, "I'm doing it." He took the leap, and I had to follow. I didn't know whether or not I was going to die, but I jumped. Swish, thud. I was alive, my overalls were full of wheat, and my feet had hit the bottom of the bin. We were thrashing around in almost four feet of grain. Somehow we got free, looked at each other, and said, "Let's do it again." Later we would hear about the boy who a few years earlier, playing in a neighbor's elevator, had suffocated in wheat.

 LESSER BARNS

Though Pop had designed the elevator, he used a plan recommended by the county agent to build the pig barn. It was a low structure, the upper half being open on the side with the sunniest exposure. An inside alleyway gave us access to the feed troughs, and there was a feed bin at one end. The pigs pushed their way through low swinging doors to get in and out.

Pandemonium erupted when someone entered the pig barn with the slop bucket. Pigs that were outside wallowing in the mud would all hit the doors at the same time. Squealing, grunting, and pushing, they would crowd the trough. Like every farm household, we fed the pigs skim milk and kitchen scraps mixed with mash. The slop bucket was the archetypal garbage disposal, ever present in the kitchen or near the cream separator.

I hated the pigs. They were the most difficult of all animals to catch, with nothing to hold onto except the ears or legs. For a time we had a red orphan pig that thought it was a dog. When it was small it ran around the farmyard, which was entertaining to watch, but the fun ended when it got bigger and started tearing down the laundry from the wash line and digging up the yard.

Just as pigs were efficient garbage-disposal systems, chickens were excellent lawnmowers. In fact, farmers back then didn't own lawnmowers; traffic and chickens kept most of the weeds down. Chickens created more landscaping problems than they solved, however. Their droppings were everywhere, and so were their dust baths.

A dust bath is a shallow hole much like a buffalo wallow, but chicken-size. Chickens scratch in the dirt until it's the consistency of talcum powder. The birds love to "bathe" and flutter their wings in these dusty beds. Considering everything there was for a barefoot child to step in, it's easy to see why we had to wash our feet before entering the house.

Any weeds not trampled had to be cut, which Pop accomplished with the mowing machine once or twice a summer after he had cut alfalfa. He did spot mowing with a scythe. Either method left sharp stubble, another hazard of going barefoot.

About 150 hens and a complement of roosters resided in the chicken house, which was a long, low structure with screened, open windows facing south. Inside was open floor space where chickens wandered around, ate from feeders, and drank from water fountains on the floor. Double rows of nests were on the east and west walls. Raised roosts made of wire mesh occupied the north side. Every evening the chickens fluttered up to the roost and slept cozily there in a cluster. The concrete floor was covered with a light layer of straw, and the ceiling was also straw, supported by more wire mesh.

A chicken house is no place for people with allergies. One quickly learns to knock gently before entering. Opening the door suddenly creates instant bedlam, with frantic flapping of wings and resulting eruptions of straw, feathers, and droppings. In winter, when chickens are confined for long periods, the strong odor of ammonia makes breathing even more of a challenge.

On the south side of our chicken house was an eight-foot-high, wire-mesh, fenced enclosure where chickens could get fresh air on sunny winter days. Pop liked being out in the sunshine and assumed that his animals did, too.

🌿 THE WORKSHOP

Right in the middle of the farmstead, squeezed between two of the large elms, was Pop's shop. About the size of a one-car garage, it was Pop's place to create and experiment, and he spent every spare moment there. He was a bit sheepish about it because most farmers kept just a few basic tools in a small room in the barn. Even Pop's brothers-in-law and Mom were skeptical about the shop, which they considered an extravagance.

The shop held a vise, anvil, post drill, blacksmith forge, and a homemade air compressor, an ingenious device Pop built from a couple of one-cylinder gas engines, one atop the other. The neighbors may have scoffed at Pop's extravagance, but they loved having an air compressor in the neighborhood. It made it a lot easier to put air in tires than the usual alternative, a hand-operated tire pump.

Pop spent many happy hours devising clever inventions and pounding them out on the anvil near the forge. Timing was critical in blacksmith work. He would heap red-hot coals carefully around the iron he was working, crank the blower fan just the right speed in order to produce the hottest fire, then watch the iron carefully as it heated and changed in color from cherry red to bright orange, at which point he generally withdrew the work with forge tongs and swiftly placed it on the anvil. Then, with a heavy hammer, he would "strike while the iron was hot" to shape the metal.

Timing was even more important when Pop was hardening steel to make a chisel. After beating it into shape, he would heat the chisel again, watch as it cooled, and plunge it into water when it was the color of straw.

Some of Pop's inventions were unworkable — a mechanical backhoe, for example, and a power posthole digger. More often, however, he succeeded in devising practical refinements for farm implements, including a power takeoff for the binder, an easy-loading low-deck bundle wagon, and a bulldozer mounted on the Case tractor and operated by a long handle made out of a wagon tongue.

When the farm got electricity in 1935, Pop was quick to use it in the shop. Frugal as he was, he rigged up a line-shaft apparatus to power the grinder, post drill, a homemade wood lathe, and a second homemade air compressor with a single electric motor. He bought an early electric welder, which greatly expanded his capabilities. With these resources at hand, he soon replaced the elevator's bulky gasoline engine with an electric motor.

It was a little sad, really. Pop liked the old International engine and hated to give it up, but the electric motor was more practical. For years afterward, the old engine sat in a corner of the elevator. Before he turned the farm over to me, he pulled it out and broke up all the castings with a sledgehammer. He did it for me, to clear out a piece of "junk," but it must have been painful even so.

 HORTICULTURE

The vegetable garden was in Mom's domain. Every year she would tell Pop when it was time to plow the garden, and he always followed orders, using a one-bottom walking plow. First, though, he had to pull down the four-foot-high mesh fences on either end of the garden.

The plow was horse-drawn until 1937, when Pop sold the horses and began using the tractor. Once over with the plow, several passes with a harrow, and, after replacing the fence, Pop's gardening duties were done for the season.

When planting her garden Mom was very particular about the rows being straight, which she accomplished with lengths of binder twine stretched between stakes. Lettuce, peas, beans, parsley, cabbage, beets, cucumbers, carrots, radishes, and tomatoes emerged in near-perfect lines beneath the string. Potatoes, planted in large plots and mulched with straw, were considered a field crop and were Pop's responsibility. Mom's garden also included a few rows of annual flowers — petunias, four-o'clocks, and zinnias — with some peonies and hollyhocks here and there along the uncultivated edges.

The mesh fence usually kept chickens, dogs, and rabbits out, but it was low enough to give chickens a sporting chance. When the occasional hen or rabbit gained entry, Mom called us kids out for the roundup. After a great deal of shouting and trampling of foliage, we would corner an errant hen, catch her, and toss her over the fence. If she got caught again, Mom would clip her wing feathers.

A garden bursting with luxuriant produce, like laundry hung out early on washday, reflected a woman's competence. It was customary for summertime Sunday visitors to inspect the farm after *faspa*. The men checked out the barnyard, and the women went out to the garden where extravagant compliments would alternate with seemingly innocent remarks. "I just don't know what to do with all my beans and tomatoes this year," a visitor might say while eyeing Mom's stunted beans. Especially vexing were Grandma Penner and Aunt Lizzie's biweekly inspections. Aunt Lizzie had a habit of casually alluding to Grandma's horticultural triumphs on this same plot of ground. Pop always went along on these tours; otherwise, with Mom frequently obliged to bite her tongue, there were bound to be long, embarrassing silences.

Rivalries aside, Mom held her own in the garden. Totally dependent on rainfall, success was never certain. Planting and hoeing were hard work, requiring every moment she could spare, but Mom's garden invariably did well enough to provide fresh produce in the summer and a year's supply of canned vegetables. She taught her children well how rewarding "sweat of the brow" could be.

A row of giant American elms bounded the driveway on one side, and another row, which overhung the claim shack and later the machine shed, divided the farmyard. Our swing was a tire on the end of a twenty-foot rope suspended from an elm near the house. The trunk had a protruding "knee," a nice place to sit and daydream. That tree and the others fell to Dutch Elm disease in the late 1950s.

There was a wooded area Pop called "the vineyard." There had once been grapes there, but they had died off and elms had grown in their place. My sisters and I called this spot "the park," and we built twine playhouses and roads for our tricycles and bicycle there. At first the roads were merely drawn with a rake used to clear away sticks and leaves, but before long that urge to move the earth, which seems to be innate in Mennonite males, led me to laboriously dig ditches and elevate the roads. From pieces of pipe found in Pop's junk pile I made culverts. I even built a "viaduct" modeled after one I had seen in Wichita on a rare grade-school field trip. I hauled earth to the project in my red Rambler coaster and spent hours racing over the roads and the viaduct on my bike, which, despite its being a girl's bike, I really enjoyed when no one else was around.

Perennially and with little success, Pop tried to revive the original orchard. It had succumbed to drought and grasshoppers in the 1930s, and I particularly remember my folks' anguish over the loss of a row of apricots, whose delicious flavor set an impossible standard for "store bought" fruit.

Year after year in springtime following the grasshopper year, Pop dug holes — big enough for me to hide in — and optimistically planted apricots, peaches, apples, plums, and cherries. Sadly, none of them survived to bear fruit, though Pop cultivated between rows with a tractor and hoped that I would hoe around the trees, one year even offering me a dollar to do so. Many times I began doing so enthusiastically, but hoeing didn't agree with me, and I never finished the job.

CHANGING TIMES

Fences segregated the animals in the farmyard. Cows and horses required barbed wire. Heavy mesh wire and closely spaced fence posts held the pigs. The fencing visible from the house was made of wood panels for appearance's sake. When Pop brought sheep to the farm, all the barbed-wire fences had to be reinforced with six-by-six-inch wire mesh; barbed wire won't deter sheep, with their heavy wool coats.

Fence repairs were an annual early spring chore. Much more difficult was building fences, a job that separated the men from the boys in a hurry. When the county widened our road in the 1930s, the pasture fence had to be moved. Pop tackled the job by himself, digging eighty postholes thirty inches deep, setting heavy hedge posts, and tamping them in solid. Drilling the first eight-inch-wide hole with an auger might have been enjoyable, but digging eighty holes was a formidable task. During the Dust Bowl the ground was rock-hard, so Pop hauled cans of water to the site. He would start a hole, pour water in it, and let it soak while he started additional holes, repeating the process again and again before actually finishing the hole. As he began a hole he could turn the auger while standing, but as the hole grew deeper he had to bend more and more until the handles were almost at ground level. It was backbreaking work.

Making the job even harder was the unbroken pasture sod. The buffalo-grass roots were deep and dense. Pop tried to invent a power posthole digger, but it wasn't a success and he ended up digging every hole by hand.

The county used two gray Model 60 Caterpillar tractors to pull the road graders. The powerful crawler tractors, pitched at rakish angles on the roadsides as they relentlessly rolled the stubborn soil, made a tremendous impression on me. They were as basic as they come: a massive X-braced radiator, a huge four-cylinder engine with no hood, and an open flywheel, all set in a frame between a pair of clanking crawler tracks. The men who operated the machines, pulling levers and pressing foot pedals, seemed to be masters of the world. Operators, tractors, and graders rumbled past the farmstead once or twice a day on their six-mile circuit, formidable harbingers of inevitable progress.

One day, arriving home from school, I saw Caterpillar tracks leading into our yard. Breathlessly I followed them and discovered Superior Township's "60" Caterpillar parked behind the big shed. I climbed over every inch of that marvelous machine, awestruck, feeling a reverence that no preacher was ever able to inspire.

9 🌿 The Animal Kingdom

Section 27 was no democracy. Pop had sole authority over our family's part of the section, but his rule was not without challengers. Roosters, in particular, thought highly of themselves, strutting proudly in their gaudy raiment to impress the harem and anyone else who might be watching. One rooster, possibly hoping to eliminate a future pretender to the throne, attacked me and wrestled me to the ground. I was only a toddler, and he was working me over with his beak and spurs when Mom came to my rescue. He had sealed his own fate, and we had drumsticks the following day.

Subtler were the tactics of the ubiquitous farmyard dog. We had a number of dogs over the years — Mikey, Bruno, Gyp, Skippy, Brownie, and others — but each felt and exercised its authority without flaunting it, letting Pop retain the illusion that he was in charge.

Dogs determined who gained entry to the farmyard. They announced and greeted or intimidated new arrivals, going into action the minute anyone crossed an invisible boundary. Some dogs were discriminating, weighing the importance of each visitor and reacting accordingly. Others approached an innocuous pigeon with the same ferocity they unleashed on the McNess man. In the end, however unwelcoming they might have been, our dogs would make a final pass across the yard, scattering chickens, before respectfully keeping their distance as we visited with those guests who had a legitimate reason to be there.

Dogs were also in charge of rabbits and predators. When we were in the fields, the dogs were usually occupied chasing jackrabbits, which were overabundant until the late 1950s. The contest between dog and rabbit was nothing like its racetrack counterpart. Jackrabbits knew the territory and tore through fences, hedgerows, rough terrain, and wheat stubble with ease, executing hairpin turns and distancing themselves from their pursuers in bursts of amazing speed. Gyp could turn almost as sharply as his prey. Legs churning, the dog would be almost horizontal as he nimbly changed direction. In wheat or tall stubble, the dogs would jump high, scanning for long ears. When the chase was successful, it ended brutally in a cloud of dust, a high-pitched scream, and a pool of blood. The dog stood with his front paws on the victim, his tongue hanging from a frothy mouth and his eyes seeking assurance that we had seen the moment of triumph.

In the early 1950s, Verna Lee and I planted a small Christmas tree grove. Rabbits were very interested in the tender young trees, which had to be wrapped in newspaper as protection from the animals. The rabbits were so numerous that I could point a rifle almost anywhere near the Christmas trees and expect to hit one. As innocent as they might appear, rabbits could destroy new shelterbelts and ravage a soybean field.

Rabbits weren't the only animals that interfered with our livelihood. We often woke to the sound of Gyp or Bruno barking and hens squawking. Pop would slip on his overalls, run to the barn, grab his little .410 shotgun and a flashlight, and dash to the aid of the dog. Usually, though, the skunk or possum had already escaped through the mulberry hedge. The next day we'd find broken eggs or a mutilated hen.

Farm dogs and cats weren't coddled or ever fed store-bought food. They lived outdoors, sought shelter in barns and sheds, and lived on table scraps and hunting trophies. They always seemed fat and contented, and we loved them, muddy coats and all.

Like dogs, cats monitored the farmyard, prowling about underfoot, pouncing on scraps, and keeping rodents and sparrows under control. Most farms had one dog and a clowder of cats. My sisters and I loved discovering baby kittens in the spring, usually alerted to their presence by meowing in a dark corner of the barn. Pop wouldn't let us play with the kittens until they could see. Meanwhile, once we discovered them, the mother would usually carry each kitten by the scruff of its neck to a new hiding place. At first I thought that was cruel, but Pop explained that the mother cats held the kittens very gently.

Taming a kitten involved a great deal of hissing and scratching. Rachel was the best at it. She would play with cats for hours at a time. Her favorite was always a little thin from all the exercise she gave it.

Cat fights could be dramatic. Sometimes I was awakened by the savage yowling of a pair of tomcats facing off in a tree. When the fight actually began, the noise sounded as if it came from a legion of wildcats rather than two relatively small creatures. One day, when two cats were fighting in an elm, one lost its grip and plummeted about twenty feet. The falling black-and-white streak landed on its feet in a cloud of dust and retreated in humiliation to safety under the shed.

Anything that had to do with milk attracted cats and flies. At milking time the cats expected a squirt or two. If we carelessly set down a bucket of milk, they were into it in a flash. They seldom got dirt in the milk, so if Mom hadn't seen the incident, there was no problem. When we slopped the hogs, the cats tried for a few sips before the pigs got there.

Our daughter Marci was a dead shot with a powerful pump BB gun, which she'd use to hunt sparrows after school. She'd lead the way into the shelterbelt, a dozen cats, tails aloft, at her heels. When she aimed, they crouched, and when she fired, they jumped. She seldom missed, and the quickest cat had a mouthful of sparrow before it hit the ground, the other cats growling enviously.

🔥 MINDS OF THEIR OWN

By the time I was old enough to be aware of how the farm operated, horses were losing their importance. We had Fanny, an old brown mare; Billy, a jet-black youngster with a white blaze; Charlie, a black gelding; and just a few others, though the barn had room for many more.

I was seldom allowed to drive the horses, but I got to guide them when Pop and I picked up alfalfa hay with a hayrack and hay loader. The trick was to keep the horses centered on the windrows and maintain a speed that the man stacking the hay could keep up with. As the rack filled, I would have to work my way up in the hay; by the time the load was full, I was at the top of a mountain of shifting, sweet-smelling alfalfa.

One day, Jake from the McCormick-Deering store brought us a shiny green 1937 International pickup truck. I was so entranced with its fancy grille, its new smell, and its electric windshield wiper that I didn't even notice our last two horses being led away. Pop had traded them for the pickup. I never missed them.

Mom had an inexhaustible repertoire of true but grisly stories about children being kicked by horses or mauled by bulls. Her exhortations to caution served only to heighten the sense of adventure I felt in the barnyard. Every farm had cattle — calves, cows, bulls, and the mysterious steers. Machines could replace horses, but they couldn't produce milk and meat. I loved going into the pasture to bring the cattle home for milking and feeding. The buffalo wallows incited me to pretend I was sneaking up on a herd of buffalo. I'd circle around the animals and start them on their way with a lot of hollering and waving of the big stick I carried, always amazed that the eight-hundred-pound animals would meekly allow a little boy to chase them home. Actually, they knew the way and needed no encouragement to go where they knew cool water was waiting for them.

Cattle and sheep tend to make trails and follow them single file. With me guiding them quite unnecessarily, our cattle would fall into line on one of their narrow crooked paths, their swaying bodies massive and dark against the red evening sky, their hooves placidly kicking up dust. Tranquil sounds — a snort, the swish of a tail, a dog's bark, the clattering of hooves on the small wooden bridge — erupted into pandemonium the minute the animals smelled fresh water. Pushing, sliding in the mud around the tank, splashing, and gurgling, they quenched their daylong thirst as I closed the gate behind them.

Sometimes a bull escaped. When someone yelled, "The bull is out," there was bound to be excitement. Fortunately, the fifteen-hundred-pound animals had no idea how strong they were, or they would have roamed free all the time.

When Pop bought the sheep, he built a woven-wire fence that he believed to be indestructible. One Sunday, Jim, the big shorthorn bull, was feeling his oats and walked right through the new fence, taking about a hundred feet of it with him. How we captured him I don't recall, though I vividly remember how Pop apprehended another wayward bull.

The neighbors had called to let us know our black Angus bull was at their place. There is almost nothing else as humiliating for a farmer. Pop grabbed

Frank Penner hauling wheat to town,
with the barn and windmill in the background.

a rope, and we climbed into the pickup and drove to the neighbor's farm. The bull was clearly in a bad mood, but Pop finally got a rope on him, which annoyed the already irate animal, and instead of pulling away he charged at Pop. Snubbing the rope around a light pole, Pop ran around the pole, letting the bull chase him until his tether was tightly wrapped around the pole.

Somehow, Pop tied the bull to the back of the pickup. I hadn't done much driving, but Pop let me drive home while he watched the bull. The huge animal did not go quietly. Wheels spinning, the little truck lurched back and forth across the road as the bull tried to exercise his authority. If there had been any bulls with similar pretensions to independence observing the episode, they would have learned an important lesson: if you don't want to be hamburger, don't chase Pop around a light pole.

As kids we let out shrieks of delight when we saw little calves, rowdily running in the bright straw covering their stable floor. Weaning calves had a room of their own, close to where the cows were milked. Teaching the little critters to drink from a bucket was exasperating but fun. The way to teach the calves was to let them suck on your finger in the milk bucket. Soon they were slurping milk right out of the bucket. The cats would prowl nearby, waiting for a spill.

Sometimes Pop would leave some milk in the mother cows he was milking and let the calves finish the milking while the cows were in the stanchions. It was a wild stampede indeed when the calves' gate was opened and they clattered down the hallway for a maternal visit.

The sheep were my favorites, but they weren't the brightest creatures. If one sheep went through a hole in a fence, they all went through, with no idea how to get home. They really got my dander up when I'd chase them back to the corral, and they'd run right past the open gate.

The artist who depicted a shepherd leading a flock of obedient sheep never dealt with Western ewes. One morning, when Pop and I were working the sheep, we had help from a preacher's son named Dale, a broad-shouldered football player whose experience with sheep was apparently limited to looking at pictures by badly informed artists. We were separating the lambs from the ewes in order to dock tails and castrate the young males, and Dale's assignment was to hold the ewes back and allow only lambs through a gate in the barn. Pop warned him that the ewes could be hard to handle. Dale only laughed, but his confidence melted as the first of the ewes came at him, airborne and chest high, and ran over him.

The buck, however, was the really dangerous one. Bucks, or rams, certainly seemed to enjoy butting people in the rear. I knew from experience that their heads were like sledgehammers. One day a buck grazed his head on a two-by-six board sticking out from a fencepost. In retaliation, he backed up about twenty feet, charged, and snapped the board in two. Another time, he and the bull got into it. The bull pawed the ground and lowered his big head. The buck backed up his usual twenty feet and came a-running. I thought the bull would throw him in the air — I'd seen that bull pick up a horse and push it away — but when the buck hit, the bull went down to his knees, regained his footing as quickly as he could, and retreated.

I was afraid of the buck and always carried my big stick when I chased the sheep — until, that is, I figured out a way to deal with him. As I mentioned earlier, sheep are none too smart. I observed that the buck focused all his momentum on a fixed point. If I held out my hand or the stick ahead of me, the buck would charge it full force, discharging all his momentum at that point and coming to a stop before he hit me.

Lambs were a different story altogether. They were social creatures, and the joy of watching them at play more than made up for the frustration brought on by their low IQs. They would run and bounce in their peculiar stiff-legged way around the ewes and feed bunks, sometimes stopping to stand on top of their reclining mothers. Lambs born out in the wheat fields in below-freezing weather would, as a rule, be running home with the flock the same evening. Occasionally, the cold was too much even for the hardy lambs. When one needed special care, we would pick it up, wrap it in a gunnysack, and carry it while the ewe followed us back to the barn.

The ewes were good mothers, but they had no way of getting a helpless lamb to its feet. Once the near-frozen lamb was in the barn, Pop would lay the ewe on its side and gently bring the lamb's cold little nose to its mother's udder. Usually a few squirts of milk directed into the mouth would stir the lamb enough to take a few tentative swallows. It was remarkable how quickly most lambs would respond to a little nourishment. Soon they would be on their feet, tails wiggling, nursing from their mothers.

Success was not always that easy, however. If the lamb didn't respond, Pop would take it into the basement, fill a five-gallon bucket with luke-warm water, and immerse the lamb. I saw lambs that seemed frozen beyond help come slowly to life that way, but, sadly, even that method didn't always work.

Sometimes it was the ewe that died, and then we had an orphan to cope with. We had a lamb, Nanny, that was left motherless, and we bottle-fed her and cuddled her like a puppy. Before we realized what was happening, she actually took on the role of a puppy. As she grew we tried to place her with the sheep, but her plaintive bleating and doleful eyes caused us to relent every time. She loved to ride in the pickup, but eventually got too big. When the ninety-pound bundle of wool and cockleburs jumped into the cab, there wasn't room to shift the gears. I'm not sure how we eventually got her to recognize who she was, but she finally ran with the flock.

❧ BIRDS OF A FEATHER

Each February Mom would start saving eggs and Pop would clean out the brooder house in order to start a new batch of chicks. The brooder house was on skids so it could be moved to a new location each year, primarily to prevent disease. Baby chicks needed clean ground to run on once they were old enough to go outside into their little pen. The brooder house was small, about ten by fourteen feet. The roof slanted to one side with the sunniest exposure being higher. The windows could open and close. A very small door opened into the pen, and a larger door for people was on one end.

Pop would scrub the wood floor meticulously with water and disinfectant and then cover the clean floor with peat litter. A low, round kerosene stove with a large circular hood about eighteen inches above the floor sat in the middle. New chicks would be confined to the area under the umbrella-like hood for warmth. These stoves were notorious for setting fire to brooder houses, however. Ours never caught fire, but the floor under the stove was charred.

When Mom had enough clean eggs, two hundred or so, Pop took them to the hatchery in Buhler. Three weeks later the chicks would come home in large cardboard boxes. The little fluffballs had to be pampered, their beaks hand-dipped in potassium permanganate and the brooder kept cozy. In fact, the brooder house was the warmest spot on the farm when raw March winds blew. The thermometer was checked hourly. Regulating the heat could be unsettling. Every change in the wind affected the damper, and the oil flow had to be constantly adjusted as the weather fluctuated.

In other respects, though, taking care of the little cheepers was delightful. After a few weeks they could go outside into their pen, though we had to keep an eye on them. Cats and dogs were as likely to eat the chicks as to guard them, and it required a lot of training to get the point across. And there was always the fear of hawks.

The chicks lived in the brooder house until they were fully feathered. At some point in early summer, their fence was removed, and they could roam the yard and even roost in trees.

Chickens and their squishy droppings were all over the farmyard during the warm months, but in winter we confined them to the chicken house. When cold weather approached, it was time to move any young fowl that roosted in trees. The tree-sitters were nearly full-grown chicks that had graduated from the brooder house. In summer we let them exercise their natural propensity to roost in trees, but by late October we rounded them up. Going out at night with lanterns and flashlights to catch these youngsters was a Halloween ritual that could be spooky and exciting, as if we were actually stealing the chickens.

We went out with chicken hooks, ladders, and gunnysacks after the birds settled down for the night. A flashlight shining in their eyes mesmerized them. We used the chicken hooks to snag the legs of those too high to reach. The captured birds would flail until we held them by the wings just behind the neck. Then we stuffed them in gunnysacks, six at a time, and took them to the chicken house, where they remained until spring. We could always tell when the hens were back on free range by the rich yellow color of the eggs on our breakfast plates.

Broody hens were a problem my sisters and I didn't understand but had to deal with anyway. There would be just one nest for each eight or so laying hens in the chicken house, and it wasn't unusual for a half-dozen eggs or more to be claimed by a broody hen — one whose instinct directs it to incubate eggs. If we found a broody hen when we were gathering eggs, we were supposed to take her out of the nest and carry her outside to the broody-hen coop, where she would be confined until she repented. Broody hens, of course, didn't appreciate our interference and pecked us ferociously. Marvella and Rachel always booted the difficult cases over to me.

 WORST CASE

Of all the animals on the farm, pigs were the ones I liked least, though it seemed for a while that I was destined to be a pig farmer. When my high school FFA project became, by default, a litter of pigs, I was indifferent. I didn't really care about the sow or her babies. What I cared about was cracklings, liverwurst, and fried ham.

It was disconcerting, therefore, to face the possibility a few years later that I might have to be a hog farmer. When Verna Lee and I got married, money was scarce. Someone had given us two silver dollars as a wedding present, and we often took them with us when we went grocery shopping, just in case. I've always been grateful that we didn't have to spend the silver dollars and that I didn't become a hog farmer when it appeared that there was no financial alternative.

I had called a federal agency that lent money to young farmers and received a bunch of forms in the mail. Filling out my name and address was easy. We lived in a small house near the main house on Mom and Pop's farm — but it was uphill work from there. The forms asked for credit references, of which, as far as I knew, I had none. Cash on hand? It didn't seem right to list the gift of two silver dollars, so I omitted them. Financial statement? We had no money; I thought that was obvious since I was requesting a loan. Farm plan? How could we plan before we knew how much money we had to work with?

The loan officer volunteered to visit the farm and help us draw up a farm plan. When he arrived, the first thing he did was inspect the farm — Pop's farm. After the inspection, without deliberation and without even asking my opinion, the loan officer pointed to the north mulberry hedge and told me abruptly that the hog house would be built there. All I had to do was sign a few papers and then hog house, pigs, and feed would be mine. I was thunderstruck. I'm not sure exactly how I declined his offer, but I was dead sure that there were already too many stinking pigs on Section 27.

🌿 EVOLUTION

From the time my forebears settled Section 27 until the 1950s, animals were an integral part of farming, not only on our land but also on most farms. The shift away from self-sustaining diversified agriculture to petroleum-dependent farming began with the disappearance of horses and proceeded so swiftly that in less than a generation local markets for farm-fresh milk, cream, butter, eggs, and meat virtually disappeared.

The idea of specialization was easily accepted. I had no qualms about plowing the pasture, even if it was the last unbroken sod on Section 27, because it made economic sense to put the whole farm into wheat, at least in the short run. The idea of a single crop and one set of machinery was attractive to me and most other farmers, especially those of the younger generation. Why be tied down by a few cows and chickens, obligated to tend to them every morning and evening? In fact, if you were going to have chickens at all, why not have 30,000 hens instead of 150? Why not feed and milk two hundred cows mechanically instead of caring for seven the old-fashioned way? And why not let someone else, preferably someone far away, raise thousands of pigs?

For better or worse, specialization soon transformed the farm, and the domestic animal population dwindled. On Section 27, by spring of the year 2000, the animal kingdom had fallen from glory, its population consisting of two cats, some roaming deer, a dozen squirrels, a few cottontails, a possum, maybe a skunk or two and a raccoon, and three people. Two annual visitors, Canada geese we call Quick and Quack, are preparing to start a new family. No rooster heralds the dawn, though innumerable finches and other seedeaters gather at our feeders every day.

The two pampered cats eat commercial cat food and go for annual veterinary checkups. They stand in for the hundreds of dogs, cats, horses, cows, sheep, and pigs that have dwelled on Section 27. But the land is far from empty. The number of creatures on the farm may in fact be about the same as it was in the early years. Deer were uncommon before the pioneer era and absent when we practiced diversified farming. Now there are so many, they are a menace to crops and a nuisance to cars on the roads. It's not unusual to see several of them sleeping in the old mulberry hedge.

House sparrows, brought from England in the 1850s to eradicate canker worms in the east, followed the pioneers westward, flourished, and became pests in their own right. (There are numerous varieties of native sparrows that are not considered pests.) During my school days the Inman High School vocational agriculture department sponsored annual pest-reduction contests that targeted sparrows and jackrabbits. We kept sparrow heads and jackrabbit ears in our school lockers until the contest ended. The resulting aroma was rather powerful.

Catching house sparrows in barns on cold winter nights was great fun. They slept in crevices and between rafters and shingles, but the ones that dozed on hay-carrier ropes that stretched from one end of the loft to the other made for the best hunting. In total darkness we would climb the mountain of hay at one end of the barn, grab a rope, and reel them in. Then, aided by the faint light of flashlights, we would grab them, pull off their heads, and stuff them in paper bags. Our gloves got pretty squishy from the blood.

A surefire way to get a few heads in a hurry was to quickly slide a shed door on its track, where there were always sparrows sleeping. The disadvantage was the messiness involved; the track rollers crushed the heads too.

Now house finches and goldfinches are crowding out the house sparrows. The finches might be as much of a nuisance as the house sparrows, but they are more colorful so we feed them. Pesky starlings and gorgeous pheasants — both introduced in North America — also reside on Section 27. On the farmstead in winter, we've observed two varieties of finches, four kinds of woodpeckers (downy, hairy, red-bellied, and flicker), black-capped chickadees, juncos, red-breasted nuthatches, brown creepers, cardinals, blue jays, Harris sparrows, house sparrows, robins, and occasionally rufous-sided towhees. Crows, turkey vultures, and a variety of hawks hover in the sky but keep their distance. Occasional pheasants, quail, and meadowlarks wander over from the nearby grassland. It was unusual to see cardinals, finches, and pheasants before the 1950s.

When sweet-smelling lilacs bloom, it's a sign that brightly feathered summer songbirds will soon appear. Early arrivals are mourning doves and blackbirds. In my mind, spring has truly arrived when I hear the song of a Baltimore oriole, though the bird itself, high in a hackberry tree, may be hidden by new foliage. Before long, a brown thrasher calls boldly from the exposed crown of a cedar. Suddenly, the farm is inhabited by a host of winged visitors: catbirds, orchard orioles, wrens, dickcissels, eastern kingbirds, redheaded woodpeckers, kingfishers, barn swallows, chimney swifts, and the elusive yellow-billed cuckoos. Really, we can hardly call them "visitors"; their claim to the place is much more ancient than our own.

Sadly, the western kingbirds and scissor-tailed flycatchers that once were numerous are now seldom seen. In years past, they took command of the highest reaches of the great elms arching over the farmyard. Every midsummer evening they would feast on bugs, bickering and chattering all the while. The scissor-tail is among the most beautiful and graceful of birds, elegant in its pearly gray coat, imposing with its long, forked black-and-white tail, delicate traces of luminous salmon pink visible on the breast and sides.

Just before dawn on summer mornings, a western kingbird would issue a tentative squeak from the mulberry hedge, joined by a few others as the light spread across the sky. By sunup, the chatter was frenetic, punctuated by a mourning dove's plaintive coo, the melodious babbling of blackbirds, the bobwhite's shrill cry, and the brown thrasher's abundant repertoire.

I sometimes recorded these performances, most recently in the spring of 1986. Then, suddenly, the charming scissor-tails disappeared from Section 27 and the kingbirds became scarce. The insects are more numerous on summer evenings, the music is fainter, and the trees seem almost naked without their garrulous tenants.

10 🌿 The Quiet in the Land

Mennonite ideology arrived intact in the New World and took up residence on Section 27 and throughout the community. It permeated relationships, ambitions, architecture, and advancement of all kinds.

My forebears the Penners, the Gaedderts, and the Lohrentzes were passengers on the *Teutonia*. The Regiers arrived later. When the ship reached the American shore in 1874 and the families made their way west to Kansas, they were a close-knit Mennonite group led by Great-grandpa Dietrich Gaeddert. They promptly established the Hoffnungsau Mennonite Church four miles east of Section 27. (The name was inspired by an immigrant's comment, on first seeing the Blaze Fork Valley, that it was a *Hoffnungsau* — a meadow of hope.)

A few years later, however, Peter Lohrentz was instrumental in establishing a "rival" church — the Hebron Church three miles to the south of Hoffnungsau — and luring many away from Hoffnungsau. David Penner followed him and became a minister in the new church. (As chance would have it, the families were later reunited on Section 27. Peter Lohrentz's daughter, Maria, married David F. Penner and became the first mistress of the Queen Anne house. Their son, Frank, married Gaeddert's granddaughter, Bertha.)

Peter Lohrentz's architectural preferences (the Lohrentz family is noted for their woodworking craftsmanship) showed up as similarities in the front façade of the Hebron Church and porch details on the Penner Queen Anne house — similar pediments over the porches, fancy brackets, and turned columns and spindles.

Dietrich Gaeddert's well-meant but domineering leadership might well have instigated the rift in the church. Gaeddert got things done, but he

Early picture of the Hoffnungsau Church built in 1898.
Note the two entrance doors — one on the left for men
and one on the right for women.

wanted to be in charge. Lohrentz and Penner weren't the only ones among the new settlers who chafed under his authority. Indeed, many derisively referred to Hoffnungsau as the "Gaeddert Church." By the turn of the century, more immigrants had settled in the area and founded churches often nicknamed for the more zealous or strong-willed in their number — the Klassen Church, Toews Church, Schellenberg Church, and others.

Differences among the churches were minor, having more to do with practice than doctrine. Personalities clashed over forms of baptism (pouring versus dunking), degrees of piety, and matters of discipline. Such disparities are understandable in the light of a basic Mennonite principle: the right of every believer to study and interpret the Bible. By the time I was old enough to go to church, the Penners had long been back in the Hoffnungsau fold, perhaps because Dietrich Gaeddert had died the last day of 1900, or maybe because the Sunday morning round-trip made by buggy was six miles shorter.

Mennonites often describe themselves as "the quiet in the land" because of the calm and peace-loving nature of their beliefs. The Penners on Section 27 were not exuberant or boisterous Christians but rather solid churchgoers who lived their religion. Talking religion was the preacher's job. In our household, my parents expressed their faith and conveyed their values by practice and ritual such as attending church every Sunday to hear the minister illuminate the word of God or Pop reading from the German Bible and talking to an apparently German God in prayer during devotions at the breakfast table. Unfortunately, the language of religion was High German and the language of our household was Low Dutch, so God's word was largely undecipherable to me.

The sober demeanor accompanying church services and morning devotions, however, clearly meant serious business. At church, the white-haired man at the pulpit discoursed loudly, sometimes tearfully, pacing and gesturing and finally raising both arms and facing the congregation. This, I knew, meant that church was over.

The pulpit was actually an imposing two-tiered dais looming over the congregation. Facing the pulpit from three sides, the sanctuary's hard wooden pews were austere by comparison. Ornate oak railings, turned columns, and capitals separated the congregation from the minister's

Pulpit area in the church prior to the 1948 fire.

sphere, where the lower platform held an elaborate lectern and three massive chairs. On either side, steps with ornamental balustrades led to the high pulpit, which was reserved for the most solemn occasions. There was a tiered open balcony above the congregational pews.

Men and women used different entry doors and, once inside, sat in separate sections — men on the preacher's right, women on his left. Of course, the arrangement freed the men from child care duties.

SEEDS OF FAITH

When I had learned enough English at school, my parents enrolled me in the English language Sunday school. I enjoyed the Bible stories — Baby Moses hidden in the bulrushes to escape Pharaoh's evil decree, heroic little David saving his flock from the voracious lion — and I was spellbound when the teacher explained how Noah had captured a pair of every kind of animal on earth and led them to safety on his ark. I mulled that over for a long time. How would he have done that, I wondered?

Full-color flip charts accompanied each wonderful story, and I was always eager to see how the pictures would illustrate our lesson. One of the flip-chart pages depicted Moses *almost* seeing God, though we were told that no one had ever seen God. In the picture, nevertheless, Moses was looking at the hem of a white robe that seemed to be disappearing behind a huge rock on Mount Sinai where he received the Ten Commandments. It looked to me, at least, as if Moses had come very close to actually seeing God.

By the time they were in fifth grade, boys and girls went to separate Sunday school classes. The congregation elected men to teach the upper-grade lessons. Otherwise, apart from the Mennonite practices of pacifism and "humble pride," our Sunday school was little different from others in the Bible Belt. The Sunday school curriculum was prescribed by the General Conference of Mennonite Churches in the United States, which generally followed the same lectionary (order of Scripture readings) as other Protestant denominations. During Prohibition there were also regular temperance lessons. Most of the teachers did their jobs well, dutifully following the prescribed lessons and teaching church doctrine and time-tested values and ethics.

Old Joe, gaunt and weatherworn, was an exception, being somewhat charismatic and independent. During the week he raised hogs, cattle, and horses, but on Sundays, glancing briefly at the assigned lesson, he thrilled young Mennonite boys with tales he had committed to memory and embellished with barnyard wisdom. We were on the edges of our seats when he told stories from the Old Testament: Lot's wife turning to stone as she looked back on the burning cities of Sodom and Gomorrah; Abraham preparing to slay his son Isaac, sprawled on the sacrificial altar, before God rescinded his shocking command. Old Joe was a fine teacher, but he skated on thin ice when it came to temperance. In spite of the obligatory Saturday evening bath, he reeked of tobacco, and some said he had wine on his breath. Yet he denounced the twin evils of tobacco and strong drink like the staunchest teetotaler. He spoke with conviction, and I believed him a hundred percent.

Whatever the cost to his conscience, Old Joe stuck to the canon — except on one occasion. It was a lesson on racial issues. Discussions of race usually dealt with black people whose salvation was in the hands of missionaries in faraway places like Africa. I had seen very few black people and only one Indian so these lessons never struck close to home. But Old Joe, after directing us to love all people, including African people, said we should also accept our black neighbors in America, adding, "though you have to admit that n___s smell, and most carry knives." Even at that age the racist remark offended me. I began to have doubts about Old Joe's veracity.

After public school ended for the summer, every weekday morning we went to the three-week vacation Bible school at Hoffnungsau. It always widened my social horizons because children from many schools and other churches attended. Before school and during the half-hour recess we played a game called "move-up," which I enjoyed because of the unrestricted participation. It was something like softball, but everyone had a turn at every position, even pitcher. There was no choosing teams; we played just for fun. If you struck out when it was your turn at bat, you became the left fielder and the catcher went up to bat. Being able to play every position was a nice change for me, a mediocre athlete who was always placed deep in the outfield when we played ball at Lake Valley.

Curtains in the church basement separated Bible school classes. The teachers were usually young farm wives who did a good job and compensated with enthusiasm for their lack of information. Men, of course, taught the seventh- and eighth-grade classes, which focused on Paul's missionary journeys. At all levels the curriculum consisted mostly of Bible history illustrated with maps, which I enjoyed enormously, though I was less enthusiastic about the memory work and the singing.

We learned that God had apparently spoken audibly to many people we read about in the Bible. Adam, Abraham, Jacob, Samuel, Solomon, Mary, Paul, and many others had all heard God's voice. There was an implicit message that we too could hear this voice — if we were "good."

I was impressed by the way Samuel had heard the Lord's voice as a boy and by Solomon's talking to God in a dream. The teacher told us that Solomon had received riches and power because he had craftily asked God only for the gift of wisdom. She implied that if we prayed for wisdom, riches would be added. I was skeptical, but from then on I always prayed for wisdom before moving on to what I really wanted — a bicycle, for example. Another teacher gave a lesson on how to pray. As if she were telling a secret, she confided to us about "three-step prayer" — first thanking God for everything we could think of, then telling God how majestic and merciful He was, and then almost casually petitioning.

For the most part, the teachers effectively taught basic biblical principles and associated them with ethics for day-to-day living. Without realizing it, we were learning the basis of our parents' faith, beliefs, and values.

WHERE IS TRUTH?

Mennonites practice "believer's baptism," which requires awareness and understanding of the commitment being made. We studied the catechism as a prerequisite to baptism when we were about sixteen years old — the "age of accountability."

When I first heard in Sunday school that a catechism class would be starting soon, it was an anxious time for me, because Pop and Mom had said nothing about it. Driving home from church in the old Pontiac, Pop mentioned that an announcement had been made about catechism and that I should go. What a relief it was to know that I'd be reaching account-ability at the same time as my classmates.

It was an awesome experience, entering the special classroom where the preacher taught catechism. The boys in the class assumed a noncha-lant attitude. Some even attempted a show of bravado as we shuffled in. The preacher, who had never even acknowledged my presence, was in-timidating. His solemnity suggested great superiority. "Here I stand," he seemed to convey, "between you, a lowly sinner, and the omnipotence of God." I didn't dare look at my classmates; we were all overwrought, verg-ing on both laughter and tears. The gravity with which the preacher instructed us and my conviction that he, like God, was infallible made the catechism experience a turning point in my life.

At school I loved science and history and did well in those subjects, so when the preacher announced one Sunday he would be talking about sci-ence, I was all ears. He began by discussing centrifugal force, which we had been studying in school. He talked about scientists' claims that if you could throw a ball into the sky with enough force, it would circle the earth indefinitely, like the moon. But according to the Book of Genesis, it was God, he said, who controlled the moon, not centrifugal force. As he con-tinued to chip away at Newton's laws of motion, he split my world in two as surely as scientists had just recently split the atom. Until then, I had believed in a fundamental and indivisible truth, just as the atom had been considered the basic, indivisible unit of matter.

The preacher was a farmer who was elected by the church and who served without pay. He was sincere and well meaning, doing his best, having taught school for a time but possessing little understanding of the sciences. But we were not then aware of his limitations. Thus his teaching had the force of gospel, and its effect on me was devastating.

Meanwhile, my fellow communicants and I continued to go to school and behave like normal teenagers, pretending to be unaffected by the transformation of our secure little world. We were in the process of being changed, the preacher told us one Sunday, and the moment the water of baptism touched us, we would experience a cataclysmic and irreversible conversion. We would be possessed with a new spirit. I looked forward to this transition, though a bit fearfully. Sin was everywhere, I could see that, but the irreversibly converted people I knew seemed to have different levels of involvement with it.

A couple of my buddies took the prospect of irreversible change very seriously. They made plans to go to the "big city" some evening and enjoy the favors of some party girls before it became impossible to sin again, ever.

A week or two before the baptism the preacher customarily interviewed each catechism student at home. He showed up at our house on a Saturday as Pop and I were loading manure with pitchforks onto a manure spreader. There I was, knee-deep in cow dung, and he wanted to talk to me about my soul. Pop and I took off our overshoes and headed for the parlor, though entering Mom's parlor as grimy as I was, it seemed to me, was just about the most heinous of sins.

The preacher's face was a solemn mask. Pop was embarrassed. Mom, who hadn't had time even to put on a clean apron, was graciously fuming. I was scared to death. We sat stiffly on the straight-backed chairs — using the plush chairs would have been even more immoral — and waited for something to happen. Never had I been in a face-to-face discussion about God and my soul.

The preacher broke the ice. "Well, Frank, are you spreading the manure on the wheat?" That started a brief discussion about the merits of manure on wheat, and I was beginning to relax when the preacher turned suddenly to me and said, "Let us pray." The substance of the prayer, I thought, was what a miserable sinner I was and how divine intervention would be needed to make something out of me. It was true, I reflected, watching manure flake off my overalls onto Mom's carpet. When the prayer ended and the preacher got ready to leave, he reminded me that on Sunday the candidates for baptism would have to confess and ask forgiveness for their sins in front of the congregation.

The public testimony was the scariest thing of all. I had seen it a few times, and the sinners in question always cried. It seemed to be the thing to do. As hard as I tried, though, I couldn't think of any sins to confess that were proper to mention in church. Sometimes I drove the old Model A faster than Mom liked, but that didn't seem worthy of the congregation's attention. I thought about Mr. Neufeld's ball of binder twine that had been released from my car on a field trip, but I didn't think that was my sin to confess.

By the time my turn came on Sunday, I hadn't thought of any sins and I couldn't muster any tears, nor could I bring myself to say I had been born in sin. That seemed to be my folks' responsibility, and I didn't see them as sinners. At the last minute, thinking of how baptism would change me, I had an inspiration. I would say that I was prayerfully waiting for the Holy Spirit to come upon me at baptism and convict me of my sins. That seemed to satisfy the preacher and the deacons.

Then the pressure was on for the following Sunday, the baptism day. When the time came, we sat in front of that awesome pulpit. The deacons appeared with basins of water, towels, and long faces — perplexing when the occasion was supposed to be so joyous — and we knelt. The minister came down from the high pulpit after much heavy praying and started the pouring on of holy water. A girl at the far end of the bench was first. He asked the same questions over and over, moving down the row toward me. Out of the corner of my eye I saw water trickle onto the floor as the boy next to me said tearfully, "I promise." I caught myself wondering if it would be proper to comb my hair when it was wet from the baptism, then tried to put such mundane thoughts out of my mind by recalling that in just a few minutes the Holy Spirit would be upon me. I braced myself to be irreversibly changed in the twinkling of an eye.

Suddenly I was aware of my own trembling response. I heard hands dipping into water and was aware of water dripping onto the floor as the hands moved toward me. I felt cold water in my hair and running down my neck and back. I felt the hands laid on me. And that was all I felt.

Life went on. I still drove fifty miles an hour to school despite the wartime limit of thirty-five. Some of my buddies still copied my test answers in American history class. The preacher never came to see me again.

🌿 MOVING FORWARD

Much as the tractor and automobile symbolized changes in agriculture and society, the pump organ represented progress in Mennonite churches. Progress meant, at various times, introduction of the English language and of salaried clergy formally trained for the ministry, as well as changes in music and in women's roles. Such developments could either disrupt or revitalize a church.

Several churches in the vicinity had steadfastly refused to have pianos and excommunicated young men who played in bands. When it came to music, Hoffnungsau was probably the most liberal Mennonite church in the area. Early in the century it placed a pump organ in the sanctuary; a grand piano arrived not long after. The church had no problem with Pop and his brothers playing in the Lake Valley band.

A woman from another church once asked Mom if we "doodled in" our preachers as a few other churches did. She was referring to the pianist accompanying the preacher's march up to the pulpit at the start of the service. Mom didn't appreciate that remark. The church pianist was always a woman, so I couldn't believe my ears when Mom told me I would be taking piano lessons.

The world wars had a lot to do with the shift from German to English in Hoffnungsau Church services. Because Germany was the enemy, it would seem that it should have been easy to introduce English language services. Many of the older women, however, even in the 1930s knew little English. Some of the mothers of my Lake Valley classmates had poor command of the language because of their isolation. In the home and among relatives and friends, the Low Dutch vernacular prevailed, and the women seldom ventured into the "English" world. The men transacted all the business, including the exchange of cream and eggs for groceries. When the women went to buy yard goods, they usually dealt with general store proprietors who spoke Low Dutch.

Thus the transition, though persistent, was gradual. First an English-language children's story was added to the service, then an occasional sermon would be in English. Before long, only one sermon a month was in German. Eventually, during the 1940s, English became the language of the church.

One Sunday during World War II, a visiting preacher told the children's story. Being of high school age, I generally paid little attention, but the kids singing "ride in the cavalry, shoot in the artillery" captured my attention. I looked up in time to see the preacher as he pantomimed the riding and shooting. The congregation was shocked and silent; never had the pacifist Hoffnungsau parishioners heard or seen such a thing. As the stony silence engulfed him, his voice trailed off. I could barely contain myself, though, at the ludicrous spectacle of this portly preacher prancing and bouncing like a horse.

As long as the Hoffnungsau community remained a closed society, women's roles were slow to change. The men were in charge, and that was fine with them and the more matronly among the women. There was something beautiful, at least superficially, about husbands and wives working in harmony, comfortable with the responsibilities that tradition assigned. There was never a question or conflict about who prepared the meals, plowed the fields, fixed leaky faucets, or fed the babies.

Since the men, including Pop, handled virtually all dealings with the outside world, Mom was resigned to her six-day-a-week job as keeper of the house. Only on Sundays did she get away from the farm, and then it was with the entire family. We all went to church for an hour of Sunday school and the hour-long service. After lunch and Pop's nap, we went visiting at the homes of our grandparents and other relatives. Sunday evening often meant another church service, again with the children in tow.

Bruderschaft (the meeting of the brethren) was an annual event considered too momentous for women to attend until the late 1930s or early 1940s. Even Pop had to mentally prepare for this daylong weekday meeting held for the purpose of electing trustees and other officials, determining church policy, and conducting other business — all taken very seriously.

Certain situations, such as the discovery that someone had committed a dreadful sin, prompted special meetings of the brethren. Having sex before marriage — more accurately, being found out — was a transgression that warranted such a meeting. After I had been baptized and had therefore become a member of this grave assembly — by that time women were also voting members — the preacher called a special meeting. After the Sunday sermon, he asked the children and others who were unbaptized to leave. After a long prayer, the preacher presented a young man who was there to confess his sin and beg for forgiveness. The man, bravely but tearfully, admitted his folly and asked for mercy. After more prayer the preacher turned to the congregation for guidance. There was a long silence, broken when one of the brethren — blessed with objectivity and good judgment — spoke up: "I move that we forgive *and* forget."

Hairstyles and apparel were within the purview of the church, which applied sanctions for women more rigorously than for men. Hoffnungsau was more relaxed about personal adornment than many other Mennonite churches, but the acceptance was hard-won. As late as the mid-1940s, many church members would shun a girl who arrived on Sunday with her hair bobbed. As many girls went on to college, however — presumably to become teachers, nurses, or missionaries — the prohibitions began to disappear. Women had gained the right to full participation by 1950, when the new Hoffnungsau Church structure had one entrance for both men and women.

Bethel College, a Mennonite institution in North Newton, Kansas, was a catalyst for changes affecting the Mennonite community and Section 27 specifically. One such change was the employment of a seminary-trained clergyman who received a modest salary, replacing the unpaid and virtually untrained preachers of years past. The man chosen was Mom's cousin, Albert Gaeddert, whom Mom dearly loved and wanted me to adopt as a role model.

Albert Gaeddert was a forceful proponent of nonviolence but not as an escape from service to God and country. He urged young men to volunteer their services to mental hospitals, in conservation work, and for other projects in lieu of military service. In 1950 my young bride, Verna Lee, and I went to see him about volunteering for a job in South America. I wanted to help industrialist R. G. LeTourneau clear the jungles, as other Mennonite volunteers were already doing. Not only had I inherited my ancestors' instinctive compulsion to clear and develop land, but I was also electrified by the prospect of LeTourneau's giant machines crushing forests into farmland.

Eagerly Verna Lee and I broached the subject with Albert Gaeddert. He rubbed his chin thoughtfully and, speaking slowly and deliberately, replied that it "might not be a good idea." It was good for some to leave for voluntary service, he said, but added that others of us were needed to serve at home. We were puzzled but left without asking many questions.

I never did understand what he meant. Until that moment, I had always dreamed of traveling to exotic distant lands. Something in me still believed in the preacher's infallibility. Because of that, and a sense that clarification would come from Above, we made Section 27 our permanent residence. Whether we "served at home," I really couldn't say.

11 🌿 Wheat

Section 27 is spectacular in June. Ripe wheat ripples in the Kansas wind, yellow heads nodding. The farmers, those who love the land, nod too, affirming the cosmic cycle that culminates with the harvest. Wheat is the staff of life, the bread that was broken like the earth it comes from. Growing wheat is a spiritual adventure.

The earth is nature's wonderful storehouse of sun energy. It was the rich soil, with its thick black humus layer, that drew Mennonite and other pioneers to the central Kansas prairie. What they couldn't have known was that not all black humus soil was the same. David Penner and Peter Balzer knew nothing of the local variations in soil types when they chose their tracts in the Blaze Fork Valley.

According to the U.S. Department of Agriculture soil survey of McPherson County, Section 27's soil is predominantly Ladysmith silty clay loam with patches of Goessel silty clay. Such soils — characterized by poor drainage, slow permeability, and a high shrink-swell factor — produce excellent crops but make tilling, seeding, and harvesting somewhat difficult. When dry, the soil plows hard; when wet, it becomes hopelessly muddy. The nearby Crete-Smolan soils are easier to farm.

Until the 1970s the moldboard plow was the principal tillage tool used to prepare a wheat seedbed. The first plow to turn Section 27's soils was probably a walking plow pulled by two or three horses. A sulky or a gangplow would soon replace it, succeeded in 1905 by an eight-bottom plow pulled by a 22-45 Hart-Parr tractor. After all the heavy sod had been broken, smaller plows and lighter, faster tractors were sufficient.

My great-grandfather, David Penner, planted the first red kernels of hard winter wheat in the southeast quarter of Section 27, Superior Township. From my father's rare reminiscences and from old-timer friends who recall first-person accounts, I've glimpsed the spirit of adventure with which prairie pioneers broke the sod, drained the wetlands, laboriously harrowed and planted with horses, and brought in the first triumphant harvests. Only with reluctance, however, would Pop talk of farming with horses — plowing with a sulky plow, walking behind a drag harrow on stubborn clods, sowing with a drill — though he was exuberant when describing the huge Avery and Hart-Parr tractors in use after the turn of the twentieth century.

More than plowing or sowing, however, and more than driving tractors, harvesting fulfills the spirit of the wheat farmer. I am fortunate to have experienced the binding and threshing process, now obsolete. Though steam engines were no longer used in my time, there was still drama in the spectacle of toiling men, sweating horses, swirling straw, cantankerous machinery, and undependable weather — with temperatures approaching a hundred degrees one day and storms threatening the next.

The yield — bushels in the bin — was crucial, but while laboring, we gave little thought to the outcome; only exertion and skill seemed to matter. Everyone worked feverishly and took pride in their craftsmanship. Bundle pitchers performed with all the concentration and dexterity of professional athletes. The job required a kind of gracefulness as well as strength. With a single smooth movement, the worker had to pierce the bundle with a fork and pitch it with a practiced twist so it would land head-end first at the feet of the stacker or in the wagon. At the threshing machine it was a cardinal sin to throw a bundle crosswise or butt-end first into the feeder; either mistake could clog the machine. The most highly valued workers could set a bundle stack, fine-tune machinery, scoop grain, and display a hearty appetite for fried chicken when the work was done.

The financial return was important, but the real joy came from a job well done. The idea of just accumulating money was alien to Pop and his contemporaries. They worked to provide a livelihood and build a strong community. A solid, well-kept farmstead, straight fences, and fat cattle outweighed the amassing of money. One Harvey County farmer was offended if his farmstead didn't have the highest tax valuation in the county, implying he had the best farm. I knew an old-timer who refused to sell his wheat when the price went to five dollars a bushel in 1975; he said the price was

The Penner threshing rig, about 1910.

too high — that it would ruin the farm economy. He was right. Farmers and bankers used high wheat prices in their financial projections. When President Jimmy Carter declared an embargo on wheat, grain prices plummeted and the farm economy was devastated.

🌾 THE BINDER

Harvesting with binders (a reaper that tied cut wheat into bundles) started before the wheat was ripe. The ideal time was the subject of much debate, but it was generally agreed that the wheat stem should show a lot of green and the kernels be rather soft. After being cut, the wheat ripened in the shocks. Early harvesting was one advantage of using a binder rather than a header or, later, a combine.

Pop would get the binder out of the shed weeks before harvest, replacing parts and sometimes making modifications. One year he converted our McCormick-Deering binder's drive mechanism from ground drive to power takeoff drive. In the early 1940s, we pulled the binder with a rubber-tired Case tractor. I wasn't yet a teenager, so Pop had to put an extension on the tractor's hand clutch so I would have enough leverage to operate it.

The Case, of course, had no power steering. It started with a hand crank, and the open power shaft ran under the seat between the operator's legs. Pop always warned me to be careful; if the shaft caught your overalls cuff, it could undress you faster than you could say ouch and would probably wrap your leg around the shaft. Pop always rode on the binder, busy with a lot of levers, adjusting cutting height, setting the reel, and centering the twine on the bundle.

There was something magical about the binder — the chatter of the sickle, the meshing of the gears, the click clack of the knotter as it tied and threw out the bundles, the reel gently slapping the divider board with each revolution. When everything was working right, the aroma of fresh-cut straw and the rhythm of the binder could mesmerize the tractor driver. If, as often happened, I fell into a reverie as I drove, I wouldn't hear Pop shouting for me to stop when the binder missed tying a few bundles. Understandably perturbed, he began carrying a bamboo fishing pole in the binder's horsewhip socket, vigorously tapping me on the shoulder with it when he needed to get my attention.

Binders were often cantankerous. The canvas conveyor belt would slip or jam, chains would fall off sprockets, and knotters would refuse to tie. Pop was an expert binder man, but he frequently exercised some very explicit Low Dutch persuasion to make the machine work. He used to say that the only machine worse than a wheat binder was a corn binder and that the devil shouted for joy every time a corn binder was sold.

A crotchety old boozer in Inman, Pete Epp, who had a way with sewing machines and binders, was often called in when all else failed. Some claimed that Pete "fixed" a balky knotter by throwing dust on the mechanism when no one was looking, which might well have worked. A knotter had to grip the twine firmly, so if it had worn smooth or had oil on it, a coating of grit might have been helpful.

Troublesome as the binder could be, I loved pulling it and watching the wheat emerge in neat bundles. Making the corners of the field was the best part of the job. You had to drive the tractor beyond the corner and then turn a sharp left so that the binder grain wheel rolled backward. With practice you could almost make a square corner. Eventually the field of standing grain would narrow noticeably, rabbits and pheasants making hasty egress to seek safety somewhere else.

When the binding was done, the bundles in the field had to be gathered by hand and set up in shocks. It was backbreaking work. A shock was six to twelve bundles set against and around each other, heads up, looking like little tepees as they dried out in the field. After a week or two they would be loaded into bundle wagons and hauled to a threshing machine or stacked for threshing later on.

Shocking wheat, like other harvesting chores, was something of an art. You would grab two bundles near the string and set them, heads up, against each other, repeating the process until you had made a proper shock. It was important to set the bundles down sharply into the stubble and to form straight rows so that the bundle racks (wagons) could work efficiently. Lifting a bundle often disturbed the temporary shelter of mice, rabbits, and snakes that had taken refuge there on a hot day.

Shocking oats was easier than shocking wheat; the bundles were lighter, but slippery and difficult to "form up." Shocking barley was unpleasant because the spiky beards scratched arms and hands.

In the thresher era, shocking grain was the most labor-intensive operation on a farm. Itinerant laborers, especially during the Depression, were generally available to help with the job. They'd wait on benches along the streets of small towns for farmers to come by, look them over, choose two or three, and take them home. During the 1930s and 1940s, we seldom used "hobos" because the binder-harvested acreage had dwindled to what Pop and the regular hired man could handle. The combine was harvesting most of the wheat by then.

Still, Pop and many other farmers used binders and threshers even when it was evident that combines were more efficient. They did so partly from habit and tradition but also because they could harvest a week to ten days earlier. Moreover, wheat in shocks was relatively safe from hail, and Pop believed that threshing-machine straw (which retained more chaff) made better livestock bedding than straw picked up with a baler following a combine.

In an era when the work of farming was done more by men than by machines, the threshed straw stack was a family-farm icon. A new bright yellow straw stack might be twenty feet high. Loose and airy, it looked fragile, but if properly formed, it could withstand wind and rain. A new stack was a tempting playground, but no one was permitted on the stack until it had settled, because indentations allowed rainwater to soak in. In wintertime, after the straw had settled and cattle had eaten deep caverns into the stack, it was the coziest spot on the farm, attractive (though dangerous) to children and secluded enough to serve as a trysting place for young lovers.

❦ THRESHER COMING

In my early childhood, threshing day was almost as good as Christmas. When Mom and Selma, the hired girl, started frantically butchering chickens, digging potatoes, picking beans, and baking pies, I knew the threshers were coming and began to watch for the threshing machine as soon as I fastened my overalls in the morning.

Mom was expected to have an abundance of food ready when the thresher crew arrived, though when that would occur was always uncertain. Serving a hefty meal on demand for fourteen men would be a challenge today; in those days it was especially difficult. There was, of course, no refrigeration, not even an icebox. It might be one hundred degrees outside and hotter inside, with wood-fueled cook stoves fired up. By mid-afternoon, Mom would be frazzled and irritable, muttering in Low Dutch something to the effect that the *schlopmetsa* (sleepyheads) would come in time to eat but too late to work.

At four o'clock the workers would expect the customary *faspa*, a comparatively light lunch. One year the crew was especially late. Mom had prepared a *faspa* of sandwiches, sweet pickles, cheese, cinnamon rolls, cookies, prodigious amounts of iced tea, and cream puffs — and nobody showed up. She was really fuming.

At about six that evening, a hayrack pulled by two horses arrived and clattered across the yard without even stopping. Johnny Pauls, the driver, shouted in Low Dutch, his voice shaking as the steel-wheeled rack bounced, "I must hurry to load up; the machine is almost here." And indeed I could hear the big Case tractor's straight exhaust. The bundle pitchers, we learned, had had *faspa* at the last job.

Bruno the dog and I wore ourselves out running from one vantage point to another. First we ran down the field driveway to check on the man with the hayrack, who was working furiously to have a load of bundles ready for the thresher. His three-tined fork moved like lightning, stabbing bundles of wheat out of the shocks and pitching them up into the rack. Meanwhile, another rack was moving into the field.

Bruno and I rushed back to the yard just in time to see the threshing machine, pulled by a big gray tractor with bright red steel wheels, coming into view on the road. This was no joy ride for the driver. Even at a mere three miles an hour it was a gut-wrenching job to hang on to the jarring mass of solid iron as the steel-lugged wheels bounced on the hard road. Fortunately, we lived on a dirt road; steel-wheeled tractors weren't permitted on pavement. The tractor's sharp lugs pockmarked our driveway as the rig crossed the yard and entered the field. The front tractor wheels had sharp skid flanges to make turns possible in soft fields, but it took a strong man to turn the steering wheel as the flanges dug into the earth.

The rush was on. Late as they were, the crew intended to thresh a lot of wheat that day. More horses and hayracks were arriving from the west.

Pop hastily cranked the Model T Ford truck to haul the threshed wheat. Our horses were already hitched to a wagon to help with the grain hauling. Joe, our hired man, was shirtless and stretching his arms and shoulder muscles; he would scoop the wheat into the bins with a heavy steel shovel.

I rode in the Model T with Pop to watch the threshing begin. Pop told Mr. Pauls, the threshing boss, where he wanted the straw stack, and from then on Mr. Pauls was the boss. Setting up the thresher was like a precision drill. Everyone had a job and worked at a breakneck pace because there was no pay for setup time. After testing the wind direction, Mr. Pauls positioned the thresher and stopped while a man at each corner hurriedly dug a hole for the wheels to drop into. Then the tractor lurched forward, the machine dropped into place, someone pulled the hitch pin, and the tractor was free. Johnny Pauls, the boss's son, had his rack waiting, filled with wheat bundles, and would replace his father on the tractor.

Lining up the tractor to the thresher belt required a deft touch, and Johnny was clearly aware of his favored position. When he pulled the throttle all the way back and jammed the hand clutch into gear, the tractor moved forward and made a wide turn, skid flanges churning the dirt, to face the thresher. As the giant belt was being unrolled, Johnny skillfully moved the tractor back and forth. With his tongue in his cheek and one eye closed, he sighted along the tractor belt pulley and the main thresher pulley, maneuvering the tractor until the alignment looked precise. Then, while workers put the belt on the tractor pulley, Johnny backed up until the belt was tight.

The thresher began to hum, but suddenly the belt flew off the tractor pulley and lashed out wildly. After another attempt, the alignment was successful. Soon the Case engine was running full throttle and the exhaust, pointing straight out of the manifold, spit fire and thunder. The thresher was humming like a hive of contented bees, and Mr. Pauls, standing on the thresher's feeder house, waved the first full rack into position.

Handling the rack was no job for greenhorns or green horses. The driver pulled up alongside the thresher, so close that the bundles touched the whirring belts and pulleys. The horses, perilously near the big belt, moved forward till the rack was in position near the feeder.

Another crew member, who had been turning some mysterious cranks and levers, swung the thresher's big blower into position to make the straw stack. Pop had been unloading the water jugs — stone crocks with wet gunnysacks wrapped around them — and pushing to get the truck and wagon under a spout to catch the grain.

Water out of a stone crock was the most delicious liquid in the world. I tried to imitate the field hand's way of grabbing the crock's leather strap, raising the jug so it rested on his elbow, and guzzling the water, much of which escaped and ran down the front of his shirt or soaked his bandana.

I noticed that some men would drink and then walk off or slip around the tractor and stand with their backs to us. Curious, I followed one of them and almost got a sprinkling. Embarrassed, I ran away behind the straw stack and almost lost my way in the blinding cyclone of swirling straw coming from the thresher's blower.

Overalls and long-sleeved work shirts, blue or black, were standard apparel. The older men always fastened the top shirt buttons — to keep the dust out, Pop said. He believed that long-sleeved shirts were cooler than short-sleeved on hot summer days. Once your shirt was soaked with sweat, any breeze had a cooling effect. Deodorant and antiperspirant were unheard of. A few men wore "half-pants" — overalls with the bibs cut off. Some actually looked dashing with their red bandanas tied loosely around their necks.

The working of the thresher was a mystery to me. Men on either side of the feeder at the front end threw the wheat bundles into the machine. Pop told me it was very important that the bundles go evenly into the thresher headfirst. I wondered why Mr. Pauls stood on the feeder house, watching as the feeder chain pulled the bundles into the chomping maw. Pauls was always barefoot, no matter how hot the steel feeder house became. Soon everything was going fine — the bundles were disappearing, dust was flying, the tractor governor kicked in, and the engine got louder. Threshed straw shot out of the blower and a stream of wheat came out of a spout into the truck bed.

Out in the field more hayracks were being loaded. By the time the first rack was empty, the sun was going down. The driver hollered to Mr. Pauls, "Do you want another load today?" Pop and Mr. Pauls glanced at the cloud bank in the west, and Mr. Pauls said, "Yes, we must work late." The driver, looking unhappy, started back into the field. As a full rack pulled up to the machine, Mr. Pauls came down from his post momentarily to talk to Pop about a late supper. Suddenly the thresher grunted, the engine slowed almost to a stall, and the big belt flew up in the air. Mr. Pauls turned toward the bundle pitchers, Pete and Slim, but they were staring at the clouds.

Looking grim, Mr. Pauls ran to the tractor and throttled it down, then returned to the thresher, opened the tin doors at the top, and started pulling straw out of the feeder housing. It was a nasty, dirty job.

No more racks were loaded that day. Only the filled ones could be threshed after the delay. On Pop's orders, I ran home to tell Mom the crew would be here for supper in a half hour. "How many?" she asked. I didn't know. She set the table for fourteen.

Soon horses and hayracks were arriving on the yard. The horses, unhitched at last, guzzled water from the stock tank. Sweaty horses blowing and snorting, jingling harnesses, the thumping windmill, lightning-charged clouds piling up in the western sky, and the wind changing course and blowing cool — I reveled in the familiar yet strange sights and sounds and smells.

Joe told me I'd better "close" the windmill since the wind was picking up. I felt pretty important, though I could hardly turn the crank.

The old truck came rattling into our granary, Mr. Pauls sitting in the cab with Pop, the field pitchers on the running boards. Mr. Pauls and Johnny decided to hurry home across the road before it rained. Slim also evidently wanted to beat the weather home. He clattered across the yard on his hayrack, standing bare-chested, face grim, and whipping the horses with his reins. Most of the men would sleep in the barn for the night.

About then I got real busy. Mom had me fill milk pails with water at our house pump. I filled them and set the buckets on a bench where wash basins, towels, and gray bars of Grandpa's Pine Tar soap were lined up. This was all set up outside on our kitchen porch.

These threshermen washed with gusto, plunging their heads right into the basins and washing faces, ears, and hair; splashing all over themselves and the floor. Not everybody changed water; usually two or three men used the same water. Pop had hung an old mirror on the wall, and everybody made a great show of combing their hair with our comb.

I was the last to get cleaned up. I wasn't used to washing that way. I sputtered and gasped for air when I plunged my head into the gray water, but I really liked its sweat-salty taste flavored with pine tar soap.

As I was drying my face, I overheard Joe laughing and telling a man named George how Slim had slugged down the thresher by throwing in some bundles crosswise. "Ole man Pauls fired him before supper," he said.

What was left of the crew had supper. Mom, naturally, was miffed. She stayed in the kitchen while Selma served the meal. And what a meal it was — chicken drumsticks from our big Rhode Island Reds, fried cured ham from the oat bin, mashed new potatoes and gravy, corn on the cob, fresh beans, dumplings, dill pickles, and slabs of rye bread with homemade butter. Mom had baked two kinds of pie, apple and apricot. Most of the men had generous portions of each.

It was getting dark early and spitting a little rain, so Pop lit a few lamps. Someone told us about a hired man so angry after getting fired that he had tied down the safety valve on a steam engine, escaping unharmed before the engine blew. A couple of horses were scalded to death and one man was badly burned in the incident, which had taken place east of Buhler about ten years earlier. I pictured Slim out there in the dark, rain in his face, lightning all around, racing down the road in his hayrack.

After supper the men headed for the hayloft in the barn to bed down for the night. Pop and Joe grabbed the milk buckets and went to the barn also; they still had cows to milk. Mom and Selma had dishes to wash and the next day's breakfast and lunch to plan. Baby Rachel, Marvella, and I were put to bed early as the thunderstorm moved in.

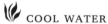 COOL WATER

By the time I joined the threshing crew a few years later, tractors had replaced horses. At first it was my job to move the tractor forward as the field pitchers loaded the hayrack behind it. While I waited, I listened to their conversations, which were mostly about girls unless one of the older men came by. Then the topic changed to Roosevelt or dust storms, which interested me more than girls.

I became a full-fledged member of the threshing ring just as binding and threshing became obsolete. The last time we threshed wheat the old-fashioned way on Section 27 was the year after Verna Lee and I got married. We had the straw stack not far from the house.

For twenty-five years, starting in the late 1930s, I did most of the plowing on the Penner half of Section 27. In the early years, since the soil was hard I pulled only a two-bottom plow, which cut a thirty-two-inch strip. At about four miles per hour, it took about four hours to plow five acres. In spite of the slow pace I enjoyed plowing. There was so much to see and think about — neighbors plowing on the other side of the fence, thunderheads building up in the west, pheasants, rabbits, skunks, and coyotes — and there was no limit to my daydreams of an exotic life ahead. The only time plowing seemed tedious was before dinner and *faspa,* when I watched for the open windmill signal to come home for dinner or the old brown Pontiac bringing *faspa.* Sometimes it seemed as if Pop had forgotten about me; using the tractor's shadow to estimate the time, I often thought it was later than it was. When I finally saw the dinner signal, I would unhitch the plow and drive the tractor home for dinner and to refill the gasoline tank.

Faspa was brought out to the field around four. Usually it was Pop who came out, and he'd make a few rounds while I ate, sitting on the ground on the shady side of the Pontiac or the pickup.

There was always cool water in a stone crock, wrapped in a wet gunnysack and sheltered under some straw or a large sunflower at the end of the field. Every time I went past that little jug, I'd say to myself, "Maybe next round I'll stop and have a drink." It was comforting to know it was there.

Thunderstorms could arrive with little warning, and I always debated when to head for home when a storm threatened. I'd watch to see what the neighbors were doing; it would never do to be the first to run home. Mom, I knew, would want me to come in at the first flash of lightning; Pop, on the other hand, wasn't one to give in easily to the weather. Then there was my own pride to consider; after all, Richard Halliburton would never let a little storm keep him away from adventure.

Storms generally came out of the northwest. When rain obscured the Inman water tower — about four miles away — common sense told me to hurry home, but I usually tried for one more round. Often the eight minutes gave the rain enough time to overtake me. Getting caught in a drenching rain was actually something of an adventure, though tame by Richard Halliburton standards.

I formed a shelter by lifting the plow, turning the tractor at a right angle to the rain's direction, and taking cover behind the leeward tractor wheel. Then I could only wait until the downpour — often accompanied by pounding hail just inches from my face — and the thunder and lightning had dissipated. After my adventure in the rain, I'd climb back on the tractor and race home (in high gear, at eight miles per hour), slipping and sliding in the mud and leaving six-inch-deep ruts in the stubble.

So quickly, in fact, did water turn our hard Ladysmith soil to mud that once when Pop was out on the east road in his 1929 Chevy, a sudden shower caused the "gumbo" (as we called it) to roll up on the wheels until it stalled the car. Uncle John, driving his Model T Ford (which had higher clearance and open-spoke wheels), came over to tow Pop out of his predicament.

In the dry 1930s, giant cracks appeared in our alfalfa field. Pop was mowing alfalfa with two five-foot horse mowers hitched behind the Case tractor when one mower, caught in a fissure, nearly tipped over. Other crevices were deep enough to hide a pitchfork standing on end. Once the rains came again, the cracks disappeared, recurring to a lesser extent two decades later. Soil engineers attributed the cracking to "a high shrink-swell factor"; we called it all sorts of other things.

The tillage chore I most enjoyed was harrowing. Newly plowed fields were rough and cloddy, so after the first rain we used the harrow to break up the clods. The job went quickly because the harrow took a wide swath and the tractor could pull it in road gear. Late on a calm summer day clouds of dust would rise behind the harrow and hang in the air, milling and swirling in fantastic patterns as the tractor pulled the harrow back and forth across the field.

 SIMPLE GIFTS

Everything a farmer has and is goes into growing wheat. Seeding is an act of faith. The farmer controls what's controllable and trusts the Universe for the rest. Wheat farming is an exercise of faith and courage.

It's about the craft of preparing the seedbed, dropping seeds at metered intervals, covering them with earth, and gently firming the ground. It's about the art of making straight-as-an-arrow drill furrows and sweeping curves along terraces. Wheat farming is both spiritual and sensuous — the smell of fertile soil and its texture, the taste of grit in the air, the welcome sight of tiny sprouts of green, and the music of wind and rustling grain.

12 🖋 For Better or Worse

Section 27 was a hard taskmaster. Gumbo and alkali soil defied the plow, combines bogged down in waterlogged fields, hail flattened ripening grain. The land's pitiless demands took their toll on a farmer's spirit.

The devastation of the Great Depression and the Dust Bowl era, however, left only faint scars on my family. Mom and Pop had always been prudent, which not only protected them from financial ruin but also enabled them to build a house and granary, buy a tractor and pickup truck, and feed and clothe three children. They were debt-free, they owned the farm outright, and they had money in the bank. Pop even bought eighty acres during the Depression, though rather than farming it, he compassionately leased it back to the farmer who had been forced to sell.

My sister Marvella was born in 1932, when I was three; Rachel arrived three years later. How Mom and Pop managed to have babies at regular intervals I never knew. Life was simple: church and visiting on Sunday, washing on Monday, chores every day, and other activities according to the season.

The Dust Bowl caused barely a ripple in our complacency. We were two hundred miles east of the epicenter and received enough rain for marginal crops. Selling our produce supplied cash for necessities, so proceeds from the wheat crop, however meager, were disposable income.

Experiencing a dust storm was awesome, however, even if it didn't destroy our livelihood. One summer morning when I was about five, Pop was feeding the pigs in the old pig barn and I was nearby, playing in fine, dry dust and watching it splash up like a fountain between my wiggling toes. The morning was bright, but the air was electric and the blackbirds in the mulberry hedge were ominously agitated.

Mom called from the house, her voice quavering. As I looked up, I saw a foreboding black cloud towering in the west. I ran to the house with Pop right behind me; the world went dark. Mom gathered us around the kitchen table. For a while it was dead calm, punctuated by the unnaturally loud tick of the mantel clock. No one spoke. The darkness seemed to suck the light from the kerosene lamp.

Then the wind caught up with the dust and moaned through the cracks in the window frame. Dust filtered into the room, someone coughed, and Mom held Marvella and me tightly.

Unlike tornadoes, dust clouds are propelled by straight winds, not necessarily with great velocity. During the long years of drought, soils in the Dust Bowl — the western parts of Kansas, Nebraska, and Oklahoma, eastern Colorado, and the Texas Panhandle — became so powdery that almost any wind sent them swirling into the sky. Storm clouds originating in Oklahoma carried a red tinge across the plains, while those from western Kansas were gray. A 1934 Dust Bowl storm covered buildings in New York City and ships at sea with an ashy film.

A severe windstorm could strip an unprotected field down to plow depth, representing a tremendous volume of fertile topsoil. One acre-inch of topsoil weighs about two hundred tons, and this was multiplied many times when layers of earth from entire counties became airborne.

❦ ENDINGS AND NEW BEGINNINGS

Pop, whose memory went back to around 1905, never mentioned any troubles occurring on the farm before the 1930s except flies bothering the draft horses at work — irritating enough, certainly, but hardly calamitous. He seemed to regard early farming as having been less stressful, whether because there were more men in the family to share the work or because his memories of plowing with big sodbusting tractors and of threshing extravaganzas were colored with a young man's exuberance.

Other changes rocked the Penner family in the late 1920s, however. Peter married and moved to his own farm. David L. died of polio. Grandpa David F., his wife, Maria, and their daughter, Elizabeth, moved to Buhler where Grandpa died in 1928. Thus Mom and Pop, who were wed during that turbulent period, suddenly found themselves operating the Penner farm, and Pop's role changed from that of a subservient youngest son to that of an independent farmer.

Gone was the cumbersome twenty-two-thousand-pound Avery tractor that for Pop represented the "golden years." In its place was a comparatively scrawny tractor, a forty-one-hundred-pound Wallis. Pop had loved the Avery but eventually admitted that the faster, nimbler Wallis plowed as many acres in a day with three bottoms as the Avery had with eight bottoms. Still, he was nostalgic about the Avery, which had a large sun-shielding canopy and which he and his brothers had taken turns driving. Plowing with the Avery required two men, one on the tractor and one on the plow, while the newer, lighter-weight tractors were a lonely one-man operation.

Not that driving the Wallis was a joyride. It rolled on steel wheels with five-inch steel traction lugs, and the exhaust came straight out of the manifold at ear level, making for an ear-splitting, gut-wrenching, bone-crunching ride even at three miles an hour. Apart from that, and the fact that the connecting rod bearings on the crankshaft required adjustment at least every other day the Wallis was in use, it was a pretty good tractor for its time. There were hand holes in the side of the crankcase for the operator to reach through to adjust the bearings. Since many farmers made the adjustment out in the field, usually after dinner to give the engine a chance to cool, a lot of dirt would find its way into the engine.

Like most other farmers, though, Pop didn't really mind the inconveniences that went with tractor farming. It was, after all, a great improvement over horse farming. With comparative ease, the moldboards churned stubble into the rich-smelling black earth. A steel-wheeled tractor would almost guide itself from one end of the field to the other once the right front wheel was in the furrow. In fact, I often saw our neighbor, young Johnny Pauls, jump off the moving tractor and chase rabbits with his dog until the tractor approached the end of the furrow.

When Section 27's heavy gumbo dried out, however, the fun was over. When you pulled the rope to drop the plow into the ground, the plowshares often just skidded along the surface. Then you had to make a sweeping turn and start over — not an easy thing considering how hard those old tractors steered. If the plow failed to penetrate the ground again, you moved some levers to adjust the depth and then, when it broke through, you had to quickly reach back and readjust the moldboard to normal depth, keeping one hand on the steering wheel as the tractor moved forward. It was a dangerous maneuver, requiring all the strength you could muster. Those who fell off the tractor were too embarrassed to tell about it — if, in fact, they survived. Uncle John, a portly man, fell off one time and rolled under the plow, miraculously avoiding the coulters, which could have sliced him in two. He was so badly bruised it was impossible not to tell the truth about what had happened.

The sticky soil on the edge of the old lake bottom was especially difficult to plow. When it was too wet, it stuck to the moldboard and clogged the plow. When it was too dry, it was almost impossible to penetrate. There was little leeway between the two extremes. Pop used to say that if it was too wet to plow before dinner, it could well be too dry afterward.

Harvesting after a rain was extremely difficult on such flat land. The old pull-type harvesters — binders and combines — worked their way around the field with the horses or tractors off to one side, moving on stubble cut the previous circuit. Thus it was hard to dodge a wet pothole. You could hardly delay harvesting, though, when your neighbors were cutting wheat or oats on ground with greater slope.

Pop's first combine was a big twelve-foot-cut Nichols and Shepard. Heavy and clumsy on its steel wheels, the combine required three men to keep it going — one on the Wallis to pull it, one to tend it, and the third to haul grain on the Model T Ford truck. The combine couldn't be used at all when the soil was wet — and it seemed as if rain always came with the harvest — so the hired help, having nothing to do but loaf, wasted a lot of time.

Pop, thinking he'd learned his lesson, bought one of the smallest and lightest combines made — a one-man Woods Brothers on rubber tires — and a rubber-tired Allis-Chalmers tractor. Though the combine cut only a five-foot swath, Pop thought it could compensate for its size by being mireproof and fast.

But you can't fool Mother Nature, nor was her ally, Section 27, taken in. Harvest came, but no rain, and of course no mud. There was also very little wheat. It was almost comical to watch Pop racing around the field for almost half a day before he filled the combine's little thirty-five-bushel bin. Wheat yields during the dry years were as low as five bushels an acre. On the bright side, there was no need for an extra man to haul wheat.

The Allis-Chalmers was one of the first rubber-tired tractors in the community, and the neighbors were skeptical. It was great for putting up hay and pulling the little combine, but it was a fiasco in front of a plow. Having no wheel weights, the tractor had a slippage problem so acute that a rear wheel once spun out on a juicy sunflower, leaving Pop unable to move in either direction. A neighbor plowing nearby with a steel-wheeled tractor pulled Pop's tractor off the mangled flower and, no doubt, told everyone about the humiliating incident. The next year Pop bought a rubber-tired Case tractor with wheel weights and larger wheels. Within five years, every farmer in the area switched to rubber tires.

In 1940 Pop gave up on the little combine. It seldom rained during harvest anymore, so muddy terrain hadn't been a problem. Most of the neighbors were using twelve-foot-cut Baldwin combines, so Pop compromised and bought a nine-foot-cut Baldwin, a new model with no front wheels. The tractor supported the front of the combine. Originally, it still required a man on the combine, but Pop ended up modifying the arrangement by installing an electric lift (made out of old Ford Model A starters) so he could control the header from the tractor.

By now I was old enough to help at harvest time. Pop built a ramp in the elevator so I could drive the pickup onto it and dump the wheat without having to do much scooping. It was fun driving the pickup to the field, stirring up clouds of dust along the well-worn route. I was proud that we had a pickup to haul wheat; many of our neighbors pulled a four-wheel trailer behind the family car.

When I got bored, I rode in the combine bin while Pop was filling it. Usually, though, I waited in the pickup and had the motor running when the combine approached so I'd be ready to drive under the unloading spout. If the wheat was standing tall, the fields were dry, and the harvest was generous, Pop was happy. Often, however, things weren't so rosy.

 MUD

Almost as soon as Pop bought the Baldwin, a string of rainy harvest years began. From my vantage point atop the pickup cab, I'd watch

Pop's tractor spin down in a low spot. He'd try, usually unsuccessfully, to back up. Then, since the combine had no front wheels, the only thing to do was jack up the combine hitch, pull the drawbar pin, drive the tractor around to the back of the combine, fasten a heavy chain to the combine and tractor, pull the combine backward to a dry spot, then do the whole thing in reverse — jack up the combine front end, rehitch, and try to find a spot dry enough to get the combine around the field. Every time this happened, Pop had to drive the tractor through uncut wheat, ruining part of the crop.

The mud was inescapable, though Pop usually scouted for a dry route, testing the soil by stomping on the ground with his heel. If it didn't leave a big imprint, the ground would support the combine. Still, he would get stuck time after time before he found a dry area or gave up for the day. Lost time meant more weeds, which grew fast in the ripe wheat and which would quickly disable the combine by wrapping themselves around the beaters. The only solution to weeds around the beaters was to open the combine, crawl inside with a knife, and cut the weeds away.

With the outside temperature approaching 100 degrees, the inside of the combine was a furnace. Pop had plenty to say to the devil in the Low Dutch vernacular, telling him just what he thought of him. In English it would have been considered cussing, but there seemed to be a special dispensation to say all kinds of things in Low Dutch.

These encounters with the devil took a lot out of Pop, and when he finally made it around the field to the pickup, he would be weary and disheveled. Then, if I got off the right track driving the load of wheat off the field and got the pickup stuck, his frame of mind was all the worse. In either case, neither of us spoke as we unloaded wheat.

The next year Pop rebuilt the front wheels of an old tractor and put them under the Baldwin's front end, a big improvement. As was always the case when he worked on projects in his shop, Pop made do with what he had on the farm.

In 1948 he bought another tractor, a little Farmall B, and when it was muddy during harvest, I would follow the combine on the Farmall. If the combine got stuck, it didn't take long to hitch the back of it to the Farmall and help Pop reverse out of the mud.

Frank Penner cutting wheat, about 1948.

A few years later, the advent of the self-propelled combine took a lot of the aggravation out of harvesting, but there were still plenty of things to fret about. To bring a stand of wheat within a few days of a bountiful harvest and then see it threatened or snatched away was heartbreaking. Sometimes, when the harvest was under way, the wheat standing tall and ripe, an ominous cloud bank would appear in the evening sky, often bringing rain during the night. In the morning sun, the giant elms, oaks, mulberries, and the garden were refreshed, reflecting a dazzling green while the wheat lay soggy and flat. Then the chattering of the kingbirds felt like an affront.

Even if the fields dried before the weeds took over, struggling in the mud exacted a price from me and I'm sure more so from Pop. Hours and hours in the mire, anger alternating with despair, tarnished the golden harvest when finally achieved. A few times I heard Pop, in unguarded moments, lamenting our farm's location in the Blaze Fork bottoms and the attendant difficulties that upland farmers were spared. He even dared to suggest that some of Section 27 should never have been plowed in the first place.

You really can't appreciate someone else's experience until you've walked a mile in his shoes or — in the case of a farmer — ridden a mile in his combine. Upland farmers little understood the valley farmer's plight. When Preacher Voth eloquently thanked the Lord for the blessed rain and the bountiful harvest one Sunday morning after we had just experienced an especially maddening delay, it cut deep.

Pop was one of the first to sign up for a soil conservation plan when the McPherson County Conservation District was organized in the late 1940s. An early survey of the western portion of the east half of Section 27 indicated a minimal slope: one-tenth of 1 percent from south to north. The conservationist told Pop what he already knew — that without extensive and costly grading it would be almost impossible to eliminate the bothersome wet spots that made harvesting so difficult. A shallow farm-through ditch recommended by the conservationist helped some but never came close to getting rid of the problem.

A major flood, of course, could wipe out the crops of many farmers in the Blaze Fork basin. John Schrag's Big Basin drainage project west of McPherson early in the century continues to be the key contributor to floods on the north half of Section 27. The later meddling — channelizing and diking the Blaze Fork waterway and test drilling for oil (the cause of numerous sinkholes) — just made things worse. Even though the dikes might save most of the valley from severe flooding, weak spots in the system produced localized misery, and the sinkholes were responsible for most of the weak spots. The Dust Bowl era was a decade-long respite from floods, but in the 1940s they returned with a vengeance.

 SURVIVAL

Uncle John and Aunt Sarah Unruh lived just northeast of Section 27. Grandpa David F. had set them up on 160 acres after Uncle John failed twice to establish a grocery store during the Depression. Optimistically, they rented an additional 300 acres, moved the house where Mom and first husband David L. had lived to the highest spot on the quarter section, and remodeled the house and built a barn. For the first decade on the farm, rain was sparse for the Unruhs, but they hung on tenaciously, waiting for rainfall.

Whatever remained of the Unruhs' enthusiasm after years of drought was drained completely by the floods that followed. The dike between our land and theirs usually held on our side, so floods would cover only what had originally been the Old Lake. The Unruhs weren't so lucky. One year, when the dikes broke near their place, Uncle John called for help, saying the pigs were swimming in the yard. A Red Cross rowboat reached them from the north but wasn't much help. A farmer had to use a horse to pull the boat back to dry land against the wind. Neighbors came in a horse-drawn wagon across flooded fields and helped catch the pigs but had nowhere to go with them. Besides, the wagon box kept floating off the running gear.

Pop cranked up the high-wheeled Case tractor and hitched up a two-wheel hayrack he had just built. He had worked the Unruh farm as a boy, and he knew it well. Even with everything under water, Pop knew where the highest ridges were. Finding the road wasn't easy — for a half mile it was under water, along with the deep drainage ditch alongside it — but Pop could see the bridge railings ahead and used them as a guide. He got to the Unruh farm by midmorning, helped move furniture and household items to the top floor, loaded all the pigs in the rack, and was home before dark. Coming home, the tractor's front wheels were covered with water, the belt pulley was spinning in water, and Mom was at home pacing and fretting.

John, Sarah, and their three boys managed to have a few successful crops, but then the flooding returned. By the time the two older boys were in college, Jean, the youngest, and his wife, Leona, were living in the Unruh farmhouse with Uncle John and Sarah. Leona was about to have a baby when the floods came again. This time there was great concern for her safety when acres and acres of water surrounded the house.

Somehow they survived, but Jean made a desperate decision. With the wheat crop gone, he took his dad's combine, borrowed money for a new Minneapolis-Moline model U tractor, mounted a wooden box on the combine to carry oil and grease and a few items of clothing, and took off for Texas with the rig. Custom combining was in its infancy then. Only a few other local men had tried it. It was risky with no jobs lined up and only the combine to sleep under. The platform overhang on the Baldwin was on the left side, so Jean had to drive on the wrong side of the highway to make room for passing cars. In farm country it was understood that when you met a Baldwin combine on the road you moved to the left side, but Jean was going a lot farther than just down the road and in unfamiliar territory to boot. He had chosen the Minneapolis because it had the fastest road gear — about thirty miles an hour.

One Inman man, apparently as desperate as Jean, made his own tractor from an old truck, pulled his combine to Texas, and harvested his way north to Montana. There he sold the combine, driving back to Kansas on the open tractor and passing more sophisticated vehicles, including a Greyhound bus full of astonished passengers, at sixty miles an hour.

After Jean returned, the Unruh families moved to two upland farms near Halstead. No trace remains of the farmstead they left behind.

 BRIDLE PATH

After a few years of drought in the 1950s, the flooding resumed and often overran the dikes in our vicinity. Shortly after Verna Lee and I were married, when we were farming with Pop and Mom, I walked out to inspect a flooded area and met up with a neighbor named George, an old cowboy, who had the same intention. His place was surrounded by water, and he suggested that we make our inspection on horseback. My riding experience consisted of a few short outings on a pony, but I hid my apprehension.

He was gone a short time and came back with two horses. My heart sank when I realized they had no saddles. I watched George leap onto his horse; and, doing just what he had done, I was able to mount mine. We rode around the big sinkhole on the elevated road, which was under two feet of water, guided by weeds poking up along the edges. After crossing a bridge with its railings barely visible, we turned east on the township road.

All the roads in the area were elevated and served as dikes, albeit ineffective ones. Next to the road we were on was a drainage canal; the water was probably seven feet deep on one side and fifteen feet deep on the other. For a solid mile the road was under water. Our only reference point was the railings of the Blaze Fork bridge at the halfway point. The water grew deeper until the horses' bellies were skimming the water. Even George sounded a little anxious when he hollered at me to stay in the middle of the road. Finally, the horses were swimming.

"Can you swim?" George yelled.

"No," I shouted back.

We had to go on, George said. After we'd gone a mile on the road, the water became shallower. George suggested that we check on Jake Ediger and his family. As we neared the Ediger farmstead, the water had deepened again. I waded to the door and knocked, and Elma, the youngest daughter, responded. She was knee-deep in muddy water in the kitchen. She and her dad were waiting out the flood, she said, and he was in the barn milking the cows. Fortunately, Jake hadn't cleaned the manure out of the barn for years, so the milk cows were in only a foot of water and he could, with careful maneuvering, get a milk bucket under them without water slopping into it.

Jake told us that he and Elma would be fine, so George and I headed home. By this time I was pretty unnerved, so when George suggested riding around the section to avoid the deepest water I breathed a sigh of relief. Years later he told me he'd been worried when I said I couldn't swim. That's

The Penner dog, Bruno, wading in the floodwaters on the northeast
corner of Section 27. The fence posts shown in the middle right-hand side
of the picture demarcate the route and depth of the water that neighbor George
and Milferd encountered on their horseback trip in a 1950s flood.

when I told him I'd never been on a big horse before. "We were lucky," he said.

During this flood, about 200 acres on Section 27 went under water. Dad (instead of Pop, I started calling my father "Dad" when Verna Lee and I married) accepted the situation as stoically as always. Floods or no floods, each year he cut all the wheat, no matter how long it took. Some years he finished cutting the mud holes as late as August. Finally he made a deal with the drainage district: it would no longer repair our dikes; we would no longer pay drainage taxes. The district went for the deal because fighting the floods was a losing proposition. Besides the Big Basin problem, more channelization and new farming practices upstream continued to exacerbate the flooding.

The Blaze Fork wasn't the only waterway to flood the Penner farm. The drainage ditch entering from the south was also overwhelmed by progress — more acres under cultivation and faster, more efficient drainage systems — though from the west and south rather than the north. One winter day runoff from melting snow completely filled the ditch. That night the wind changed, blowing bitterly cold from the north. In the ditch, ice formed and choked the channel while water continued to flow underneath. Water and ice piled up in the barnyard corral, backing up into the barn itself and forcing the cattle to struggle pitifully with every step. To make things worse, Rachel developed rheumatic fever, and Pop had to pull the old Pontiac through the ice with a tractor to get her to the hospital. He bore it all patiently, as always, but later admitted that it was the most difficult time he ever experienced on the farm.

Springtime often brought its own set of annoyances, including hailstorms. The worst one came just a month before Verna Lee and I were to be married. I was installing a kitchen window in the little house we would live in when the sky turned dark with a distinctive blue-green cast. I had just put the glass into the frame when hailstones, propelled by a brisk north wind, started pounding the window. I opened it, pushed the screen through the opening and held it over the glass. I saved the window, but my hands took a beating.

In a matter of minutes, most of our wheat was beaten into the ground. Strangely, the hail damage ended at the east road, and the neighbor's wheat was standing tall the next morning. After inspecting the crop, Dad decided enough wheat — about 30 percent — remained to make an attempt at harvest worthwhile. Because damaged wheat ripens unevenly, we decided to windrow it with a binder. We planned to take the elevator canvases off the binder, thereby letting the wheat fall to the ground in windrows. After the grain had dried, we would pick it up with a combine.

On June 6, a few weeks before it was time to windrow the wheat — and three days before our wedding was to take place — I had an emergency appendectomy. In the 1950s, that meant a week in the hospital and a week of recuperation at home. Verna Lee sent cards explaining the delay and postponing the wedding until June 25. Almost three weeks after the surgery, I was still a washed-out puppy, but Verna Lee was a beautiful and radiant bride.

After a one-day honeymoon I helped Dad windrow the wheat. My incision hurt with every turn of the tractor wheel, but the loss of the crop was more painful to me. Dad just kept going.

Sometimes, though, adversity made victory over the elements especially gratifying. One day, baling alfalfa, we raced frantically with the weather. A custom baling crew was about to finish a field as clouds began building in the west. The crew loaded the bales directly into a wagon towed by the baler. As the last bale was tied, we watched as heavy rain obscured the water tower in Inman and approached the farm. We hitched the bale wagon to the little Farmall tractor and sped to the farmstead. Raindrops were falling as we reached the open shed. We unhitched, and all the men helped push the wagon into the shed. It was sweet indeed to hear rolling thunder and the drumming of rain on the tin roof, knowing that the fragrant hay was safe in the shed.

13  Simple Pleasures

Almost everything we needed could be found on Section 27 — on or beneath the land or occasionally above it. For sustenance, shelter, even entertainment, we had little reason to travel far from home.

One winter evening, when Pop had taken me out onto the north porch at bedtime (as was our custom), I saw the aurora borealis for the first time. I must have been about four because we still lived in the old house. As I was unbuttoning my overalls, I looked up, and there they were in the northern sky — luminous streamers dancing upward into cold starlit space. I watched the spectacle in awe bordering on fear. Pop explained matter-of-factly that we were seeing the northern lights.

We stood in the darkness for a while, spellbound. No manmade lights competed except the gentle glow of the kerosene lamp in the kitchen window. Masses of stars, dwindling as they approached the dark horizon, framed the mysterious, shimmering purples and violets. Not at all comprehending what I saw, I nevertheless sensed a connection with eternity.

 HOME COOKING

The days brought their own wondrous delights. Dinner — the main meal, eaten at noon on the farm — was almost as magical as the northern lights when Mom served summer borscht or Rhode Island Red rooster drumsticks. Called *somma borscht* (summer borscht), the soup was a tantalizing blend of garden greens, including weeds like curly dock. The full recipe included cooked ham soup bone, new potatoes, diced onions with green tops, dill, parsley, beet tops, Swiss chard, and, after it was cooked, a liberal dollop of sour cream and pinch of pepper seasoning. The recipe is really just a starting place; somma borscht is an art form that allows free and creative expression. Mom added barley and scouted the farm for other tasty ingredients.

I always made a pig of myself eating somma borscht. I loved it to an extreme. This was before the days of counting calories, and an exuberant appetite was a compliment to the cook. I remember eating bowl after bowl of it, asking Mom how I would know when I was filled up.

Rhode Island Red rooster drumsticks were just as good. These were not the bland, puny facsimiles found at chain-store meat markets today. These juicy morsels came from animals that grew to bold roosterhood in our farmyard and that were carefully nurtured with the succulent end product in mind. Fried on the old wood cookstove with Mom adjusting the damper or adding another stick, the erstwhile rooster evolved into a hungry boy's delight. Mashed homegrown potatoes and dumplings topped with brown gravy, garden-fresh green beans, and generous slices of rye bread spread with homemade butter complemented the perfectly cooked poultry. My routine was first to eat a drumstick, then a thigh, then the gizzard and heart. Mom always ate the legs (the bony part extending from the knee to the feet); I couldn't believe she liked them. Marvella didn't like chicken, so Mom always fried some ham, too, and generally I ate some of that. Pie always followed.

Somma borscht and drumsticks weren't daily fare, but regardless of what was served, summertime meals were large to provide fuel for strenuous physical work. On our farm, even during the Great Depression, there was no relationship between food and money. A little sugar, some flour, salt, pepper, and other seasonings were all we needed from town to eat well. When blizzards closed in, it was such a good feeling to see colorful rows of canned food on the cellar shelves — beets, beans, corn, tomatoes, meat, and assorted fruit. Hanging from the ceiling were pork sausages and liverwurst — a great breakfast treat — and in the barn there were hams and bacon either curing in a barrel of brine or hanging in the oat bin. We grew our own potatoes, too. Though I can't recall where they were stored, I remember the large plot of potatoes covered with a straw mulch out in the field.

A break-action single-shot BB gun was my ticket to adventure land. The moment I picked up that gun, I was Sergeant Renfew of the Royal Canadian Mounted Police, or Buffalo Bill, or any of a number of other heroes I had read about in the old *Youth's Companion* magazines I found in the attic, the *American Boy* magazines Pop ordered for me, and Osa and Martin Johnson's and Theodore Roosevelt's African adventure books.

When I carried my trusty gun, the winter fields of Section 27 became snow-covered Canadian wilderness; in the summer, the landscape was the African veldt where lions crouched just out of sight. Actually, the gun was far from trusty. The only thing reliable about it was its magical ability to transform the Kansas countryside into exotic regions or untracked wilderness. As far as firepower was concerned, it was useless. Once, I managed to fluff up a sparrow's feathers. Wimpy as it was, however, I always adhered strictly to Pop's rules about acceptable targets and fired only at sparrows, starlings, and jackrabbits.

The winter cold — often hovering around zero degrees — with its biting wind and drifting snow, and the treeless landscape made it easy to transport myself to the tundra and emulate my Canadian Mountie hero. Faithful Gyp, running by my side, became Renfew's husky, scouting for signs of our quarry's whereabouts. Once beyond the mulberry hedge, I could, by looking only to the north, see no sign of human habitation. Even a slight haze or drifting snow obscured the nearest farmstead, almost three miles north. Here and there, sorghum stalks and two mulberry trees in the fence row dividing Penner and Balzer land were all that pierced the white canopy. The solitary pair of gnarled trees were objects of wonder, having survived lonely battles with ferocious winds and summer lightning. Their scarred trunks and broken branches told the tale while mounds of earth beneath recalled the laborious digging of badgers. A derelict robin's nest, precariously situated, hung overhead. After paying our respects, Gyp and I continued on our journey.

Occasionally a jackrabbit would burst out of its grassy retreat under the fence. Gyp, oblivious to the cold, would rise to the challenge and chase the animal halfheartedly. They would disappear, but Gyp would soon return, tongue hanging out, declaring victory. Snowbirds — perhaps snow buntings or horned larks — would zoom in on us, flying in perfect unison. Their swoops were exquisitely choreographed, white bellies flashing as they wheeled in the air. As they descended and settled down on the snow, only their brown backs were visible.

Thinning clouds raced overhead and a pale winter sun, low on its southern trajectory, broke through but added no warmth. The wind picked up, plucking snow from the fields and slipping it under the fence to lie in drifts among the weeds and grasses. Soon the countryside disappeared behind an opaque white curtain, while overhead the sun played tag with wispy clouds. I decided even Renfew would have looked for shelter. I headed home with my back to the wind.

Some years later, when I had a single-shot .22 rifle, I would follow the grassy banks of the drainage canal intent on finding cottontails, thinking I would skin them and sell them as my Lake Valley classmates did, but that never happened. Cottontails were plentiful and it wasn't unusual to scare up quite a number, which were easy prey when they ran a short distance and then stopped to see what was going on. Like the other boys, I made a wire hook, which hung from my coat pocket, to haul the carcasses. I'm sure Mom didn't appreciate the blood all over my clothes, but she never complained. Although my intentions were to make a fortune off of rabbit skins, I always ended up burying the dead rabbits in a posthole.

In the spring and summer I did African safaris. It was rather difficult in a Kansas wheat field to conjure up Roosevelt's lions, tigers, and wildebeests, but on long walks to the sinkhole, almost a mile north of the house, I let my imagination run wild and eventually the African carnivores materialized, along with their prey.

As absorbed as I was in my adventures on the veldt, I still managed to notice the spring and fall flights of ducks and geese. Later I learned some high flyers were sandhill cranes. They could be distinguished by their rattling "garooo-a-a, garoo-a-a," a sound much like that made by a stick strumming the turning spokes of a bicycle wheel.

After a rain or spring thaw, walking across the fields was a matter of dragging one foot after the other in the mud. I usually wore four-buckle overshoes, and sometimes the mud would suck the overshoe, shoe, and sock right off my foot. I soon found that walking in shallow water was easier than slogging through the mud, although it was more challenging to pretend I was walking beside a covered wagon on the Santa Fe Trail after a storm.

Often my tramping destination was a ditching machine, also known as a dragline, that sat idle near the big sinkhole when it wasn't being used to build dikes. The dragline had tracks, a long boom, and a digging bucket suspended from a long cable. It could reach down into the drainage ditches, lift a load of earth, turn, and dump its cargo on the dikes. I was enthralled with it. If no one were around, I would climb almost reverently up onto the tracks or the framework. In my wildest imagination I never dreamed that I would someday operate such a wonderful machine. Once, when the cab was unlocked, I sat at the controls, awed by the size and complexity of it all.

🍃 THAT MOMENT

There is a little spot on our farm unscathed by plow or fire for over sixty years. Only rust and decay have altered a relic here that harks back to a moment of time evoking memories that stir my soul.

While a poet may laud that perfect day in June, I experienced such a perfect moment one day in April as a little boy in overalls — a warm sun low in the west, honeybees humming amidst lilac blossoms, and cattle jostling and lowing on a dusty path. Life was good. The last day of school was near at hand (it closed in mid-April); soon I would be free to roam barefoot in the long rows of mulberry trees, groves of elm, and the pasture with my dog, Gyp, and single-shot BB gun.

The pastoral setting of that moment was forever imprinted in my mind: rambunctious cows and calves returning from a day of grazing lush green wheat, eager for the cold water awaiting them near the barn; the crisp call of a bob-white and the repetitious song of a brown thrasher atop a tall elm; an orange flash, a returning Baltimore oriole; and the new canopy of pristine leaves, already providing some welcome shade. Even the poignant aroma resulting from cattle on wheat mixed with dust and sweat is a pleasant memory.

My job after school was to bring the cattle home from the fields and to pen them up in the corral. The milk cows were heavy with milk, udders

Remains of the old corral gate.

dripping, and frisky calves were running ahead and butting heads. The gate opening was a bottleneck, where bulky bodies collided and fence posts were tested to the limit.

That "perfect moment" still so clear in my mind occurred as Gyp was barking the last cow into the corral. The gate was a wooden affair, one end hinged to a large hedge post and the other riding on an old steel wheel. No grease ever graced the point between hub and axle. As I pulled on the wood gate frame, the wheel squeaked and moaned in protest. That sound sealed the moment. That rusty wheel and attached remnants of rotting wood and memories are a legacy I will leave undisturbed to my grand-daughters till the last bit of iron rusts away.

A quarter century later, on a cold, sunny winter afternoon, I walked along the bank of the pasture ditch with my little children — nine-year-old Murray, six-year-old Marci, and Beth, who was four. Running through the pasture, the ditch was barren of trees except where it made a big turn. There some old cottonwoods and low brambles offered shelter. Elsewhere grasses and weeds were tall enough to have trapped some snow, so Murray and Marci frolicked in the drifts. Poor little Beth Ann (she prefers to be called Liz now) valiantly tried to follow them, but the snow was almost up to her waist. Most of the time I carried her.

In the bend where the ditch turned east, we found an eight-foot-deep dry channel devoid of snow or grass. Facing the warm sun and shielding us from the wind, the little canyon made a cozy retreat for cuddling, sharing a candy bar, and telling stories. The sun turned the bare earth from brown to gold. Transported by imagination and sunlight, as I had been so many times on that landscape, Marci exclaimed, "Let's build a house here." Eventually we did — a towering tree house that overlooked our snug winter hideaway.

14 🌿 The Barn

Tumbling in the haymow on a wintry Sunday afternoon was about as much fun as Mennonite children were permitted. On the other hand, I'm not sure it's possible to have more fun than that. A whiff of cured alfalfa hay brought instant spring. You could almost hear the dickcissel's song and see horses pulling a creaking hayrack filled with fresh, green alfalfa even as a cold winter wind whistled by outside.

My sisters and I played in the barn for hours on end. We'd scale the ladder to the loft, then struggle up, up in the loose hay — sinking to the waist with each step — and climb to the peak, only to drop with abandon, tumble through the hay to the floor, and jump up, laughing, to do it all over again.

Most barns were a maze of corridors, doors, ladders, and dark rooms — perfect places for children to play hide-and-seek or build caves in the hay. It would have been hard for us to believe that the fragrance of the hay, the lovely patina of wood rubbed by dozens of cows, and the old lantern hanging on a nail would be only a grandpa's memories in several generations.

In the summertime swallows attached mud nests to the ceiling joists above the calves and cows. The birds would swoop in and out of the barn catching flies, squeaking noisily, especially if a cat was near.

Every spring, mysteriously, kittens appeared in one of the barn's remote corners. I'd listen for their squeaky mewling and then follow the sound, to be rewarded (when my eyes had adjusted to the dark) with the sight of a squirming patchwork of fur — black, white, gray, and sometimes tan — bodies wriggling, blindly but instinctively, toward their mama. If the mother was one of our tame cats, she would stay and nurse them where they were born, allowing me to play with them after their tiny eyes had opened. The feral cats, however, usually moved their kittens, once discovered.

North view of the Penner farmstead barn in the 1920s.

No place seemed safer than the barn. A blizzard might tear at the land, snowdrifts piling up where the wind whipped around the structure; but at dusk, when all the animals had been fed and bedded down on bright straw and the doors shut tight, all was well. Even wartime anxieties disappeared in the barn, where familiar noises — cattle crunching on hay, softly lowing or simply breathing heavily and rhythmically, and sheep bleating — brought a deep sense of peace.

SCHOOL OF LIFE

The milk cows, returning from the pasture at the end of the day, were trained to march into the barn and poke their heads into their assigned stanchions, where oats awaited them. It was my job to squeeze between the cows and secure the stanchions with wooden blocks. I had to work quickly or the cows would get away. I was little, the cows were very big, the floor was slick with manure, and the barn was in semidarkness. It was scary, exciting, and satisfying all at once.

When the six red shorthorns, each weighing some nine hundred pounds, were safely in their stanchions, Pop would milk by the light of a kerosene lantern hanging on a nail. On winter evenings, as snow melted off the cows' backs, steam would rise and water often dripped into the milk bucket.

After we got electric lights, I helped with the milking. I sat on a little wooden stool, my head pressed into the cow's side as I squeezed milk out of the teats. I usually took a beating from the animal's tail, which might have a mudball clinging to the tip, adding insult to injury. In the summer, flies annoyed the cows, and the beatings were more severe. I took it out on the flies by squirting them down into the milk and drowning them. Any harm done to the milk, I thought, would be undone when we poured the milk into the cream separator through a cotton strainer.

Usually I hobbled (fastened the hind legs together) the cows I milked because nothing made me madder than for the cow to step into the bucket or kick it out of my hands. Hobbling a cow was something of an art, with a little luck thrown in. The person doing the hobbling, working from the cow's right side (the milking side), was very vulnerable when reaching under the cow's belly to put the hobble on the left leg. I always tried to get the cow's tail caught between the hobble and her leg, but that was not always possible.

We kept feeder cattle in the barn as well, and it was also my job to pitch alfalfa down to them as they lounged in their big pens. I would climb the ladder and feel my way to the dark haymow, groping for the string to turn on the single electric light. My intrusion would disturb any sparrows or pigeons that happened to be there, and they'd flap around blindly in the dark. Often there would be a little screech owl sitting on the hay-carrier rope. I didn't mind the screech owl, but one day climbing into the loft I came face to face with a monkeylike visage. It scared me momentarily. Pop, responding to my excitement, climbed into the loft and said it was a barn owl.

As safe and comforting as the barn could be, it also held excitement and harbored secrets. Animals were born and died in our barn, skunks lived under the wood floors, and the large room filled with old machinery was redolent of "olden times." It was in the barn that I was introduced to death. One morning at breakfast overhearing Pop and Mom whisper about a cow that had just died, I crept out of the house, made my way to the barn, and peeked into the cattle pen. The huge black animal was lying almost upside down, its straight legs angled upward. I realized death was a terrible thing. Birth didn't impress me much more when I saw a cow in labor with legs sticking out in the back. I wasn't prepared to accept that as pleasant either.

The barn was a school of life in more ways than one, and we learned by watching and doing. When a barn door broke, I learned basic woodworking by helping Pop fix it. I developed physical coordination with a pitchfork, and knowing that the animals — sheep and cows — depended on me for food instilled responsibility. Instead of gymnastics, cleaning barn stalls built muscles. My sisters and I didn't have to be taught about the food chain or shown where a loaf of bread came from. We could see with our own eyes that food came from cows, chickens, pigs, and the garden. We carried milk from the cow to the cream separator and then to the butter churn, and when it emerged as butter we spread it on homemade rye bread. Butchering pigs and steers didn't seem cruel to me; it was the way it was.

 BARN TALK

A woman's domain was the house; a man's, the barn. During the week, men would do their visiting in the barn; they had no business in the house. Young as I was, I could see that men acted differently in the barn than they did in the house on Sundays. In the barn, for example, I would never stand downwind of Uncle George. In the house, Uncle George blew his nose into a handkerchief; in the barn, he pressed one nostril with his thumb and emptied the other onto his free index finger, deftly flicking the mucus onto the ground. I wondered how I would ever learn to do all the things men did.

Barn conversations were different too, but I never got to hear much of it because as soon as there were cusswords or the topic turned to women, Pop sent me out to carry water to the chickens.

Cattle traders were regular visitors to our barn. Every time Pop sold an animal to one of them, he would promise Mom afterward that this was the last time he'd do business with them. For the most part they were devious old men driving old cars that pulled rickety two-wheel trailers outfitted with stock racks. The way the cattle trader operated was simple and semi-unscrupulous. He would buy an old cow or steer from a farmer the day before the weekly cattle auction in Hutchinson, leave the animal penned in his trailer overnight, water it heavily in the morning to add weight, and sell it at the sale barn before noon. If he had guessed the animal's weight accurately, and if the price per hundredweight were up, he made a few dollars.

The cleverest of the traders was old Pete. He had mastered the art of bamboozling farmers out of their cattle and could break down the most stubborn resistance, even from someone as practical and hardheaded as Pop. One evening he arrived at our place at milking time, when, he knew, all the cattle would be near the barn. Pop told Pete flatly that he had nothing for sale, but Pete assured Pop that he wasn't there to buy, he just wanted to see Pop's fine cattle. With that he limped off to the corral, using his cane for support.

After looking around in the corral for a bit, Pete came back to the barn and found Pop and me milking the cows. Pete made small talk for a while, complaining about President Roosevelt, chatting about nothing in particular, and remarking offhandedly that cattle coming in from the Flint Hills pastures would soon be driving prices down. Pop's guard went up, but Pete went on to say that he'd never seen such a fine bunch of cattle as ours and then hobbled out of the barn, his cane tapping noisily on the wooden floor. Pop breathed a sigh of relief, but it was premature. The tapping got louder again, and there was Pete, shouting to Pop — almost as if it had slipped his mind — "Say Frank, did you notice the udder problem on the old red cow?" Within twenty minutes Pete had the cow in his trailer and was pulling out onto the road.

Once he'd been taken in, though, Pop wasn't about to be outfoxed again at the bank. The trader would give Pop a check for the animal, and Pop would hold the trader's check for a day or two. The auction barn would then pay the trader by check, and Pop would show up at the bank on the day that the auction barn's check cleared. A day too early and there would be no money in Pete's account and a day late and the money would have been spent on someone else's tired old bull or ailing cow.

Memories fostered in that old barn remain, and I love to share them with a new generation that may never know the tranquillity found under its rafters.

15 🌿 The Valley of the Shadow

War is an abomination to Mennonites. They abhor it and refuse to take part in it. It's not a matter of cowardice, because many have paid a bitter price for their conviction — torture and death. Rather, a conviction to pacifism serves as a basic tenet of faith. So it was with the inhabitants of Section 27 and their neighbors of the faith.

Refusal to serve in the military was one of the reasons the Mennonites left Russia. They were led to believe that in America they would be exempt from conscription. As fate would have it, however, the land they occupied had only recently been violently wrested from the Plains Indians. Encroachment of settlers and railroads, treaties made and broken, and decimation of the buffalo population had given the Indians little alternative but to fight for their land, culture, and livelihood. While George Custer and other standard-bearers of the Indian wars were still engaged in their campaign of conquest, the Penners and Balzers arrived in McPherson County, possibly without an inkling of what the abandoned buffalo wallows signified.

Almost a century later I asked my father and some of the other old-timers what they recalled hearing from their elders about the "Indian situation." Dad and the others simply said that there had been no Indians in the region when the settlers arrived. I remember Pop pointing out an Indian to me on the street in Hutchinson when I was a little boy. I asked why the Indian was wearing no coat on such a cold, blustery day, and Pop replied that Indians were immune to the cold and could live outside just as animals did. Pop was not a mean-spirited man, but he reflected the ignorance and insularity of his culture.

The immigrants' rural ways of life and comparative isolation distanced them from the warfare on the western plains. The language barrier, the railroad's sales propaganda, and the struggle to survive in harsh and unfamiliar surroundings reinforced their lack of awareness. They would have been surprised to learn that in Stafford, Kansas — only seventy miles southwest of Section 27 — during the Spanish-American War in 1898, a local delegation executed a vagrant passing through in a railroad boxcar because he spoke only Spanish. They simply assumed he was an enemy.

🌿 SAFE AT HOME

Section 27 and its people apparently felt little direct impact from the Spanish-American War, but World War I was another matter. Throughout the nation the call went out for maximum farm production, and plains farmers responded by planting on every inch of prairie they could plow. In the emergency, no thought was given to how such drastic cultivation might damage the land, though the consequences would be tragically evident during the dust storms of the 1930s. On Section 27 most of the sod had been plowed prior to this time except for the Old Lake, which still stymied the Penner/Balzer drainage efforts. However, the war fervor imprinted a subtle line of separation between the pacifist Mennonites and their "English" neighbors.

Frank Penner, my father, turned eighteen during World War I and was waiting for orders to report for service when the armistice was signed. As a conscientious objector, he would have reported to his assigned post and been given noncombatant duties. At the time, my uncles told me, rumors abounded that some COs endured grave digging assignments for their own mock executions by firing squad. The only time Pop spoke to me of this traumatic event in his life was when he gave me his army-issue safety razor kit for my inaugural shave.

Even in the era of World War II, sheltered enclaves like Section 27 were about as far removed from the clouds of war as any place in the world. Without minimizing the dangers faced by many Kansans (including General Eisenhower) — or the suffering of families whose loved ones were wounded or killed — for those fortunate enough to remain at home, Kansas seemed safe and the war was felt mostly as an inconvenience.

There was rationing, of course. We had to present ration cards or stamps to buy gasoline, tires, sugar, and other food products. When Pop went to register for a gasoline permit, the elderly clerk, who knew Pop well, directed him to sit down and then demanded his name. Pop started to laugh, but then, seeing how she reveled in her importance, soberly said, "Frank L. Penner." She pecked away on her upright typewriter, then looked up and asked the make of his car. "Pontiac," he replied.

"Make of pickup?" she asked.

"International," Pop answered.

"Make of pickup, please," she repeated. Once more Pop said, "International."

"I need the manufacturer of the vehicle, not where you think you might drive it," she retorted. "What is the make of your pickup?"

"International," Pop said helplessly, almost laughing in spite of himself.

"No, no, no!" she shouted. "Is it a Ford or a Chevy or a Dodge? What is it?" Pop was despairing of his ability to inform this woman, who obviously didn't know much about trucks, when the truck dealer himself walked into the office.

"Jake," Pop called over to him, "what is the make of the pickup you sold me?"

Jake looked at Pop incredulously. "Why, don't you know? It's an International," he said.

Embarrassed and somewhat miffed, the clerk filled out the rest of the form, not troubling Pop with any more questions.

For us, rationing was less a hardship than a matter of coping with red tape. Indeed, many people believed that much of the rationing was a form of propaganda. Equally vexing was the nationwide thirty-five-mile-per-hour speed limit. The Model A Ford I drove to school was capable of twice that speed, though the speedometer was so unreliable I never knew exactly how fast I was going.

The Pontiac, on the other hand, drove much more smoothly, and thirty-five miles an hour seemed absurdly slow. The Pontiac's speedometer registered slower than the actual speed because of its weird rear tires. Since the ration board had authorized new tires for the pickup but not the car, when the Pontiac's tires went bad Pop put a set of old pickup tires on the rear and bought new tires for the truck. It was a little embarrassing to drive my friends around in a car that always felt like it was going downhill. After the war, those oversize tires simply refused to wear out, and Pop never bothered to change them.

Even obsolescent sulky plows, grain binders, and old tractors went to war as scrap iron. Pop had a warm spot in his heart for these old-timers, envisioning them as a source of material for inventions he was working on. In his spare time he would meticulously take them apart, saving the bolts and sorting the iron for further use. During the war, however, it was considered unpatriotic for a farmer to keep scrap iron. Rather than argue with anyone, he let go of a lot of fond memories and historical treasures, including vestiges of a 1920s Heider tractor — fenders, wheels, and giant gears.

The 1942 halt in production of civilian cars, trucks, and most farm tractors left us stranded with old vehicles. Thanks to Pop's thrifty ways, we owned a 1930 Model A, a 1935 Pontiac, and a 1937 tractor and pickup, while most of my friends drove newer cars. I was jealous at the time, but soon after the war ended and new cars were still scarce, people with 1941 cars would sell them at inflated prices. Many did, and while waiting the year or so required before their new cars would be delivered, they drove around in old cars, which made me feel better. Pop didn't sign up for a new car or tractor when the opportunity arose, preferring to wait until prices dropped. In 1948, without a word to anyone, he bought a Kaiser demonstrator.

❧ THE CONFLICT WITHIN

During the war I was slow to realize that most of the able-bodied eighteen- to thirty-year-old men were away and that Pop himself, who was forty-three when the war began, had a draft number. Most of the Mennonite men who left went into Civilian Public Service (CPS) in lieu of military service, though a few joined the armed forces.

CPS jobs open to conscientious objectors ranged from soil conservation and forestry work to health care. Young men were building dams with bulldozers, parachuting into forest-fire fighting areas, tending cattle on cargo ships headed for Europe, and working in Veterans Administration and mental hospitals. I wanted to go with a group taking tractors to Russia and demonstrating them there, but I was too young.

Outside our immediate community, being a conscientious objector was unpopular. Beyond being called "yellow-bellied," Mennonites were sometimes refused jobs, although a McPherson grocery store that turned down Mennonite applicants quickly reversed its policy once the owner saw how many customers he lost.

It was understandable for people to be resentful when their young men were risking their lives while COs worked in comparative safety and comfort. But the young men I knew were less afraid of going to war than of being ridiculed as cowards. Toward the end of my high school years, when the draft was imminent, I wasn't sure which way to go. My parents and the preacher guided me toward alternative service, but I was also influenced by my adventurous literary heroes and by magazines and other publications that depicted German and Japanese people as evil and sometimes grotesque. I found comfort in the idea that our enemies were something less than human beings and therefore it might not be wrong to kill them. It was easier for me to think of the Japanese as monsters than the Germans, and I actually thought for a time that if it were guaranteed I could fight the Japanese and not the Germans, I could join the army with a clear conscience.

When the time came, however, I found that Pop had, as usual, taken care of everything. I signed some papers and a few days later received a letter confirming my status as a conscientious objector. It wouldn't have mattered; the big bomb was dropped, the war ended, and that was that.

THE LAND ENDURES

In World War II there were tangible villains. It wasn't until after the war that the atrocities committed by the Nazis were widely understood, and learning about them was enough to persuade me that I could have fought against such an enemy. But in the Korean War — which began on the day Verna Lee and I were married — the enemy was an ideology, not an evil emperor. Communism was practiced in Russia, so Russia, a U.S. ally just a few years earlier, had also become an enemy. I had a lot to learn about the ways of the world, but even then it all seemed like politics to me. As the conflicts shifted to Indonesia and the Middle East, the reasons for fighting seemed less and less clear and the political and economic interests more and more evident. I saluted the heroes who served and reproved the leaders.

The Vietnam era, in particular, was a troubling time, and those on the battlefields weren't the only ones who felt the shadow of evil. Through it all, the still waters and green pastures of Section 27 remained a source of comfort and strength.

16 🌿 A New Generation

I vividly recall the fist time I saw Verna Lee. I was in Inman near the Duerksen Garage (where I often had my Model A fixed), watching a bright bevy of high school girls walk down Center Street. Among them was a skinny freshman in a plain dress, her straight hair pulled tightly back. Her country simplicity, almost stark against the comparative sophistication of the other girls, called to mind my own insecurity early in high school.

Verna Lee Enns grew up on an apple farm in the sand hills of western McPherson County. Of six girls born to Dietrich (Dick) and Anna Enns, she was the youngest by nine years. Poor Dick often seemed to be overwhelmed by Anna and the older girls. On the other hand, he probably enjoyed the feminine attention.

Dick planted an orchard — apples, peaches, cherries, pears, and apricots — in the 1930s and put his heart and soul into nurturing it. The orchard flourished, and people came from all over to buy the delicious produce, especially the apples. Dick took great pleasure in recalling the days when his girls and he would pick the fruit, even in the hot sun. Ruthanna, however, recalls days when Adena sat in the shade with her mother taking in the money while the older girls worked in the orchard. It was Verna Lee's job to pull wagon loads of apples to the shed with the family's little John Deere.

On Armistice Day in 1940, an unusually sharp frost killed the entire orchard. Though the weather had been mild that fall, Dick had seen the potential for disaster in the late green foliage on his beloved trees. The sap was still flowing on the night of November 11 when Dick's forebodings were realized as temperatures plunged dangerously. Surveying the disaster the next morning, Dick held out no hope — unlike Anna and the girls — for the orchard to green up in the spring. His fears were well grounded; spring brought no return of tender leaves or fragrant blossoms to the stricken fruit trees.

Dick shifted production to wheat, watermelons, and cattle. Years later I helped my brother-in-law, John Willems, make firewood out of what remained of Dick's orchard. At the time I had no idea what anguish still smoldered in Dick's failing heart. Preoccupied with Section 27's hailstorms and floods, I little appreciated that, while hail took away only a single year's wheat crop, the destruction of an orchard could ravage the best years of a man's life.

🌿 BUDDING ROMANCE

After first seeing Verna Lee near the Duerksen Garage, I gave no more thought to the skinny girl with straight hair until my senior year when I noticed that she had disappeared and that a rather shapely and attractive brunette was using the same name. About that time my friend Leland suggested I find a girl for a double date with him and his steady girlfriend, Esther, to see a play at Bethel College. The dating game was still a great mystery to me, and the idea of asking a girl for a date was terrifying. Pop and Mom had never talked to me about "relationships," and I was too uncomfortable with the subject even to ask Pop for the use of the car. Never at home, in school, or at church had I heard any discussion of puberty or dating.

Floundering between ignorance and desire, with Leland's persistent encouragement, I summoned the nerve to ask Verna Lee for a date. To my amazement, she said she would be happy to go with me. The *Hoosier Schoolmaster* was hardly a romantic production, but the evening set me to thinking about my date in a very different way.

I told the folks that I had gone to see a play in Newton with Leland and that Esther and another girl had gone along. Mom approved of my going to a Bethel College function. The folks assumed I would go to college there, and Mom still dared to hope that I would take a lot of religion courses and become a preacher. But other than commenting on the play, they said nothing about the evening, oblivious to my social needs, though I was completely absorbed with them. I had no social graces, no money, and, most important, no car, except the old Model A Ford, which had no headlights.

Our isolation on Section 27 became painfully apparent. I had been happy to accept things as they were, as long as home remained the center of my world. I hadn't minded not having a new car and not going to restaurants. Those things had seemed frivolous, and, besides, during the war everyone drove old cars, and gasoline and tires were scarce.

Suddenly my world turned upside down. I realized that other kids were going to picture shows, ball games, and picnics. All at once Delbert's and Leland's folks had new cars. To top it all off, Verna Lee was driving a new 1947 Chevy to school.

The deadly mix of hormones, wanderlust, and ambition made Section 27 look pretty shabby all of a sudden. Chattering kingbirds and fragrant alfalfa fields lost their charm. My frustration found a target in the old brown 1935 Pontiac. What point was there in asking a girl who drove a new car to go out in our old heap with suicide doors, a patched fender, and truck tires on the back wheels?

Miracles do happen, however. As luck would have it, I was the one who retrieved the mail on the day a letter from Verna Lee Enns arrived. I hid it in my shirt as I ran home, plunking the other mail (probably just the *Hutchinson News*) down on the kitchen counter and running upstairs to my room. My heart pounded as I tore the letter open. I had never had a letter from a girl. In fact, I don't remember having received any mail at all except for my draft card.

The words really didn't matter. I think it was one of those "how are you? I am fine" letters, but the idea of a real live girl thinking about me was exhilarating. She mentioned that maybe we would see each other at a Sunday evening community church service in Inman Park.

What to do? How to reply? She had used fancy stationery, and I knew we had nothing like that in our house. I had to talk to her — but how?

 OVERTURES

I had heard other boys say they called girls on Sunday evenings from "Central," the telephone office in town. When I worked up enough nerve to ask Pop if I could have the car on Sunday, his disconcerting reply was that if I wanted to go to the evening church service in Inman, we could go as a family. Plunging blindly onward, I somehow managed to convey that I wanted to go by myself. He apparently caught on (having been a callow youth early in his own courting days) and gave me permission to use the Pontiac.

Thus it happened that late Sunday afternoon I joined the line of boys waiting to use Central's telephone. I felt a kind of moral support from the other boys — we were in the same boat — but it was all so public. The Central operator knew what we were up to, and I could see that she was listening in. When my turn came, I walked into the little booth, closed the glass door, picked up the receiver, and, with a trembling hand, turned the crank. I watched the switchboard operator as she said, "Number, please." This was the moment; "1908," I replied, signifying line 19 and phone 8.

The phone rang twice before a man's voice said, "Hello." Summoning all my nerve, I said, "Is Verna Lee home?" Abruptly the man asked, "Who is this?" I was caught off guard, but I managed to stammer my name. "I'll call her, " the man said.

Verna Lee picked up the phone and we talked briefly. She said she wanted to see me too, but that she had to play the piano at the community church service. I could take her home afterward. Wow! I had a date, at least for part of the evening.

During the service, I hardly knew what was going on around me. I was aware of little apart from the pretty pianist accompanying a rather somber men's chorus, and I could hardly wait to be with her.

On the drive to her house we chatted comfortably about school and home. Very suavely (I thought) I suggested that the evening had been all too short. She said she had an eleven o'clock curfew, so we drove around and talked some more.

I'd heard boys talk about "parking," so when the time seemed right I asked Verna Lee if she'd mind stopping for a while. As it happened, we were on a little-used road, but she didn't mind. The Pontiac, for all its faults, had a comfortable bench seat. Verna Lee slid close to me, and at last, very casually, I put my arm over her shoulders. It occurred to me that the whole dating thing was easier than I had expected.

I was still wrestling with the problem, however, of where to go on a date, unfamiliar as I was with movies, restaurants, dances, and ball games. I'd been to one movie with the 4-H club and then quit 4-H, having concluded that the movies were too worldly. My parents weren't directly responsible for my prim attitude and had never forbidden any social activities. The combined influences of Sunday school, catechism, overheard adult conversation, and lack of encouragement, however, were more potent than parental rules could ever have been.

Verna Lee opened my eyes to a new world. She and her sisters had friends and interests beyond my experience. The family went to town once a week just for fun and ice cream, her sisters took her to movies, and they ate in restaurants and took family vacation trips to other states. To my astonishment the family had a social life beyond relatives and church functions.

🌿 LEAVING THE NEST

That fall Pop and Mom sent me to Bethel College, a Mennonite school of higher education. For the first time in my life I was away from home. Outside the womblike protection of Section 27, I was a lost soul, taking refuge in dreams of faraway places, vaguely thinking of becoming a journalist or a writer, fantasizing about adventures like those of Richard Halliburton. I was two people: a naive country boy and an aficionado of science, history, and literature. Neither identity helped much in dealing with day-to-day reality.

Most of Bethel's male freshmen that year — 1947 — were discharged conscientious objectors or military veterans. Some were battle-scarred. One was an ex–Nazi soldier, and the talk sometimes became boisterous and menacing.

A sophomore, a Hoffnungsau boy whose father was a deacon, approached me one day and suggested we go to town in his car. As we drove the mile to Newton, he lit up a Chesterfield and offered one to me. Lamely, I declined. When we ended up at a pool hall, I knew I had flunked my first social relationship at Bethel.

I loved most of my classes, however, and did well academically, though I shied away from social situations by going home every weekend. My worlds were so disconnected that Verna Lee seemed as unreal as Halliburton and his adventures. Meanwhile, Verna Lee was a senior at Inman High School, and her family was building a new house in Hutchinson.

The winter dragged on. I made a few friends, some of them girls, but with no car and little money I felt stymied. I spent a lot of time with a student who shared my lack of direction, until the day — when we had been exchanging our tales of woe as usual — he asked me if I had ever thought of killing myself. Startled, I almost shouted, "No! Why, have you?" He acknowledged that he often thought about it. I dropped him like a rock.

As spring approached, I heard the siren call of the Blaze Fork Valley and dropped out of school when the term ended in March. Pop was building a new hay wagon, and the aroma of wood chips was irresistible. But I quickly became lonely and depressed at home. Life on the farm was suddenly different. Leland was already married, and other friends were seeing girls. Once again, my social prospects were dim.

Pop had a little extra money, and I knew he had it earmarked for a car. Sure enough, without even consulting Mom, he came home from McPherson one day with a 1947 Kaiser. The crumbling Pontiac was mine now, but I held out hope for a newer replacement until the Hoffnungsau Church burned down, and Pop immediately contributed money to rebuild it. He had made a large donation, he told the family, adding that he had intended to pay me enough for farm work so I could buy a new car. Now, though, we would have to tighten our belts.

Even a few months away from home had made me more assertive, however, and eventually I worked up the courage to ask Pop if I could use the new car on Sunday evenings. "You have the Pontiac to drive," he said. "Why do you want the Kaiser?"

It was hard to explain in Low Dutch what I had meant to tell him for a long time. Nevertheless, much to my own surprise I blurted out in the vernacular, "I would like to go see Verna Lee." His reaction surprised me even more: "That's Dick Enns's daughter, isn't it?" he mused. "I think they are nice people."

With that tacit endorsement I began seeing Verna Lee often. She enrolled in Hutchinson Junior College that fall. Verna Lee and I romanced in English, of course, and in the languages of smiles and growing affection, whatever their names might be. I guess love really *is* blind; she seemed just as happy to ride in the old Pontiac as in the Kaiser. Since she played the piano for the men's chorus, we spent a lot of Sunday evenings in church.

I tried Bethel College again that fall and lasted another six months. My heart just wasn't in it. For reasons I still don't understand I avoided courses that might have helped me become a writer — English composition, grammar, even typing.

I went home every weekend and drove forty miles from Bethel College to Hutchinson every Wednesday night to see Verna Lee. We would drive around awhile, park, cuddle, and talk. Both of us were circumspect about "proper conduct." We had a wonderful time just talking. I must have bored her almost to tears going on and on about my dreams of adventure. For the first time in my life I felt comfortable expressing my doubts, fears, and goals. One frosty moonlit night as we snuggled in the car, cozy and contented, I proposed marriage. She was taken aback, naturally. We were pretty young, she said, and she'd have to think about it. Fortunately the next time I saw her, she made the right decision. Her answer, to my great joy, was yes — on the condition that we wait a year. She was wise; we had a lot of bridges to cross.

When I told Pop and Mom about our plans, they were as stunned as Verna Lee had been when I proposed. After regaining their composure, they said some kind things, and then Pop asked where and how we planned to live. I simply replied that we planned to wait a year, and Pop thought that was a good idea. Verna Lee was eighteen and I was twenty, considered young for marriage even then. Mom was first married at twenty-six, and Pop was twenty-eight at the time, so they saw no reason for us to rush things.

Verna Lee and I dated regularly and followed the local customs for betrothed couples. We went to supper at the homes of uncles and aunts, to family reunions, and to church functions on Sunday evenings. Where we went didn't matter to me as long as I could have an hour alone with her. Sometimes we parked on a sandhill road north of Hutchinson. On one such occasion we were talking quietly when there was a loud thump on the back of the car. There had been reports of voyeurs annoying couples in the area, so I was prepared. The Kaiser motor roared to life the instant I turned the key. As I released the clutch and stepped on the gas, the car literally leaped forward. Whatever man or beast had jumped on the car quickly found himself face down on the road.

 NESTING

Our plans were beginning to take shape. I had lined up a job as a welder in a Hutchinson factory, and Verna Lee intended to get a job after she graduated from Hutchinson Junior College in the spring. Then we'd rent a small house and live on love. But Dad (as I had begun calling him), realizing that the prospect of both cheap labor and a Penner dynasty on Section 27 was slipping away, announced one day that he had purchased a vacant house nearby and that "we" were going to move it onto the Penner farmstead.

Such arrangements were fairly common. Leland and Esther were living in an old house on one of his father's farms, and Delbert's father was moving a house onto their property for a similar purpose. It had even been done on Section 27, and to Dad it made perfect sense. Traditionally, a young unattached man was often referred to as a *benjel* or *jung,* a "boy" who had no standing and whose opinion didn't matter. I'm sure Dad still thought of me in that manner. Opinions aside, I was completely dependent on the folks for funds. Instead of giving me a wage or a crop share, Dad had been doling out money to me as needed.

In any event, Dad's way was the way it would be. Verna Lee accepted the new plan with the grace and poise she has displayed ever since. As it happened, she was enrolled in a college course called "The House" that dealt with decorating and furnishing a home, and she welcomed the challenge of applying her knowledge to the little one-and-a-half-story dwelling.

The first time I saw the house was on a cold January day in 1950. No one had lived in it for years, and layers of dust covered everything. It had neither plumbing nor wiring. Dad merely said that it was a "real solid house" and would move easily.

We picked a spot about a hundred feet southwest of the folks' house and squared away digging lines for the foundation. I learned a lot working with Dad. I admired his building skills, and he began explaining things to me. No power trenchers came to our aid; I dug all the foundation footings

8 inches wide and almost 30 inches deep with a sharpshooter spade. We used a little cement mixer to make our own concrete. It took two shovels of gravel, one shovel of cement, one-half bucket of water, and another two shovels of gravel to make one batch. We dumped the mix into a wheelbarrow and wheeled it to the forms we had set over the footing trenches. I actually enjoyed that part of the work.

Moving a house was a complex project, however, with hindrances such as narrow bridges and telephone wires to consider. The mover placed planks on the bridges to lift the house above the railings, and a telephone man drove ahead to raise wires as needed.

When the house arrived at the site, the mover boss turned to Dad and said, "Now, do as I tell you, and you'll save a lot of money. Go to the chicken house and catch a fat hen, put her in a sack, and give it to the Bell Telephone man. I mean it, do it now."

A bit sheepishly, Dad went to the henhouse while the truck was maneuvering the house over the foundation. He did exactly as the mover boss had instructed, and nothing was ever said about the one-hundred-dollar fee Bell usually charged for going under long-distance wires.

Once the house was on the foundation, the Enns and Penner families went to work. Verna Lee, her sisters, and her mother stripped layer upon layer of wallpaper and paint. Dad and I framed up a wall and built cabinets for the kitchen. I had taken a basic electric wiring class at Bethel, and, with advice from a local electrician, I wired the house myself. Outside, Dad and I made concrete porch steps, a short sidewalk, and a U-shaped driveway and placed a privy in the mulberry hedge.

After the dust cleared from the carpentry work, the women refinished the woodwork, papered the walls, painted the cabinets, and hung the curtains. Using her recent education in decorating, Verna Lee was both creative and thrifty. I found the Enns women's skill and vigor a bit intimidating.

Nevertheless, our combined efforts paid off. It was gratifying to see how, while we'd been working hard and enjoying it most of the time, the house had been transformed. It was clean and bright and cozy, and it would be ready for our wedding, June 9.

So we believed. Calamity struck in the form of a devastating hailstorm. The wheat crop was nearly destroyed — quite a blow for Dad, especially

Milferd and Verna Lee's honeymoon cottage in 1950.

since he was financing us all the way with cash reserves already depleted by recent flooding. Even so, he gave us eight hundred dollars to furnish the house.

Then, I developed appendicitis and had emergency surgery on June 6. Dad, in typical fashion, called Verna Lee only when the operation was over and I was recovering. She rushed to the hospital to see me, unconcerned that plans for the entire wedding were now in limbo. Although Verna Lee and her sisters had been planning and arranging and sewing for weeks, they cheerfully sent out cards announcing that the wedding would take place on June 25, which allowed me a week of recuperation in the hospital and a week at home in bed.

On June 25, 1950, in a little Mennonite church in Hutchinson, we were married. Verna Lee was so beautiful, walking down the aisle on her father's arm in the stunning dress she and her sister Adena had made; she took my breath away. On the same day, half a world away, war broke out in Korea. Married one day later, I would have been drafted.

The hail and the hospital stay and the fact that I was flat broke anyway meant that I had made no honeymoon plans. We spent the day after the wedding exploring Coronado Heights, a high scenic outcrop near Lindsborg. For me this was actually an adventure. Not only had I never been out of Kansas, but the triangle formed by McPherson, Newton, and Hutchinson had been the perimeter of my travels before that day. Other than the few months at Bethel, I had never been away from home overnight or eaten in a restaurant. Verna Lee, on the other hand, talked of California and Colorado trips she had taken with her family. She seemed so sophisticated that I felt painfully unworldly by comparison, and for many years I was very uncomfortable in public places. In any event, we were home in our little cottage at the end of the day. Dad needed me for the delayed hail-damaged harvest, so two days after the ceremony I went off to the fields, and Verna Lee, breaking Section 27 tradition, helped out by driving the tractor and stacking alfalfa bales.

Thanks to her, the little house was a cozy home right from the start. We joked about running water as we carried buckets from the "big house." Diligently I kept the weeds down in the path to the privy. In the fall we moved a little wood-burning stove into the dining room for heat, always regulating the fire so that the kitchen and bedroom would be warm without the dining room being too hot. Just before the wedding we traded the old Pontiac for a cozy 1942 Nash coupe. I still think it was one of the cutest cars ever built.

I settled quickly into the routine of working with Dad on the farm. We expanded our operation, farming 120 acres west of Inman that Dad and his sister Elizabeth owned. Though my loyalty to Section 27 never flagged, I found the upland soil west of town a pleasure to farm — easy to plow and free of the potholes and alkali spots that were so troublesome in the Blaze Fork bottoms.

About three years after our wedding, Murray was born. Anticipating bushels of baby laundry, we had installed modern plumbing. I hand-dug trenches and laid pipes that tapped into the folks' water supply about 150 feet from our house and dug a hole for a septic tank. Dad and I made the concrete tank using our small cement mixer. The biggest job, however, was turning the pantry into a bathroom.

Marci was born in 1956. By then Murray had already worn a path to Grandma's house, and it wasn't long before Marci began scampering after him. By that time we had moved the children upstairs. A narrow stairway with a treacherous curve led to a pair of small rooms with ceilings that slanted up toward the middle. Verna Lee, practical and creative, made the rooms cozy and cheerful, and the children loved them. A grate-covered hole in the floor supplied heat from the stove below.

In 1958 Beth was born and completed our little family. She was too young when we moved into the main house to remember our first home, but the rest of us have happy memories of the little cottage: Murray and Marci playing with colorful hula hoops and Marci outlasting Murray every time; sitting on the porch swing in front of a trellis covered with red roses; Murray playing with a red truck in a sand pile; and reading *The Swiss Family Robinson* to the children, the four of us huddled in one bed under a thick blanket, listening to the cold wind moan outside and imagining that we were the Robinsons, lost on a faraway island.

Beth was still a baby when Dad had a minor stroke and retired from farming. He recovered fully, but back then we assumed stroke victims had

The Penner stable of cars in 1950:
a 1942 Nash and a 1947 Kaiser.

to be extremely cautious about exertion for the rest of their life. The folks had a house built in Newton and moved there in late 1959.

I had been contracting land-leveling jobs to supplement my farming income. We sold my outfit, took over the payments on the farm, and moved into the main farmhouse, which is still our home.

The property, we soon learned, was haunted, though it didn't take long to discover the identities of the ghosts who would flutter out from the kitchen cabinets, the three patriarchal oaks, even the fence posts. They were Mom's and Grandma's ways of doing things — canning peaches and butchering chickens — and the legacy of generations of Penner men. Most of the spirits were benign, but others tried to imprison us in the past.

Our first thought was that we should leave the farm and build new lives in a place where we could realize our own ambitions. Then, to my great relief — as I really did not want to leave Section 27 — Verna Lee came up with the ideal solution: we would make alterations to the house and land, physical changes that represented our own values, tastes, and ideals.

We remodeled the house; razed the barn, the hog house, and the chicken barn; planted trees and lawns; replicated a prairie; and dug a pond. We thanked the spirits for their wisdom and hard work, and we promised to honor and build on their traditions without being bound by them.

Overcoming deep-seated inhibitions, I consented to taking the kids out to eat on Sundays. We took family trips to places like Six Flags in Texas, Great Smoky National Park in Tennessee, and the Black Hills of South Dakota. In the Black Hills we followed a guide through Jewel Cave, which is so narrow in places that we had to scoot on our stomachs. I was worried about Beth, who was only five, but when we finally emerged and asked her how she had liked the cave, she replied, "When I grow up I want to be a spelunker."

The Penner ghosts had been subdued, and back on Section 27 prairie grasses were growing once more.

17 🕯 Living Off the Land

During the early years of our marriage, floods and hailstorms on Section 27 eroded the farm's income, so I wasn't making much money working with Dad. Though our expenses were modest — we lived rent-free and shared garden produce with the folks — we wanted to be more financially independent. So Verna Lee went to work at a grocery store in Hutchinson and I began doing what was known as "custom work."

At first I worked with my brother-in-law John Willems, who was an experienced tree trimmer. He had a pickup, we split the cost of a chain saw, and we got a job right off for a utility company near Newton cutting trees and Osage orange hedges under power lines. The company paid six dollars an hour for the two of us and the chain saw, and we earned every cent and more.

It was wintertime, and we wore heavy coats. The protection they provided from thorns more than compensated for their bulkiness. The Osage orange thorns were about an inch long and needle-sharp. Dragging the saw, which was running, we had to crawl under thorny branches to the base of a tree, set the thirty-pound saw against the trunk, and press the throttle. It was possible to cut the tree in a minute or so, but the saw invariably went into a bind. The trees had to fall only one way, so it was up to the second man to free the saw by pushing the tree over with a pole.

I spent a good part of every evening squeezing thorns out of my legs, but I enjoyed the work and took pride in learning the skills involved. Still, the best part of the day was lunchtime. Verna Lee packed sandwiches, a drink, cookies, and — best of all — hard-cooked eggs nestled in pepper, salt, and melted butter. John and I took exactly an hour off to eat and talk.

The camaraderie of hard work and lunchtime conversation was the start of a lifelong bond.

Unfortunately, my skill with the chain saw was required on the farm all too often as many of the large American elm trees succumbed to Dutch elm disease. The oldest and largest elms started dying in the 1950s.

🌱 PIONEERING

In the early 1950s, farm magazines such as *Successful Farming* and *Farm Journal* began publishing articles about chemical weed control. Spraying 24D was being touted as an effective way to control weeds in crops and pastures. I was so impressed that, with very little additional information, I decided to go into the business. I bought a 1935 Chevy for thirty-five dollars and converted it into a self-propelled spray rig. What a sight it was, with its yellow wire wheels, its top cut off behind the windshield, and a fifty-five-gallon drum laid on its side where the back seat had been. Two pulleys and a belt protruded from the grille, and a power shaft ran to the back of the car, where it drove a war-surplus B-17 bomber fuel pump. A homemade spray boom, a bunch of hoses, and gallon cans of 24D and pesticides completed the outfit — the first field spray rig in the area.

I tried it out at home in the pasture, which overgrazing had left vulnerable to common ragweed and pasture thistles. Maintaining a steady speed of five miles per hour while the old Chevy bounced and lurched through buffalo wallows wasn't easy, and Dad was skeptical about the project — until the ragweed dried up within two weeks.

My best customers were cattlemen in the sandhill pastures near Hutchinson. Using DDT, I used the rig to spray the cattle for flies. What a mess. Me with my water/DDT wand and about forty head of unruly range cattle in a little corral stirred up quite a slurry of flies, sand, and manure. Using a high-pressure handgun supplied by a one-hundred-foot hose from the Chevy, I'd mix right in with the animals until they and I were drenched.

Some of the cattle had pinkeye, and the cattlemen believed that DDT would cure it, so I concentrated on the eyes. The bulls were aggressive, but getting blasted between the eyes with three hundred pounds of pressure turned them right around.

Milferd's first commercial venture, a homemade spraying rig.

The operation worked pretty well and I made a little money, but the price was high. Red spots appeared on my neck and soon turned into open lesions. Various ointments didn't work. In fact, the sores spread quickly, so I was placed in semi-isolation in Grace Hospital in Hutchinson. I didn't feel sick, but seeing how apprehensive the nurses were made me uneasy. Finally, the tests revealed that I had blastomycosis, a bovine disease that in rare cases could infect humans.

After three weeks in the hospital, during which time there was some improvement, I went home, but I had to wear a medicated bandage around my neck for several months, which was irksome out in the dusty fields. I complained to the doctor, and in exasperation he agreed to "try something new," which turned out to be a strong light — "Stronger than hell," he said as he plugged it in, "but we have to do something." He aimed a thing that looked like an engine timing light at my neck, leaned back as far as he could for safety, and pulled the trigger. The light was bright but, as at my baptism, I felt nothing, though the doctor assured me that once again I'd been saved. Before long, some scars on my neck were all that remained of the ordeal, although I refused to spray cattle from then on.

Field spraying for weeds was often a frustrating affair. The sprayer tips were very small and line filters were unheard of, so the nozzles were continually clogging up. If they weren't cleared right away, the uneven application of weed killer would be conspicuous in a few days, when strips of vegetation remained green while the rest of the weeds turned brown. Out in the field, the only practical way to clear an obstruction was to remove the nozzle, put it up to my lips, and blow — an annoyance made worse by the lingering aftertaste of DDT, 24D, lindane, methoxychlor, and chlordane.

When I sprayed insecticides, the nozzles didn't have to be cleared as often; there would be no telltale strips of green weeds among the brown. Since the insects I was spraying for — chinch bugs, green bugs, aphids, and grasshoppers — moved around in the field, precision was less important than the quantity of insecticide applied per acre. Thus I could keep working as long as most of the nozzles were open.

I finally replaced our Chevy spray rig with a used Jeep, which was a very practical vehicle for the spraying business. With the spray boom removed we had a lot of fun with the Jeep, racing and climbing over the dikes that encircled the sinkhole on the northeast corner of the section. At that time the sinkhole appeared as a sort of natural amphitheater. The road, which had been rebuilt on higher ground after the sinkhole developed, overlooked the seven-acre depression; the side rails of the old steel bridge were still visible when the water was low.

One Sunday, on the way home from church, Verna Lee, the folks, and I noticed an unusual number of cars heading north on the sinkhole road. That afternoon, when Verna Lee and I drove out to the sinkhole in the Jeep, there were at least a dozen cars parked on the rim, doors closed and windows up. It turned out that a neighbor had reported seeing a thirty-foot snake playing in the water, and the story had found its way into the *Hutchinson News,* which nicknamed the alleged monster "Sinkhole Sam." The drawing that accompanied the newspaper story looked a lot like popular representations of the Loch Ness Monster.

Verna Lee and I decided to investigate. In the roofless Jeep we plunged down the steep incline and followed the shoreline — flaunting our disdain for Sinkhole Sam — skirting the mudflats that could bog down even a four-wheel-drive Jeep. Reaching the far shoreline uneventfully, we drove out of the sinkhole and raced home across the fields. Some time later a couple of fishermen reported seeing Sam, but if there were other sightings, I never heard about them.

The Jeep's width — it tracked perfectly over rows of milo spaced at forty inches — made it ideal for spraying row crops. When Murray was four, I started taking him along when I sprayed milo fields in June and July for weeds and chinch bugs. I thought he was probably bored much of the time, but he laughed delightedly when we crossed shallow rivulets and spattered water and mud all over ourselves. Grandma wondered whether the spray drifting into the open Jeep might be harmful to Murray, but I assured her there was no risk.

Business was booming when I contracted with Kansas Gas and Electric Company to spray brush under its rural power lines in five counties. It was a two-man job, one to drive the Jeep and the other to walk along the right-of-way spot-spraying the trees and brush with a handheld applicator pressured up by the Jeep. In heavily foliated areas the driver also sprayed with a second hand gun. On the hottest summer days we cooled off by spraying each other with the defoliant chemical "245T," later known as "Agent Orange" in Vietnam.

Defoliation was proving to be an efficient way to clear unwanted vegetation. After Blaze Fork Creek was channelized to expedite the flow of water, trees along and in the creek were considered a nuisance. Several drainage districts hired me to kill all the trees in the channel.

Even in the Jeep, negotiating the Blaze Fork was difficult. We drove either on the piles of dirt that formed the dikes or, when the creek was dry, in the channel. I got a thrill out of driving the Jeep down the steep embankments, and I got to know every foot of the Blaze Fork intimately.

When the book *Silent Spring* by Rachel Carson appeared in 1962, it made me angry. I thought the author's opposition to herbicides and insecticides was unwarranted. Wasn't I living proof that the chemicals were harmless? The book, however, set me to thinking, and shortly thereafter our family doctor suggested that I might be flirting with disaster. I thought back to my blastomycosis days and began to wonder. We questioned whether there was any relationship between the decrease in kingbird and scissor-tailed flycatcher populations and the use of farm chemicals.

❧ IDEALISM VERSUS REALITY

Having inherited the urge to drain and develop land, I dreamed of working with bulldozers and earthmovers. Financially it was out of the question, or so I believed until I saw an ad for an Eversman land-leveling machine at a reasonable price. I very much wanted one, rationalizing that it would solve the pothole problem on our land and that I could earn money doing custom work with it. To my surprise, Dad was in favor of it and suggested asking his sister, my Aunt Elizabeth, for a loan. She was willing to help, so with her five hundred dollars I bought it and took possession of the thirty-foot-long machine. Paired with our M Farmall tractor, it did an excellent job of making seedbeds for alfalfa and wheat and leveling the deep furrows left in our fields by the Hart-Parr and Avery tractors repetitively plowing around and around many years ago. My custom work — leveling land and spraying for other farmers — became a substantial part of our income.

My expectations for the Eversman, however, were a little too high. It was more of a land plane than a leveler in the heavy earthmoving sense of the word and was not the machine required for soil conservation work. A bulldozer was essential, I told myself, to construct terraces and ponds — important elements of conservation farming — though I was never sure whether I wanted a bulldozer to practice conservation or wanted to conserve land so I could own a bulldozer.

Most of my enthusiasm for conservation farming came from reading Louis Bromfield's *Malabar Farm*. Under the spell of Bromfield's idealism, I saw myself as something of a bulldozer-borne crusader for the conservation ethic; I'd take care of the details later.

To usher in conservation farming on Section 27, I bought a used Caterpillar D4 diesel with a dozer blade and, to haul it, a rough 1942 two-ton GMC truck. On the truck there was an oilfield bed with a very steep loading ramp. I was elated, though I hardly knew what to do with the rig, my experience being limited to driving the township's dozer for a few hours.

My first job came almost immediately, however, and seemed easy enough — a farmer wanted me to dig a pond. When I got to the job site, a man from the Soil Conservation Service was staking out the pit pond's dimensions. He could tell I was a greenhorn, and he patiently explained the project. I went straight to work, expecting miracles from my little dozer. Though I was pushing mammoth dirt mounds, the pit wasn't getting much bigger. There was a vast difference, I quickly learned, between loose piles of earth and bank cubic yards — the original soil in place — and between soil types. The job was in southwestern McPherson County, within a mile of where Verna Lee grew up. Unlike Section 27's "gumbo," this soil was of the sandy-loam type that predominated west of the Little Arkansas River.

By the time the conservation service man returned a few days later, I thought I had nearly finished the job. With infinite patience, he taught me how to check grade with a little hand level and urged me to be more precise in establishing dimensions. Like many other contractors at the time, I knew very little about conservation practices, and we were indebted to the conservation people for their cheerful willingness to coach us along. Gradually, with their help, I mastered pit ponds, terraces, waterways, and even concrete terrace outlets. (As it happened, our farm was so flat it didn't require the standard conservation work, though the Soil Conservation Service recommended digging some shallow drainage ditches.)

The midfifties drought brought irrigation to McPherson County and the surrounding area. An earthmoving contractor from Nebraska began leveling land for irrigation in McPherson County. There being no local competition, I just had to get into the business. The distinction between soil conservation and land development began to blur in my mind, and I bought a five-cubic-yard scraper that my Caterpillar could pull.

When Clarence Froese, who farmed east of Inman, asked me to level forty acres for him, I didn't even know what to charge for the job. For guidance I turned to Gene Bohnenblust, who headed up the Soil Conservation Service in McPherson County. I worked with Gene and his staff to stake out the field in one-hundred-foot squares. Then the conservation people established the relative elevations and went back to the office to perform some complicated calculations.

The conservation service developed a cut-and-fill chart for me to follow so that when the field was leveled, the earth would be distributed to produce a uniform grade. An error tolerance of only plus-or-minus one-tenth of a foot was allowed. Since the stakes were at one-hundred-foot intervals, I had to exercise a lot of judgment.

The U.S. Department of Agriculture offered farmers financial help for irrigation projects, paying a percentage of the fifteen-cents-per-cubic-yard cost of having dirt moved. For Froese's job, a little over eight thousand cubic yards, I would receive twelve hundred dollars. In the fifties this seemed like a lot of money. My little scraper, rated at five cubic yards, carried only four cubic yards when compaction was considered, thus I was earning about sixty cents per load. I had to keep a very steady pace to make my eight-dollar-an-hour goal.

It was tedious, dusty, and bone-jarring work, but I loved it. My little steel-tracked Caterpillar performed well; I would load in low gear, then shift manually to fourth gear for the four-mile-per-hour haul. And I always had the field lunch packed by Verna Lee, and evenings at home with her and the children, to look forward to.

In 1958 Murray was starting school at Hillcrest, a country school located by chance on the same hilltop as the original Lake Valley School was from 1874 to 1879. Though Verna Lee took time to help Dad and me with the plowing, tilling, seeding, harvesting, and haying, we hired additional help so I could continue the spraying and earthmoving work. Land-leveling and conservation jobs were plentiful, and before long I needed a larger tractor and scraper.

In 1960, after Dad's mild stroke (when, according to the prevailing wisdom, we assumed that his working days were over), I sold all the earthmoving equipment to devote full time to farming our half of Section 27. I did, however, continue with the agricultural spraying business. The folks sold their land west of Inman to pay cash for the house they built in Newton.

It didn't take long, however, before I again felt the ancestral call to dig, clear, and drain. I bought a Ford industrial tractor with a backhoe "just to keep busy in slack seasons." Then I needed a truck to haul it. Then a salesman offered a great deal on a little Allis Chalmers dozer and one of the early John Deere motor scrapers. And, of course, a motor grader was essential for finish work. Since I had a motor grader, why not build terraces? Before I knew it, I had hired some help and we were doing conservation work in four counties, as well as digging basements, leveling land, and preparing sites for poultry houses. I converted our granary — removing the elevator mechanism, the grain bins, and the second floor — into a place to work on heavy equipment.

One of our customers had chosen to situate his three-hundred-foot-long poultry buildings on steep slopes. This part of Kansas is comparatively flat, but he probably preferred the rolling terrain because the land cost less and drained better than level land. Whatever his reasons, we loved to see him coming. The work was lucrative, often requiring six-foot cuts on one end of the site and a corresponding fill on the other end. Meanwhile, I was learning the craft of surveying and designing building sites, drainage ditches, and irrigation fields. As the business grew, our farmstead became a rendezvous for tractor operators. Every morning a row of pickups was parked along the empty sheep corral fence.

 CHANGING TIMES

In 1968 I brought in additional owners and we incorporated as Penner Earthmoving. Though the business moved to Inman four years later, our family continued to live on the farm. Willis Harder, a Moundridge farmer, rented and worked the fields. Otherwise, Section 27 was practically deserted. The only animals were a few cats and a dog. Besides the main house (where we had lived since the folks' move to Newton), we used garage and storage space. The rest of the buildings were vacant. Our honeymoon cottage had been sold and hauled away in 1962, and the Balzer house on the west half of the section had burned down.

Similar transitions were taking place on the four sections surrounding Section 27. Instead of an average of three or more working farmsteads per section as there were during the first half of the twentieth century, only four working farmsteads remain at the century's end. Two of these farmers supplement income with other work, and the other two are near retirement age. Three farmsteads have been totally abandoned and cleared, although nine residential tracts have been added.

Contributing to the shift in population were changes in the mechanical aspect of farming occurring in the 1960s. Early in the century, after the era of the large sodbusting tractors, tractors were downsized but made more versatile. The three-plow-capacity Wallis that my Dad had and the ubiquitous model "D" John Deere are examples; however, horses were still used for row crop and haying into the 1930s. Generally speaking, at least in our area, every farm had a three- or four-plow tractor, and progressive farmers began replacing the horses with additional, even lighter-weight, row crop tractors. The capability of these tractors limited farm size to two or three quarter sections. These were generally diversified family farm units.

Then in the early 1960s, tractor capabilities expanded rapidly. More tractor horsepower and technological improvements such as advanced hydraulics, four-wheel drive, and cabs made longer working hours possible and increased an individual farmer's production potential dramatically. Ancillary farm machinery such as combines and planters progressed at the same rate.

Other radical changes in the business of farming affected Section 27 also. Fertilizers, improved seeds, and irrigation raised the yields per acre three- and fourfold. Thus fewer people, working fewer days, produced more grain. Section 27's wheat harvest, which traditionally had lasted for weeks, was finished in two days in June of 2000. As a result, population dynamics on Section 27 and four sections surrounding it changed.

Penner Earthmoving, responding to the transitions in agriculture, ripped out fencerows and hedges, drained marshland, cleared abandoned farmsteads, and leveled large tracts for irrigation. Personally, I enjoyed any job that allowed me to operate our heavy Caterpillar D7, which was equipped with a bulldozer. One day, as I was blissfully ripping out a quarter mile of hedgerow, I noticed a man taking pictures and stopped to talk to him. He proceeded to berate me for violating a "pristine prairie remnant," though in truth the Osage orange trees I was destroying were not native to Kansas; the area, in fact, was practically devoid of trees before settlers arrived. Still, I saw his point.

In the early 1970s, most of my work involved surveying and designing irrigation fields. Using my own methods, I became proficient enough at calculating the required cuts and fills — working without the aid of calculus or a computer — that I could have a motor scraper working in the field an hour after the surveying was done.

With respect to our own land, however, we didn't know if there was enough water under Section 27 (which was very near the western edge of the Equus Beds) to make irrigation feasible. Finally I suggested to Dad, who still owned the land, that we irrigate part of the section. After mulling it over for a while, he conceded that it might be a good idea and suggested we talk it over with "an expert." Stunned and offended, I dropped the subject and never raised it again. In fact, I worked out a deal — with Dad's approval — to sell the northeast quarter of Section 27 to Gordon and Carol Schmidt. (Gordon later hired one of my competitors to level the east eighty acres for irrigation.)

More and more, our work supported the development of large irrigated farms and intensive poultry, hog, and cattle operations. The principle of maximum grain production, without regard for long-term consequences, got a boost from worldwide food shortages during the 1970s. Land prices doubled and tripled, and we converted grasslands and wastelands to cornfields at every opportunity. To clear catalpa groves near Hutchinson, we attached a massive clearing blade to our largest Caterpillar tractor. The trees, planted some time around the turn of the twentieth century, had been used to make fence posts, but by this time catalpa was no longer considered good fence post material.

We cleared ten acres a day, in some cases grinding the stumps with a three-hundred-horsepower rotary tiller. Our tractor could cut trees eighteen inches in diameter at a steady two miles per hour. A stinger at the leading edge of the clearing blade split and cut larger trees with a few extra moves. To protect tractor and driver from being crushed, we built a heavy steel frame — impervious to even the largest of trees — over the tractor.

Navigating this fifty-five-thousand-pound juggernaut that crushed everything in its path was a thrill that overruled aesthetic and environmental considerations. I once remarked that by sawing, spraying, and bulldozing I had killed more trees than anyone else in Kansas.

🌿 TURNING POINT

Eventually I became a partner in a large pivot-irrigation dealership. Not only was it satisfying work — setting up one irrigation system after another and knowing crop production would triple — it was very profitable. Consequently, in 1977 we dissolved Penner Earthmoving and sold all the equipment at auction.

As grain prices continued to soar, farmers had no trouble finding money to buy farm equipment. Government and private lenders alike believed that the booming farm economy was stable, and loan officers helped farmers revise their financial statements to reflect increases in land-value and grain-price projections. Many a farmer of moderate means emerged from his bank a paper millionaire and eagerly headed for the nearest equipment dealer. Wheat prices neared five dollars per bushel, and experts projected seven dollar wheat down the road.

The end of the decade brought an end to the euphoria. In 1980 President Jimmy Carter declared a grain embargo against the Soviet Union in response to its invasion of Afghanistan. Within days, grain prices and land values tumbled. Maximizing grain production, just yesterday a noble cause that provided food for the hungry, was today a political football, and Congress was much more concerned about the "grain surplus" than about the hungry. It was perplexing and demoralizing. How could a popular crusade have become a disgrace overnight?

I lost all enthusiasm for selling irrigation systems and leveling land. Aldo Leopold's "land ethic" was making more and more sense to me. His land ethic is summed up in his quotation in Stewart Udall's book *The Quiet Crisis,* "We abuse the land because we regard it as a commodity belonging to us. When we see land as a community to which we belong, we begin to use it with love and respect."

Exploiting the earth was making less and less sense. It was time to make amends — not only to the land but also to friends and family. I sold my half of the irrigation business to my partner and began looking for a way to return something of what I had taken from the land.

A generation goes, and a generation comes, but the earth remains forever.—Ecclesiastes 1:4

18  The Cycle of Life

Six generations of the Penner family have made their appearance on the land we know as Section 27. It seems like only yesterday when, with childish delight, my sisters, Marvella and Rachel, and I picked mulberries from the grove that our Great-grandfather David planted before the turn of the century. Just a few days ago, two generations later, our granddaughters, Sofia and Paulina, shook the ripe fruit down from the very same trees.

Green beans still grow in the garden. Verna Lee and her sister, Ruthanna, stemmed some last night as we visited, and the resulting bean soup was delicious, just as it has been for a century. And the plow and the great blue heron, still icons of agriculture and nature, represent a continuing dichotomy.

So, is it true, as the writer of Ecclesiastes says in his treatise on vanity, that "there is nothing new under the sun"? Has a century of time wrought any change at all on this little plot of ground called Section 27? Are all the changes brought to our land "vanity" in the context of the universe, or is it, perhaps, possible that the everlasting cycle of time and regeneration is progressive and gradually moving on to a higher plane? Whatever the theological and philosophical truths may be, the twentieth century brought many and profound changes in human terms to Section 27 and its environs.

THE NEW WAY

The pioneer's moldboard plow, symbol of conquest and struggle, is relegated to museums, and even its modern counterpart is seldom used on Section 27. Most of the farmers in the vicinity are shifting to a stubble mulch or no-till agriculture, which minimizes soil tillage. Both methods leave most of the previous crop's residue on the soil's surface to reduce erosion and nutrient loss from rain and wind.

Stubble mulching requires tillage with disks or field cultivators, implements that do not turn over the soil like a plow, but a disadvantage of these is the buildup of undesirable annual grasses over a period of years. Generally, a moldboard plow is used every four or five years to turn under the undesirable seeds.

No-till farming disturbs the soil less than stubble mulching since the soil is sliced open by a planter or drill only far enough to drop the seed in the ground. A possible problem with this method, however, is that weeds are totally controlled with chemicals. In theory, no-till farming appears to be a good solution to erosion, but many farmers question the wisdom of long-term chemical usage. I have my reservations also.

Another solution to the erosion and the chemical buildup is being advocated and developed fifty miles north of Section 27 at the Land Institute near Salina, Kansas. Its founder, Wes Jackson, suggests that we look at the original prairie as a model for sustainable agriculture. He explains that the prairie is a polyculture, that is, a diversity of plants growing in an interrelated fashion. Jackson is seeking to produce a mix of perennial plants that, like the prairie, sustain themselves and yet can be harvested as cereal crops. Such a discovery, of course, would reduce energy inputs and solve the erosion problem. Imagining Jackson's theory put into practice, I can envision, once more, a tranquil, pastoral life on the prairie lands.

As I write this last chapter of Section 27's history, the wheat harvest is nearing completion. Grandpa David F. would gaze in utter amazement at the harvest machinery if he were here. Charging through the ripe grain, modern combines — cutting thirty-foot strips — thresh between five hundred and nine hundred bushels of wheat an hour, about as much grain as David's threshing machine threshed in a day, not considering the time spent binding and shocking the grain. In the Dust Bowl era, Frank's five-foot-cut combine threshed at best forty to fifty bushels an hour.

Somehow, farming seems more impersonal now, a step removed from the land. Seldom does an operator come down from the cab to feel the chaff in the air or the friability of the soil or to inhale the scents of harvest. Within a cab the air conditioner, the radio, and the whine of hydraulics overcome the voice of the meadowlark. The setting sun merely signals the time to turn on an array of lights, not a time of repose. Something seems lost. Late one afternoon, I discovered that the truth of the matter is not that simple.

In a nostalgic exercise of reverie, I plow a small tract of land I have set aside for myself. I take the old Ford tractor that I bought the year Liz was born, 1958, and attach a three-bottom plow. The tractor has no cab; I'm out there with the elements — mosquitoes and all. The seat is steel with just a little spring and the power steering doesn't work. I drop the plow, but it just slides over the dry gumbo; it takes some manual adjusting to get it into the ground. Before long I'm plowing.

I feel a deep satisfaction in seeing the plow rolling the black soil over the last crop's stubble; I can see results, and I like the smell of the fresh soil. The wind is calm; the dust hangs in the air, colored orange by the low sun in the west. Mysteriously, eastern kingbirds and barn swallows discover the insects I'm stirring up. They glide gracefully through the air, yet when they see their elusive prey, they turn and dodge, aggressively making their catch.

The little diesel struggles with the load, and I notice the heat gauge climbing. I want to finish before dark because rain is forecasted. Indeed, in the southeast, thunderheads build, spreading purples and oranges high in the sky. Generally, clouds in that direction pose no problem.

A baby rabbit runs ahead of me in the furrow, scampering furiously. It reaches the end of the furrow and runs into a fencerow before I catch up. A sudden change of wind cools the air.

The clouds from the southeast move in fast, jagged bolts of lightning piercing the darkening sky. I still have a couple rounds left to finish the field, and the heat gauge nears the red zone. This experience reminds me of boyhood days on the tractor.

Should I finish the field in spite of the elements or play it safe? Of course, I keep on plowing, exhilarated by the race, as swirls of dust dance across the field. Rain only a mile away and the heat gauge holding steady just below the red, I have only one more round to go. Finally in darkness, lit only by lightning in the eastern sky, I finish the job with rain pelting me as I drive the tractor into the shed. What more fun could a seventy-year-old man have? But, I think, if my livelihood depended on farming, I would want a cab on the tractor.

 MUSINGS

Generations of people, crops, animals, and even inanimate objects such as machinery have been caught in Section 27's circle of repetition. The assumption always seems to be that each new generation's endeavor is wiser, better, and bigger. I wonder what the great-grandpas' (Penner, Gaeddert, Lohrentz, and Regier) judgment would be about all the changes? If my father, who observed Section 27 from the dawn of the twentieth century to its sunset, were here to express himself, I know he would say, "Why always bigger?"

I recall how bitterly disappointed I was on one occasion when I told Dad how large and powerful my new Caterpillar tractor was and how much it cost; he barely acknowledged my enthusiasm and talked instead about his 1915 Avery as if they were equal. I didn't understand his feelings or his point of view then. I recall his saying later that when a man has enough land or possessions to make a comfortable living, the remaining opportunities should be left for younger farmers.

Dad persistently questioned two clichés in vogue in the late seventies when I was selling irrigation systems: "If you're not expanding the farm you're going under" and "The bottom line is all that counts." Both philosophies were foreign to the first three Penner generations in America.

Earlier voices and spirits envelop us on Section 27. They tell of steadfast faith, dauntless courage, and the tireless ambition that drove our ancestors to subdue the prairies and build our homeland. At the same time they speak of unquestioned dogma — the earth is ours to subdue and have dominion over, unbending tradition — the plow must turn over the earth, and zealous piety — we are the righteous.

Another voice also resonates on Section 27; it emanates from the land, and as a lonely little boy, daydreaming under the ubiquitous mulberry hedge with Gyp at my side, I felt the immanence of the land. In Sunday school, when the mystery of Moses and the burning bush was presented, it seemed perfectly natural for me that God, as one with the land, assured

Moses that "I am that I am" from a shrub. As I grew older, however, it was easy to let dogma, economic obsessions, and social peer pressure overwhelm the message.

For years, the bulldozer was my idol. It was a symbol, as was the plow for Grandpa David, of my power and prestige. It represented my ancestral instinct to clear and drain the land. Then, as that fickle icon rusted away, it dawned on me that there might be more to my heritage than just blindly reaching for more land, more possessions. Voices attuned to the land — from the Psalmists' "beside the still waters" to Thoreau, Leopold, and Jackson — warned of making conquest the only value. These voices, however, appeared to me to chase unattainable dreams until two profound experiences changed my perspective.

In 1969 a very traumatic event separated me from the bonds of dogmatic and pious traditions. In the throes of a political campaign, a Mennonite preacher, leading a fundamentalist antidancing and antisex education group, informed me that he and his cohorts would destroy me to attain their goals. (In the late sixties a virulent antisex education campaign, under a religious guise, spread across the country.) The preacher told me, in a clandestine midnight meeting, that they would crucify me. Indeed they tried.

Apparently, statements I had made privately and as a Sunday school teacher regarding stewardship of the land and concepts of time and space led them to consider me a threat to the status quo. It was painful to see friends and neighbors go along with these tactics. Soon my self-esteem was shattered, and I was questioning my own credibility. I reacted with shock, a period of anger and rebellion, and finally enlightenment. It took me years to rebuild my spiritual life, but in the final analysis that event was the best thing that ever happened to me.

This episode pulled me out of a narrowly focused world into a more open-minded view of people, land, and nature as one community. It became clear that the real meaning of dominion over the land meant stewardship and included restoration, that tradition was not to be blindly followed, and that right thinking was not limited to our Dutch-speaking enclave.

The second experience was more personal than political. Following my heart attack in 1989, little Alyssa, my first grandchild, brought into focus a dream I had long pursued as she visited me in a hospital room. Not quite two years old, she bounced into my room to show off her new shoes. So beautiful she was, with a big bow in her hair, so full of innocent joy over nothing more luxurious than her new shoes. I loved her dearly. Her visit and my flirtation with death set me to thinking of the real values life has to offer.

After they left, I dreamed of leaving her a safe and beautiful world. I thought of a winter wonderland experience I'd had recently at the Quivira Wildlife Refuge. A gentle snow of large soft flakes was falling in absolute silence. Then, overhead, almost obscured, a flight of Canada geese passed so close I could hear the whisper of their wings and their soft honking conversation. It was clear that the magic of mornings like that was a legacy I would strive to leave for Alyssa and the children of the world.

REINCARNATION

By midcentury, the original wetlands, Section 27's and those surrounding it, were becoming a source of irritation and strife to those who had spent generations subduing them. Once drained, after a brief season of bountiful crops, they turned into conspicuous failures. Just north of Section 27, Uncle John and his family suffered mightily for several decades on their lowland farm. The soil that had adapted to cord grass and bulrushes did not yield readily to the plow. Being the lowest land in the area, they were the first to flood when dikes failed, and plenty of blame was passed around for that.

All that remains of Uncle John's habitation is an old water pump I just rediscovered the other day, standing forsaken in the tall grasses. This would be near the spot where Uncle John shot a rabid skunk. Dad was there to see it. They assumed the skunk was rabid because it was out in the daytime, not afraid of anyone, and walking in circles. John ran for his .22 repeater and fired as the skunk neared the barn. He missed and the skunk started running toward him. He fired and missed a number of times, finally bringing it down near his feet. Even Dad, imperturbable as he was, betrayed excitement when he told this story.

Thirty-five acres of Penner farmland on Section 27 in the Old Lake Bed fared no better than Uncle John's farm, but we had enough higher ground

A last relic of the Unruh farmstead.

to get by. In the late 1940s, Dad proposed to a few drainage district members that we abandon efforts to farm the Old Lake Bed and use it as a flood overflow. The idea was rejected at the time because it was too radical. The purpose of the district, they said, was to drain land.

Years later, in the 1980s, while working on *Kansas Journeys,* I was reminded of the economic value of the Quivira National Wildlife Refuge and the Cheyenne Bottoms State Refuge. Not only did these great assets to our environment impress me, but gradually I also realized that a similar potential treasure lay hidden in my own backyard. As a former spraying and earthmoving contractor, I was acutely aware of the drained Big Basin and the former Chain of Lakes extending from Conway south for seventeen miles to Farland Lake and our own Old Lake. Like prairie seeds dormant in the earth for years, Old Lake, Farland Lake, the Big Basin, and the Chain of Lakes were waiting to be free.

I was very excited about my discovery but assumed that others had come to the same conclusion. On several occasions when I met with Kansas Wildlife and Parks officers, I mentioned the phantom refuge in McPherson County. I even broached the subject with a Nature Conservancy official. They were not aware of this potential wetland. By May of 1991, however, the Kansas Department of Wildlife and Parks requested signatures on a recommendation form to establish the McPherson Valley Wetlands. (One other private citizen and a number of prestigious organizations completed the list.)

Today, the McPherson Valley Wetlands (MVW) are a reality; almost one thousand acres of wetland property adjoin Section 27. Furthermore, another two thousand acres, including segments of the Chain of Lakes and the Big Basin west of McPherson near Conway, are under development. Once more, millions of Central Flyway travelers — ducks, geese, and shorebirds — are making the MVW a stop on their annual trek to the northlands. I hope the great blue heron smiles as he wings his way over the expanding marshes.

The practical advantages of the MVW are immense: controlling floods, recharging the Equus Beds, filtering nitrates and other contaminants from the water, and removing marginal land from competition in a surplus-driven market. The reestablishment of a waterfowl stopover, the restora-

A look at the restored wetlands, once known as the "Old Lake"
when Lake Valley School was organized in 1874.

tion of natural wildlife habitats, sport hunting, and bird watching also provide strong reasons for the MVW reincarnation.

For many people who live and farm in the MVW area, the advantages are not so clear-cut. Many farmers have roots in the land that go back four or five generations, and they have personally engaged in the struggles of converting marshland to farmland. Their emotions are mixed on the subject. The MVW, however, strictly adheres to a policy of purchasing land only from willing sellers.

Eventually nine thousand surface acres may be restored as an MVW project. For perspective, this project should be seen as many smaller tracts of marginal bottomland scattered among eighty thousand acres of farmland. Section 27 anchors the south end of this chain of lakes and shallow marshes. It is doubtful that any existing farmsteads will be affected by the MVW; no doubt, a segment of Section 27 will soon be a part of it.

🌾 CROP REPORT

Today, Section 27 lies serene under a warm summer sun with fluffy cumulus clouds floating in a blue sky. The last combine just departed from the fields, and in typical farmer fashion a smile hides the yield statistics. About 375 acres were harvested. Several tractors are pulling tandem discs — the stubble mulch process — in preparation for next year's crop. One tractor is red, the other green, the colors signifying the brand names. The green for John Deere and the red for Case hark back to the 1840s when John Deere and J. I. Case began building plows and threshers. The names of tractors my Dad enjoyed so much — Hart-Parr and Avery — vanished from the farm scene long ago.

A Valley irrigation system sprays one thousand gallons of water a minute on a 140-acre field of soybeans on the northeast quarter. The lush green beans stand in rows straight as the flight of an arrow and clean of weeds and grasses. This is a no-till operation with chemically controlled weeds.

Another green tractor is planting about forty acres of rather late milo in the Old Lake Bed. Last week on the southeast quarter, a field of milo was cultivated where the herbicide failed, and a small patch of alfalfa was cut and baled. What is new here is that the large, one-thousand-pound bales are wrapped in plastic for protection. To round out the crop report, a mix of prairie grasses grows in three corners of the irrigated field.

A shelterbelt, an old shed, and a decapitated windmill are all that remain of the Balzer farmstead, leaving ours as the only viable farmstead on the section. The Big Sinkhole is still expanding, gradually creeping southward, creating a visible dip in the road. Beavers build dams on the north side of the section in the drainage ditch, much to the dismay of several neighbors — one calling for dynamite.

The south drainage ditch cutting through our farmstead is overgrown with cottonwood, elm, ash, and mulberry and attracts deer. The ditch is lined with trees, but I have managed to keep a twelve-foot channel open. Once the trees form a shading canopy over the ditch, no new growth — trees or weeds — occurs in the channel.

All but a few of these trees have grown up since the late 1970s. As long as we had cattle, they kept all the woody growth under control. After the cattle and sheep were sold, I kept growth down with the bulldozer and by spraying 245T. Once the bulldozer and spray equipment were gone, I let the trees grow and maintained the channel center with a chain saw. This decision turned out to be the best ecological solution.

Two venerable cottonwoods survived the cattle and the bulldozer. The one in the bend where the ditch turns east became Marci's tree house abode. About four feet in diameter, it had a large hollow in the trunk where raccoons lived. Through this cavity ran a barbed wire, nailed to the tree when it was small. For years Marci begged to have a tree house built there; I, being the hardworking provider, thought the project too frivolous. Finally, when she was a high school senior, she said, "Dad, I'm going to build it."

By whatever means she dragged boards and tools a quarter of a mile and started building ladder steps. My heart melted, but I was almost too late. I saw that I had never taught her the rudiments of construction. Soon she let me help. Those days up in the cottonwood with Marci are days I wouldn't trade for all the bulldozers in the world. The house was crude, but she was smiling. Just a few years ago a small twister destroyed the tree.

 THE PENNER FARMSTEAD

June 28, 2001. The Penner farmstead on Section 27 is doing very well. From my window I see a myriad of yellow prairie coneflowers floating over our tall grass prairie. Western kingbirds and Baltimore orioles, resplendent in their bright colors, cavort over the prairie in search of bugs for their babies in the elm tree. An eastern kingbird hovers low to the ground, waiting for the right moment to snatch that delicious bug. A mourning dove is softly cooing in the background. It is gratifying to see that a pair of western kingbirds has returned to the farm after long absence.

Our two 2-acre prairie plots, after a succession of weeds, have matured into what appears to be a stable ecoculture. We planted the oldest, a tall-grass prairie replica, in 1983. We seeded tall bluestem, switch grass, Indian grass, and little bluestem into the plot along with a mixture of indigenous forbs. Maximilian sunflowers tend to dominate, but coneflowers, purple prairie clover, pitcher sage, and goldenrod are doing well. The little bluestem does not compete well with the taller grasses in this prairie plot. It is interesting to note that forbs were always part of the prairie ecosystem.

In our mid-grass prairie plot, planted in 1993 with grasses prominent in prairie lands with moderate rainfall, the little bluestem dominates over wheat grass, buffalo, and grama grasses. It is significant that on the edges of the plot where we mow, buffalo grass takes over. Forbs are not as noticeable there; seeded gaillardia, blue flax, chicory, and lupine have almost disappeared. Purple prairie clover, lead plant, white yarrow, round-head lespedeza, western salsify, native coreopsis, and coneflowers are on the increase. As with the other prairie, Maximilian sunflowers are very numerous. Common milkweed and daisy fleabane, possibly originating from dormant native seed, are multiplying in both prairies.

We have another tract and some driveways that were seeded to only buffalo grass. With occasional mowing, the buffalo grass easily crowds out everything else. Can we assume this was the case in the natural prairie where the buffalo clipped the grass short?

We burn these prairies every three or four years. Small as these tracts are, the flames generated are awesome. Burning seems to favor the taller grasses over the forbs here, but timing may be a factor.

The mix of mini-ecosystems on the farmstead — a pond, fifty varieties of trees and shrubs, lawns, prairie, and surrounding fields of wheat and alfalfa — demonstrate how birds and animals prefer different habitats. Meadowlarks and dickcissels prefer open space or field's edge, pheasants like the tall grasses, quail claim unmowed ditch banks, and orioles nest in drooping branches too precarious for a cat to climb.

Yesterday, on a walk along the wooded creek, skirting past a prairie in bloom, through knee-deep alfalfa, across a disked wheat field, and back to the house through the mulberry hedge, I became aware of a presence. Section 27's generations were there with me. Their essence, their genes, and their footprints across the fields were around and within me, and they were pleased with what they saw.

The dominant voice of Section 27 is subtle, not expressed in English, definitely not in Low Dutch, but rather in a universal language of the heart. Each delicate prairie flower is a poem that touches the soul. A cornucopia of newly mown hay, golden grain, and red-ripe tomatoes nourishes the body while a chorus of kingbirds on a summer morn declare the glory of God.